◎ 本书由扬州大学出版基金资助，特此鸣谢
◎ 本书获扬州大学研究生优秀课程资助，特此鸣谢
◎ 本书为扬州大学研究生教育教学改革课题成果之一，课题编号:XJGLX_005

英语教学设计与案例分析

周维杰　编著

Instructional Design for
Teaching English as a Foreign Language
and
Case Analysis

上海交通大学出版社
SHANGHAI JIAO TONG UNIVERSITY PRESS

图书在版编目(CIP)数据

英语教学设计与案例分析/周维杰编著. —上海：上海交通大学出版社,2020(2024 重印)
ISBN 978 - 7 - 313 - 19435 - 0

Ⅰ.①英…　Ⅱ.①周…　Ⅲ.①英语—教学研究　Ⅳ.①H319.3

中国版本图书馆 CIP 数据核字(2018)第 106442 号

英语教学设计与案例分析

编　　著：周维杰
出版发行：上海交通大学出版社　　　　　　　　　　地　　址：上海市番禺路 951 号
邮政编码：200030　　　　　　　　　　　　　　　　电　　话：021 - 64071208
印　　制：上海景条印刷有限公司
开　　本：787mm×1092mm　1/16　　　　　　　　经　　销：全国新华书店
字　　数：232 千字　　　　　　　　　　　　　　　印　　张：10.25
版　　次：2018 年 8 月第 1 版
书　　号：ISBN 978 - 7 - 313 - 19435 - 0　　　　　　印　　次：2024 年 1 月第 4 次印刷
定　　价：43.00 元

教学即研究

——十年磨一课

　　《英语教学设计与案例分析》这门课到今年已经走过了十个春秋,其中的酸甜苦辣只有我自己心知肚明。十年来,英语教学设计案例走过了从无到有、从捉襟见肘到游刃有余。可以这样说,这门课教学每前进一步,都离不开研究。具体地说,就是 research in instructional design, research on instructional design and research for instructional design(在教学设计中研究、对教学设计进行研究和为了教学设计而研究),因为教学设计永远是一个"没有最好,只有更好"的东西,它要求我们不断推陈出新、不断自我完善、不断精益求精。

　　2008 年冬,我接到开设《英语教学设计与案例分析》这门课的任务。当时,我是两眼一抹黑,对《英语教学设计与案例分析》一无所知。接下来,我在网上搜索相关中英文材料,开始认真研究:阅读、摘抄、思考、质疑、借鉴、内化,为开好这门课做了大量的前期准备。

　　2009 年夏,我如期为在职教育硕士第一次开设《英语教学设计与案例分析》这门课程。虽说我做了大量的准备,但毕竟没有经验,当时的教学基本是照本宣科,人云亦云,偏重英语教学设计的理论,给人以空对空的感觉。我本人对这门课不满意,学员对这门课的兴趣也不浓。课程结束后,我进行了深刻的反思,决定改变跟在前人亦步亦趋的讲法,走自己的路,尝试采用案例教学法。同年,我编写了第一个教学案例《基于"问题教学法"的 Getting the Best Value for Time 的教学设计》,该案例获扬州大学优秀教学案例,并由江苏教育出版社出版。

　　2010 年,我开始指导在职教育硕士撰写《英语教学设计》方面的硕士论文,探索教育硕士论文的新路子。同年 11 月,我参加在安徽师范大学召开的《全国教育硕士专业学位"学科教学·英语"教学研讨会》。在小组发言时,我谈及撰写《英语教学设计》作为教育硕士论文,得到了主持小组讨论会的华东师范大学的张吉生教授的肯定。

　　2011 年,我在广泛研读英语教学设计方面的论文和书籍的基础上,增加了教学设计要基于某一理念,这使教学设计上了一个新台阶。有了理念,教学设计就有了魂,有了根。就这样,《英语教学设计与案例分析》这门课逐渐完善,日趋成熟。同年暑假,这门课的一些内容第一次变成《江苏省高中英语骨干教师培训项目》讲座的内容。

　　再经过 2012 年的探索,《英语教学设计与案例分析》这门课已成为我的一大特色和亮点,并得到我院教育硕士导师的普遍认同。多达三分之二以上的导师在指导教育硕士论文时,用英语教学设计。同年,我被评为全国教育硕士优秀教师。这对我来说是个新的鼓舞、新的鞭策、新的起点。

2013 年初,我对我前几年指导的英语教学设计方面的论文进行认真筛选、推敲、润色;同时,继续指导新的教学设计方面的论文,准备把它编成《英语教学设计·实践篇》这本书。经过一年的苦战,终于完成这本书的编写。

2014 年 7 月,由我主编的《英语教学设计·实践篇》在上海译文出版社出版。这更加坚定了我对《英语教学设计与案例分析》这门课的信心。此后,我继续探索,并着手对我自己的教学设计进行全面系统的总结、反思、修改与分析。

2015 年,我主持的《英语教学设计案例库》获"扬州大学专业学位研究生教学案例库建设项目"立项。同年,《英语教学设计与案例分析》这门课程的内容第一次走出江苏,在青海西宁变成国培的内容,受到国培学员的普遍欢迎。

2016 年,我开设的《英语教学设计与案例分析》这门课程获"扬州大学研究生优秀课程"建设项目。同年,应河南南阳师范学院外国语学院的邀请,为国培学员连续做了三场《英语教学设计》方面的讲座。

2017 年 4 月,我在江苏省名师送培项目中,给连云港的高中英语教师做了一场《英语教学设计的创意》讲座。同年,我主持的《英语教学设计的创意研究》获"扬州大学研究生教育教学改革研究与实践课题"立项。

就这样,迄今为止,《英语教学设计与案例分析》这门课有三个校级项目支撑。由于这门课,我先后在青海西宁(国培)、河南南阳(国培)、江苏扬州(国培、省培、省高职英语教师培训班、市英语教师高级研修班)、盐城(省培)、连云港(省培)、东海(省培)、常州、泰州、金坛、邗江、宝应等地做了英语教学设计的 30 余场讲座,每到一处都受到热烈欢迎。

在其受欢迎的背后,就是研究,十年的研究。这里,我们不妨来看看六个教学即研究的片段。

第一个片段

这是我专门为教育硕士《英语教学设计与案例分析》的第一个节课写的一首诗,题目叫 *I'm Happy to Instruct You in This Course*。虽说这首诗仍有好多需要改进的地方,但我是用心写的、用情写的。

I'm Happy to Instruct You in This Course

I'm happy to instruct you in this course.

I hope your information it can associate

So that you will be able

To rearrange and to transform and to integrate.

I'm happy to instruct you in this course.

I hope your interaction it can motivate

So that you will be able

To discuss and to exchange and to illuminate.

I'm happy to instruct you in this course.

I hope your interest it can stimulate

So that you will be able

To self-learn and to inquire and to collaborate.

I'm happy to instruct you in this course.

I hope your imagination it can cultivate

So that you will be able

To know and to discover and to innovate.

I'm happy to instruct you in this course.

I hope your inspiration it can activate

So that you will be able

To relax and to interconnect and to create.

I'm happy to instruct you in this course.

I hope your ideal it can elevate

So that you will be able

To strive and to individualize and to culminate.

　　这首诗里有好多信息,这里我只讲其中的四个。第一,我从事教育工作 30 余年,至今仍深爱着这一份工作,从"高兴"一词,可以窥见一斑,否则我教你们这门课程不会"高兴"。因此,有时候,我在想我们不要给学生空谈什么大道理,诸如巩固专业思想之类。身教言传比什么都重要,它可以起到潜移默化、润物无声的效果。很难想象一个自己都不把精力放在教学的老师,会让他或她的学生有巩固的专业思想。第二,这首诗浓缩了英语教学设计的精髓:13 个 i,即 instructive(要有教育性),informative(要有适度的信息量),integrative(要采用综合教学法),interactive(要有互动),illuminating(要有启发性),interesting(要有趣),inquisitive(要探究),imaginative(要有想象力),innovative(要有创新性),inspiring(要能激发灵感),interconnective(要把各种东西联系起来,要打通),idealistic(要有理想),individualized(要个性化)。第三,这首诗第四段的最后一句"To know and to discover and to innovate"隐含三个苹果改变了世界。To know 是指亚当和夏娃吃了伊甸园里的苹果,那苹果树叫"Tree of Knowledge",他们吃了以后,就和上帝一样,知道了善恶,最后上帝把亚当和夏娃逐出伊甸园,来到我们现在的世界,因此,第一个苹果带我们看到了世界,让人类有了道德。To discover 是指牛顿从苹果掉到地上发现了万有引力,因此,第二个苹果,带我们了解了世界,让人类有了科学。To innovate 是指乔布斯的苹果公司,他们锐意创新,发明了一系列的苹果产品,第三个苹果带我们体验了世界,让人类有了新的生活。从某种程度说,我们的学校教育,尤其是智育,就是引导学生有所了解、有所发现、有所创新。第四,从语言教学的角度看,-ate 是五个常用的动词后缀之一。常用的动词后缀是-ize/ise, -en, -ify, -ish, -ate。在这首诗中就有 12 个以-ate 结尾的单词:associate, integrate, motivate, illuminate, stimulate, collaborate, cultivate, innovate, activate, create, elevate 和 culminate。类似的还有 liberate(解放)、deviate(背离、偏离)、decelerate(减速)、degenerate(退化)、operate(操作、手术)、vibrate(振动、颤动)、migrate(移动)、anticipate(预期、期望)、abbreviate(缩写)等,因此也可以通过这一首诗扩大学生的词汇量。

第二个片段

这是我给英语专业的一年级新生讲的第一节《英语阅读》。因为是《英语阅读》课，我就提了这样一个问题：What is reading？Reading 对于这些新生来说，可谓司空见惯，可是，要问什么是 reading，还真的一下子把他们给难倒了。他们感到语塞、茫然，有些不知所措。这可能是由于他们是新生，也可能由于这是第一节课，还可能因为他们是大班（正常是两个班合上，偶尔也有三个班合上）。此刻，我常说的一句话是："Take it easy. Let's think about it.（不要紧，我们来思考思考。）"正如孔子所说"不愤不启，不悱不发"。"愤"就是学生对某一问题正在积极思考，急于解决而又尚未搞通时的矛盾心理状态。这时教师应对学生思考问题的方法适时给以指导，以帮助学生开启思路，这就是"启"。"悱"是学生对某一问题已经有一段时间的思考，但尚未考虑成熟，处于想说又难以表达的另一种矛盾心理状态。这时教师应帮助学生明确思路，弄清事物的本质属性，然后用比较准确的语言表达出来，这就是"发"。这时，我一般暗示同学们一下，"What organ or organs will you use if you want to read?"，可以想象一下，你小时候在父母怀里或在幼儿园里，你父母和幼儿园的老师怎么教你阅读。那首先是用"eyes"。接着因势利导，"Yes. You will use your eyes. This means reading is a visual process."（是的，你会用眼。这意味着阅读是一个视觉过程。）如果不用眼睛，就什么也看不见。如果什么都看不见，就无所谓阅读了，当然读盲文除外。还要用"mouth"大声朗读。"Yes. You will also use your mouth. This means reading is a vocal process."（是的，你会用口。这意味着阅读是一个发声过程。）还要用"mind"去思考。"Yes. You will also use your mind. This means reading is a mental process."（是的，你会用心。这意味着阅读是一个思维过程。）这样，我们可以把阅读总结为"Reading is a visual, vocal and mental process to decode meaning out of the written or printed or online materials"。这使人联想到南宋理学家朱熹读书有三到，即"眼到、口到和心到"。与"眼到、口到和心到"相对应的"reading"分别可译为"看书、读书和念书"，即"看书"有"目"，表示用"眼睛"；"读书"有"口"，表示用"嘴"；"念书"有"心"，表示用"大脑"。把"眼到、口到和心到"和"看书、读书和念书"用一个字来概括，就是个"总"字。上面两点代表"眼睛"，中间是个"口"，下面是个"心"。顺便说一下，在这三个译文中，"读书"使用最广、内涵最丰富。搞清楚什么是 reading 后，我们来看看如何读书。具体地说，要读薄、读厚、读活。以后我会慢慢地跟大家谈。

第三个片段

《英语词汇学》是一门选修课，我刚开这门课时，其选修人数在 60 人到 70 人之间，在我开到第四个年头时，整个年级都选这门课，高达 150 人左右。究其因，我想可能有两个。一是《英语词汇学》这门课可以帮助学生做到 3 000 单词百日通；二是我采取了 80 分教育。这里我来谈谈 80 分教育。

1. 80 分教育的缘由

为了冲破教师、教材以及教室对学生的束缚，为了培养学生的动手能力、查阅资料的能力、概括能力、合作能力和研究能力，为日后的毕业论文写作打下一个良好的基础，我一改往日的试卷考试，取而代之的是课程小论文。应该说以课程小论文作为考试方式并不是什么新鲜事。学生一次性完成课程小论文,我批改后给学生一个成绩,就算完成了该课程的教学任务。但我发现有些学生的论文质量较差,有的甚至是从网上直接下载下来的,最后成绩不及格。我把这些不及格的学生一一叫到办公室,指出他们的问题所在,要求他们重写或修改论文。经过有针对性的指导后,有些同学写得不错,可以达到80分。这件事引起了我的思考:为什么只给少数不及格同学这样的机会呢?为什么不能给所有学生均等的机会,让学生在撰写和修改小论文中得到锻炼,从而提高进步呢?如果经过学生反复修改后可以达到80分,为什么不给他们80分呢?这样就产生了80分教育。

2. 80分教育的界定

由于80分教育是我提出的一个较新的观念,尚没有一个被大家接受的界定。我认为,所谓80分教育是一种面向全体学生,旨在提高全体学生综合素质的教育;是一种既注重过程也注重结果的教育,其中特别注重过程的教育;是一种树立学生信心,培养学生自信的教育;是一种以学生为本的和谐教育。具体地说,是某一门课程(如英语词汇学)以课程小论文的形式进行考试(或以其他考试形式),学生在撰写小论文的过程中,按照老师的要求,经过老师的耐心指导和学生的反复修改,最终成绩达到至少80分。在这一过程中,学生不是消极被动的知识接受者,而是积极主动的探索者和研究者;在这一过程中,老师应该始终用发展的和变化的眼光看待学生,用发展的和变化的理念武装学生,用发展的和变化的言语鼓励学生,使学生感到自己在进步、在发展、在前进。

3. 80分教育的方式

到目前为止,笔者实施了两种80分教育的方式。一是老师开学初就向学生讲清楚《英语词汇学》课程的要求。该课程以课程小论文为考试形式,论文用汉语撰写,长度为3000字左右。学生独立选题,独立查找、收集和分析材料,最终独立完成论文。完成论文后,交给老师,老师对学生的论文认真阅读,如果达到80分或80分以上,就不要修改或重写;如果没有达到80分,老师首先指出论文中存在的问题,如:选题太大、文不对题、过于浅显、观点不明、层次不清、语言不畅、论证不足、前后矛盾等。接下来,老师针对所存在的问题,提出具体的修改意见,例如,针对选题太大,笔者往往建议学生只研究一点:某一个颜色词、某一个数词、it、that、such、so、and、复合名词、反义词、同义词、词缀、关于hand或heart的习语等。并一一进行当面指导,大部分学生经过两三次指导后,论文可以达到80分或80分以上,有些学生修改达五次之多,才能达到要求。因为《英语词汇学》是一门专业选修课,一般情况每年选修人数在60人到70人之间,由于近年来实行80分教育,选修人数从70人上升至100人,最高达150人。如果每人按指导两次计算的话,就要300次;如果每个人按指导三次计算的话,就要450次。说实在的,对于一个教师来说,工作量太大了,有些力不从心,于是就产生了第二种方式,即以小组为单位,合作完成一个项目。笔者首先把150个学生分为25个小组,每组6个人左右,小组实行自由组合,一般以宿舍为单位,每组选一个组长,负责召集全体组员,分配工作与协调组员之间的关系。大家共同合作,集体商讨选题,分工查找资料,最后,由组长或本组擅长写作的同学执笔完成论文。本项目包括三个方面的内容:一是课程论文,用汉语撰写,长度为4500~5000字;二是每个组员所收集的材料和所做的读书笔记,主要防止学生大段抄袭或直接下载;三是一份项目小结,其中包括项目的总体计划、日程安排、每个组员的工作分工情况、整个完成项目过程中的表现情况以及每个组员的自我评价和小组评价。整个成绩由三部分组成：一是自我评价占10%；二是小组评价20%；三是教师评价70%。一般情况自我评价和小组评价都可以达到80分。而教师评价有可能达不到80分，如果教师评价达不到80分，那整个小组必须根据老师的修改意见进行修改，直到达到80分或80分以上为止。

4．80分教育的反馈

我在实施80分教育后，对部分学生进行了非结构性访谈，请他们谈谈对80分教育的看法。总的来说，他们认为这种方法是好的。有的同学认为这种方法比一次考试确定成绩更加合理、更加科学。一般考试是在考前一周突击复习一下，考过以后全都还给老师了。而要写一篇论文前后时间至少要持续五六周，有的甚至要持续九至十周。经过自己查找材料、分析材料，加上老师的指导写出的论文，印象特别深刻，不容易遗忘。有的同学认为整个项目过程比较愉悦，因为他们选择的是自己感兴趣的题目，所以他们乐此不疲，无论是在讨论、收集材料，还是在写作时都很愉快；有的同学认为这种方法锻炼了他们的能力，如：动手能力、查阅资料的能力、概括能力、合作能力、研究能力、语言表达能力和电脑操作能力；有的同学认为这种方法可以拓宽他们的视野和思维。由于不同的同学负责不同的内容，在交流过程中，同学之间相互学习、相互借鉴，他们学到了许多书上学不到的知识。还有的同学建议，建立一个网站，把学生写得好的放在上面，以便大家共同学习，共同提高，同时，可以把小组交流扩大到全班，甚至到全年级。在访谈中，我也发现有极个别同学不够认真，他们或滥竽充数，或浑水摸鱼，或坐享其成。

第四个片段

这一片段是来自《研究方法与论文写作》这门课。当时我发现我们有一些研究生，觉得自己是研究生了，了不起了，有些飘飘然。他们一进校，就忙于做家教，找课代，极个别研究生还在班上搞起了推销，心思根本不放在学习上。看到这个情况，我有些心痛。我想还是要对他们进行教育，不能听之任之，放任自流。这样就有这一片段。

同学们，我们先来看我仿写的一首小诗，题目叫 *Twinkle，Twinkle，Little Star*。

> Twinkle，twinkle，little star.
>
> You must know who you are.
>
> Once you know who you are.
>
> Your way to success is not far.

这一首诗的主题句是：You know who you are（你认识你自己）。这个主题句可以缩略成一个短语 know yourself（认识你自己）。这个短语可以再缩略为一个词 self-knowledge（识己）。"认识你自己"，这是古希腊哲学家苏格拉底的一句名言，刻在德尔菲神庙上。"认识你自己"一方面要认识自己的长处，扬其所长；另一方面，更重要的是要认识自己的短处，避其所短。不要以为考上研究生了，就了不起了，实际上，我们还有许多东西不知道，还有许多东西要学，说到底，我们还很无知。我们每个人都有两种无知。一种叫"先天无知"或"原始无知"或"自然无知"，即"primitive ignorance"或"natural ignorance"，另一种是"后天无知"或"获得性无知"，即"acquired ignorance"。

所谓"primitive ignorance"或"natural ignorance"，也就是我们赤身裸体来到这个世界时

的无知。随着我们来到这个世界，我们便开始有知，从降生到幼儿园，从幼儿园到小学，从小学到中学，从中学到大学，我们的知识不断增长，且越积越多，很少意识到自己的无知。但实际上，我们很无知。我们不妨举一个大家最为熟悉、最为简单的"一"。它的简单主要体现在三个方面：它是一切数字中最简单的数，所有数都始于"一"；它的书写也非常简单，只有一笔画；它的发音也非常简单，没有声母，只有单韵母，声调属阴平，没有如何高低升降的变化。就是这个简单的字，到今天你上研究生，你又了解多少呢？根据吴慧颖的《中国数文化》，"一"共有19个意思。它们是①最小的整数，属基数词。②由此引申为数量极少。如："一鳞半爪""一毛不拔""一无所知"。③表第一，属序数词。如："五月一日""一不做二不休"。④若干分中的一分。如："三分天下有其一"。⑤相同、同一。如："众口一词""说法不一"。⑥单一、独一。如："一家之言""一面之词"。⑦专一。如："一心一意"。⑧也、又。如："马铃薯一名土豆"。⑨某一。如："一天，家中来客"。⑩每一。如："一人发三本书"。⑪统一。如："六王毕，四海一"。⑫全、满。如："一身是胆""一如既往"。⑬极、甚。如："一早""一贫如洗"。⑭一个方面。如："一则以喜，一则以惧"。⑮竟然。如："为害之甚，一至于此"。⑯表示动作、现象突然出现。如："枪声一响""眼前一黑""一哄而起"。⑰表示情况与行为、行动与行动、动作与结果的紧相连接，相当于"刚""才"。如："天一亮便起床""一学就会"。⑱一经、一旦。如："一成不变""一蹶不振"。⑲表示动作的稍微、短暂、试行。如："研究一下""闻一闻""洗一洗"。根据《汉语大词典》，以"一"打头的词条达115页之多，共1700余条。根据现代汉语常用字字频统计，使用频率最高的首推"的"字，其次就是"一"字，居"老子天下第二"。

　　这里我们再来进行深层次的挖掘，看一看"一"里所包含的哲学内蕴。第一，简单中包含复杂。这一点我们可以从书写简单、发音简单、最简单的数字"一"却包含19个意思，1700多个词条可以看出。第二，无中生有。"一"是从哪儿来的？根据老子的《道德经》，"一"来自于"道"。就是所谓"道生一，一生二，二生三，三生万物，万物负阴而抱阳，冲气以为和"。那么，什么是"道"呢？"道"是看不清、说不明的"虚无"状态。从某种意义上说，世间的万事万物都是"无中生有"。我们人是"无中生有"；我们住的房子是"无中生有"；我们读的书是"无中生有"；将来，你们的论文也是"无中生有"。第三，风马牛相及。还是刚才谈到的"道生一，一生二，二生三，三生万物"。也就是说，万物都与三有关。既然万物都与三有关，那么，风马牛相及了。第四，窥斑见豹。所谓"窥斑见豹"，是指我们通过"一"可以了解整个汉语。刚才，我们发现我们对"一"并不了解，怎么办？查字典。一查字典发现，"一"有19个意思。其中第一个意思是："最小的整数，属基数词"。我们连"一"都不了解，那么，对"最""小""的""整""数"，"属""基""数""词"，也不了解。这样继续查字典，发现"最"又有若干个意思。这些意思又不懂，又要查字典，如此这般，经过五六次，有可能把所有的汉字全部囊括其中。这也就是我们通常所说的"一叶落而知秋""一滴水可以看大海""一粒沙可以看世界"。第五，万物归一。既然"一生二，二生三，三生万物"，那么，反过来"二也是一""三也是一""四也是一""七也是一""十二也是一""三十也是一""六十也是一""五百万也是一""十三亿也是一"。

　　原来，"一"里面有这么多东西。真是"不说不知道，说起来吓一跳"。关于"一"你了解得不多，那么"二"呢？关于"ABC"，你又了解多少呢？这时，你突然意识到你自己的无知，这就是"acquired ignorance"。这种"acquired ignorance"虽然也是无知，但要比"primitive ignorance"或"natural ignorance"高一个层次。从辩证法(dialectics)的角度看,我们刚才经历了"否定之否定"(negation of negation),即"primitive ignorance"或"natural ignorance"——"knowledge"——"acquired ignorance"。经过否定之否定,事物运动就表现为一个周期,在更高的阶段上重复旧的阶段的某些特征,由此构成事物从低级到高级、从简单到复杂的周期性螺旋式上升和波浪式前进的发展过程,体现出事物发展的曲折性。这里给大家讲个小故事。爱因斯坦获得诺贝尔物理学奖以后,变得比以往更加谦虚。他的一个学生不解,问他:"爱因斯坦博士,您已获得诺贝尔物理学奖,怎么还这么谦虚?"爱因斯坦随手拿出在一张白纸,在上画了一个大圆、一个小圆,并说道:"如果用小圆圈代表你们学到的知识,用大圆圈代表我学到的知识,看起来似乎我比你们掌握的知识多了些。但这两个圆圈之外,都是无知。由于大圆比小圆大,它所接触到的无知也比小圆多,换句话说,我所不知道的要比你们多。正因为我所不知道的要比你们多,所以我就更加谦虚。"

知道自己"无知"该怎么办? 很简单,那就是"发奋、进取、前行"。所谓"无知者无畏"中的"无畏"指的就是无所畏惧,勇往直前。从这个意义上说,"Ignorance is power."(无知就是力量。)

第五个片段

这是我翻译教学中的一个片段,是对过程教学法的研究。传统的翻译教学比较重视翻译的终端结果——译文,对学生的翻译过程重视不够。忽视学生在翻译过程中所遇到的问题,当然也就谈不上帮助学生解决问题了,这种教学方法通常称为结果教学法(product-oriented approach),其典型的上课模式是:教师首先讲解一些翻译理论或翻译技巧,然后布置一些相应的翻译练习,一般以短文的形式出现,长度在 500 ~ 1000 词不等。接着教师对学生的译文逐一进行批改。批改时,教师的注意力往往集中在学生的错误上,力求将学生翻译中的错误全部挑出并一一改正,惟恐留一个会"误人子弟",或给学生留下工作不认真的印象。最后,对学生的译文进行讲评,其中仍以纠正错误为主,偶尔也把学生中好的译文放进去。这种教学方法明显有几点不足:①教师无论在批改译文还是评讲译文时,注意力都集中在学生的错误上,容易挫伤学生学翻译的积极性,这在心理上会使学生产生畏惧、厌恶情绪。②偏离了素质教育的宗旨,素质教育的宗旨是培养学生的综合能力,即创新能力、辨别是非的能力以及发现问题、分析问题和解决问题的能力等。而这种仍以教师为中心的教学方法,学生的主体作用没有得到充分的发挥。③这种"保姆式"的教学方法既容易助长学生的依赖情绪,又容易使学生养成敷衍了事的不良习惯,译得好不好不要紧,反正教师到时候要为他们修改、评讲。④这种教学法缺乏对学生的引导,学生往往很少去对教师所改的或所讲的译文进行认真的分析和反复推敲,因而印象不深,致使教师指出的问题仍会重复出现;此外,教师在学生翻译过程中无法进行监控,若学生在翻译过程中碰到问题,教师无法及时发现并加以指导。

如果说我们把翻译比作一座冰山,学生交给教师的译文只不过漂浮在水面上的冰峰,而深藏在水下那复杂的翻译过程,我们完全没有重视。为了克服结果教学法的不足,我尝试使用过程教学法(process-oriented approach)。过程教学法建立在对翻译过程大量研究的基础上,强调在翻译过程中发现问题、分析问题和解决问题。众所周知,翻译是一个极其复杂的心理过程,涉及思维、语言等诸多因素,通常我们把翻译过程分为三个阶段,即理解阶段、表达阶段和修改阶段。理解阶段是指学生对原文的理解,这是一个解码过程,是翻译的基础。表达阶段是指学生把自己理解的内容用另一种语言表达出来,是一个编码的过程。修改阶段是指学生对照原文,反复阅读译文,看看有没有译得不畅的地方,有没有译错的地方,然后进行认真修改。这三个阶段可以是线形的,即理解—表达—修改;也可以是非线形的,即边表达边修改,或边修改边加深理解,但必须贯穿整个翻译过程。

如果把结果教学法与过程教学法做个比较,我们不难发现过程教学法增加了修改阶段。如何修改,我在教学中做了以下的尝试和探索:①同学互改;②小组讨论后修改;③班级讨论后修改。不论是同学互改,还是小组讨论后修改,还是班级讨论后修改,都是建立在个人译文基础上的交流,目的是为了互相启发,互相借鉴,加深理解,澄清问题,最终提高译文的质量。为了使全体学生都积极参与课堂活动,我把整个翻译成绩分为三块:课堂参与情况占30%,平时的练习与修改占30%,期末考试占40%。因此,不积极参与课堂活动的学生,翻译就很可能不及格。

同学互改(peer revision),我把 36 个学生分为 6 个小组,为了防止同桌之间在表达阶段互相参照,译文雷同,从而使同桌互改失去意义,我让第一小组的学生修改第三小组的译文,第二小组的学生修改第四小组的译文,第三小组的学生修改第五小组的译文,依次类推,第六小组的学生修改第二小组的译文。修改方法:统一使用铅笔,统一使用修改符号。修改符号如下:你认为译得好的句子,在下面画一道横线,并在横线后面打一个五角星(＿＿＿＿＿＿＿★);你认为译得牛头不对马嘴,有严重问题,在下面画一道横线,并在横线后面打一个×(＿＿＿＿＿×);你认为这句话的理解有问题,在下面画一道横线,并在横线后面打一个问号(＿＿＿＿＿＿＿?);你认为这句话的表达有问题,在下面画一道横线,并在横线后面打两个问号(＿＿＿＿＿＿??);你认为这句话需要调整词序,画上这样的符号"＿＿＿＿｜＿＿";你认为这句话需要省略,画上一个括号"(＿＿＿＿)";你认为这句话需要增加,画上这样的符号"∧"。在这一过程中,学生之间的交流是平等的,每个学生既是修改者,又是被修改者。作为修改者,每个学生都有权利评判别人的译文,并对其提出自己的修改意见,这对别人的译文来说是一种改进,对自己来说,既是一个发挥主观能动性的时候,也是一个学习提高的过程。作为被修改者,每个学生的译文应受到别人的评判,这时,每个学生应本着有则改之的态度。同时,如果你认为自己是正确的,还可以进行反评判。最后,根据别人的修改意见逐一进行修改。

小组讨论后修改(revision based on group discussion),我把整个班级分成 9 个小组,每组指定一名组长,组长负责协调全组成员的活动。首先,每个组员把自己的译文读给其他组员听,其他组员对照自己的译文,进行讨论,大家各抒己见,对其他人的译文提出具体的修改意见,每个人都得发言。然后,根据讨论的意见,每个人进行修改。在修改好以后,从 9 组中挑选 3~4 名代表,把各自的译文读给全班学生听,这样做的原因是有时眼睛看不出毛病的东西,耳朵一听就听出来了。全班学生再在 3~4 名代表呈现的基础上,再次修改各自的译文。

班级讨论后修改(revision based on class discussion),课前我从班上任意挑选 4 篇学生的译文打印好,上课时把它们发给全班学生,要求他们比较这 4 篇译文,指出它们各自好的地方,让学生从正面总结成功的经验,同时,更要指出每篇不足的地方,让学生从反面吸取教训。在此基础上进行讨论,集思广益,使学生真正领略翻译过程是一种乐趣和享受,最后,学生再进行修改。

第六个片段

我在教《英语语言学》这门课程时,一直使用的戴炜栋、何兆熊两位教授主编的《新编简明英语语言学教程》。正如这两位教授在其"序言"中所指出的那样:"'简'与'新'是本教程的两大鲜明的特征。"这里,我还要再补充一个特征,那就是"全",即比较全面。

我在教 Syntax 这一章时,觉得其中有几幅"树"形图画得欠妥。

比如该书第 47 页,讲述的是 X⁻ 理论,它有两条规则:

第一条规则是 XP→(Specifier)X⁻;

第二条规则是 X⁻→X(Complement)。

也就是说,这是一个三个层次的结构:第一个层次为 XP,第二个层次为 Specifier 和 X⁻,第三个层次为 X 和 Complement。而 Figure 4 – 2 的"树"形图是这样画的:

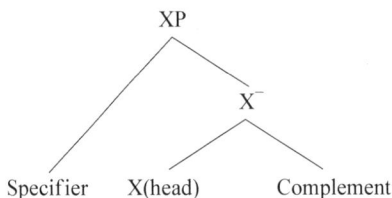

该图看不出 Specifier 和 X⁻ 是一个层次,相反,只能看出 Specifier、X 和 Complement 是一个层次。

根据上述两条规则,笔者建议将该图改为:

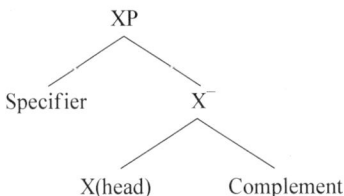

这样可以一眼就可以看出是三个层次。

该书第 52 页,Figure 4 – 3 是这样一幅"树"形图。

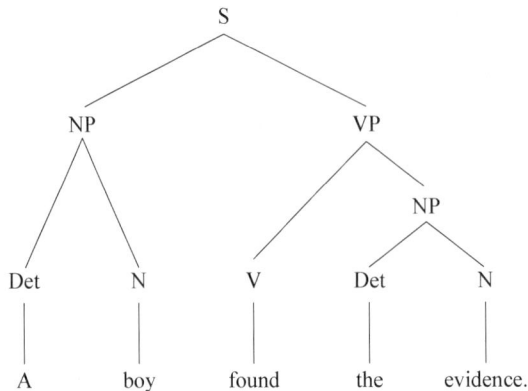

　　该"树"形图层次不清,其中最主要的问题是 VP 是由 V 和 NP 组成的,V 和 NP 应处在同一层次,而不是不同层次,因此,建议改为:

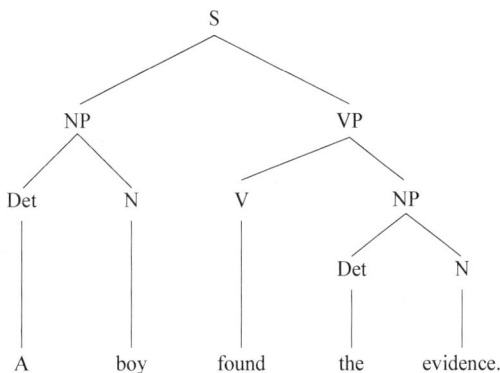

```
                        S
              ┌─────────┴─────────┐
             NP                   VP
          ┌───┴───┐          ┌─────┴─────┐
         Det      N          V           NP
                                      ┌──┴──┐
                                     Det     N

          A       boy      found    the   evidence.
```

以保证 V 和 NP 在同一层次。

　　这里我只是想培养学生的批判性思维,让学生学会思考,书上的东西未必完全正确,让他们明白尽信书不如无书。

　　以上六个片段都属于教学研究,它们包括教学内容的研究、教学方法的研究、教学对象的研究、教学目标的研究和教育的研究。我把这些片段与英语教学设计打通,成为我教学案例的一个部分。

　　本书所收集的教学设计的案例,是我近十年所教课程的教学研究的成果。内容涉及《英语阅读》《词汇学》《翻译》《研究方法与论文写作》《语言学》等课程的教学设计。这些教学设计是我主编的上海译文出版社出版的《英语教学设计·实践篇》的深化、拓展与补允。

　　本书是一本自我设计、自我分析的书,给人有些自说自话的味道。因此,设计得未必完美、未必巧妙;分析也未必到位、未必深刻,甚至还有些主观或武断,不妨把它称之为"一家之言"。最主要的目的是能与同行交流,给学生与学员以启迪。

　　在编著本书的过程中,我得到许多人的鼓励和帮助。首先要感谢俞洪亮教授对我高度信任,让我担任教育硕士带头人与《英语教学设计》这门课的负责人。正由于此,才有这本书的出现的可能。感谢他对我在探索新路子上的肯定、鼓励以及一些非常中肯和有益的意见。其次,要感谢我的学生和学员,他们用各种方法对我进行鼓励,包括当面、纸条、贺卡、短信、qq、微信、微博等:如:"听了周老师的课,胜读十年书""周老师的课让我终身难忘""上周老师的课是一种高级享受""因为老师的课,我开始重新喜欢上了英语啦""我们还没有听个够"等等不一而足。这些鼓励是对一个老师最大的奖赏。我时常在想:一个优秀的老师不一定要受到校长或院长的表扬或奖励,但一定要深受学生或学员发自内心的喜爱与欢迎。如果十年、二十年、三十年以后,还有学生想念你,谈到你当年的课就眉飞色舞,你就是成功的。当一个老师在课堂上听到学生或学员发自内心的掌声时,看到学生或学员发自内心的微笑时,你会觉得所有的付出都是值的。最后,此书在出版过程中得到扬州大学外国语学院院长王金铨教授和上海交通大学出版社张冠男主任的帮助,这里一并致谢。

周维杰

2018 年 5 月

Contents

Part One

Instructional Design of *Reading* and Case Analysis

Theme-based Instructional Design of *Parental Love* and Analysis

I. Theme-based Instructional Design of *Parental Love*

Step 1: Lead-in with a questionnaire about parental love

Before we learn the texts, I'd like to conduct a survey with two questions.

1. He loves her very much. She is very beautiful: fair-skinned, bright-eyed and full-breasted. But one day, she had a car accident. Having fully recovered from the accident, she has a few ugly scars on her face. Do you think that he will still love her as ever?

A. Certainly.　　　　　B. Probably.　　　　　C. Never.

2. She loves him very much. He is a business elite: enterprising, quick-witted and genteel. But one day, he became bankrupt. Do you think that she will still love him as ever?

A. Certainly.　　　　　B. Probably.　　　　　C. Never.

When you answer these two questions, most probably you subconsciously take these two as lovers, that is, they have a loving relationship, or we can say "he" is a boyfriend and "she" is a girlfriend.

If you change their relationship into parent-child one, that is, father-daughter relationship in the first question and mother-son relationship in the second question, what will be your choice? Surely, you will choose A. Why?

In this world, there is a kind of love which is ever-lasting and unselfish, which requires nothing in return, and which never changes whatever happens. That is parental love.

We're going to learn four texts about parental love. The first two texts are about paternal love and the next two about maternal love. Parental love can be shown through what they said, what they did and what they thought.

Step 2: Reading with a focus on how to show parental love through what they said

Let's look at Text Ⅰ first.

> My father was a lawyer with no sons, so he decided that his older daughter, Susie, would follow his career and take over his business when he died. When Susie was in kindergarten, he began to work on her: "Susie," he would say, "you will never have to worry about a thing, for I have paved all the roads for you. I have done all the dirty work in establishing a good business in law, and all you will have to do is take it over." [From Text Ⅰ]

From what her father said, we can sense the paternal love. When you read her father's words, pay close attention to the word "all" and put proper stress on it. This reminds us of what Chinese schools say: "一切为了孩子,为了孩子的一切和为了一切孩子。"

Step 3: Reading with a focus on how to show parental love through what they did

We'll look at Text Ⅱ.

> My father and I were both at the same college back in the mid 1970s while I was in class at Columbia, he was on a bricklayer's scaffold not far from the street, working on a campus building. . . .

Both the father and the son were at Columbia in the mid 1970s. The father was a bricklayer and the son was a university student. Columbia University is in New York, one of the top ten in America, something like Fudan University in Shanghai.

> In 1980, after college and graduate school, I was offered my first job, on a daily paper in Columbus, Ohio. I broke the news in the kitchen, where all the family business is discussed. My mother wept as if it were Vietnam. My father had a few questions: "Ohio? Where the hell is Ohio?". . . .
>
> "The truth?" the old man exploded, his face reddening . . . .
>
> However, after I said my good-byes, my father took me aside and pressed five $100 bills into my hands. "It's okay," he said over my weak protests. "Don't tell your mother." [From Text Ⅱ]

It is difficult for a bricklayer to send his son to an expensive university like Columbia for undergraduate program. It is even more difficult for a bricklayer to send his son to a university for graduate program. So after his son finished graduate school at Columbia, it was natural and understandable that he insisted that his son should find a decent job in a big city like New York, making a lot of money. Although America is a developed country, Ohio is one of the least developed states. That's why his wife wept as if it were Vietnam and he exploded when they heard the news that their son was going to work there. But when his son insisted that he go to work there, he relented. He took his son aside, pressed five $100 bills into his hands and asked him not to tell his mother. One thing worth mentioning is that $500 in 1980 can't stand comparison with ＄500 in 2010's, and that a bricklayer's ＄500 can't stand comparison with a lawyer's ＄500. That money took him a lot of sweat and hard labor. Besides, that's his case-dough for drink or smoke or trip or hunting or casino. The behavior "pressing five ＄100 bills into his hands" means deep and strong paternal love for his son.

Now, let's move to Text Ⅲ.

My mother called to tell me that my grandmother was dying ....

Sometimes, I kiss and hug Audrey so much she starts crying, which is in effect what my grandmother was doing to my mother all her life ....

But tonight, she is feeding me as she always does when I come, and I am eating more than I do anywhere else .... [From Text Ⅲ]

The title of Text Ⅲ is *Four Generations*. The first sentence of Text Ⅲ is "My mother called to tell me that my grandmother was dying", which tells us there are only three generations: "my grandmother", "my mother" and "me". One more generation is my daughter. So the story of the four generations is actually a story of three mothers and three daughters, in other words, my grandmother is my mother's mother, my mother, and I am my daughter's mother; my mother is my grandmother's daughter, I am my mother's daughter and my daughter. Let's look at this sentence: "Sometimes, I kiss and hug Audrey so much she starts crying, which is in effect what my grandmother was doing to my mother all her life." The two words "kiss" and "hug" here show maternal love. Besides, there is maternal love that is passed down from generation to generation, that is, my grandmother passed maternal love to my mother by kissing and hugging, who, in turn, passed maternal love to me by kissing and hugging, who, in turn, passed maternal love to my daughter by kissing and hugging. We'll move to the next sentence: "But tonight, she is feeding me as she always does when I come, and I am eating more than I do anywhere else." In this sentence, the word "feeding" shows maternal love of her mother for her. The phrase "eating more than I do anywhere else" is an indirect way of expressing maternal love. The reason why she eats more than she does anywhere else is that her mother cooks the best dishes and knows what she likes and dislikes.

Text Ⅳ is a Chinese story called *The Mad Mother*. We'll look at it.

23 年前，有个年轻的女子流落到我们村，蓬头垢面，见人就傻笑，且毫不避讳地当众小便。……

记得我读小学三年级时一个冬日，天空突然下起了雨，奶奶让娘给我送雨伞。娘可能一路摔了好几跤，浑身像个泥猴似的，她站在教室的窗户旁望着我傻笑，口里还叫："树……伞……"一些同学嘻嘻地笑。带头起哄的是小范，当他还在夸张地模仿时，我抓起面前的文具盒，猛地向他砸过去。他冲上前来掐住我的脖子，我俩厮打起来。我个子小，根本不是他的对手，被他轻易压在地上。这时，只听教室外传来"嗷"的一声长啸，娘像个大侠似的飞跑进来，一把抓起小范，拖到了屋外。都说疯子力气大，真是不假。娘双手将欺负我的小范举向半空,他吓得哭爹喊娘,一双胖乎乎的小腿在空中乱踢蹬。娘毫不理会,居然将他丢到了学校门口的水塘里,然后一脸漠然地走开了。……

由于是住读,学习又抓得紧,我很少回家。父亲依旧在为 50 元打工,为我送菜的担子就责无旁贷地落在娘身上。每次总是隔壁的婶婶帮忙为我炒好咸菜,然后交给娘送来。20 公里的羊肠山路亏娘牢牢地记了下来,风雨无阻。也真是奇迹,凡是为儿子做的事,娘一点儿也不疯。除了母爱,我无法解释这种现象在医学上应该怎么破译。

2003 年 4 月的一个星期天,娘来了,不但为我送来了菜,还带来了十几个野鲜桃。我拿起一个,咬了一口,笑着问她:"挺甜的,哪来的?"娘说:"我……我摘的……"没想到娘还会摘野桃,我由衷地表扬她:"娘,您真是越来越能干了。"娘嘿嘿地笑了。

……

娘静静地躺在谷底,周边是一些散落的桃子,她手里还紧紧攥着一个,身上的血早就凝固成了沉重的黑色。我悲痛得五脏俱裂,紧紧地抱住娘,说:"娘啊,我的苦命娘啊,儿悔不该说这桃子甜啊,是儿子要了你的命……"我将头贴在娘冰凉的脸上,哭得漫山遍野的石头都陪着落泪……[From Text Ⅳ]

如果一个女子当众小便,这个女子精神上肯定有问题,是个疯子。就是这位疯子,当她看到她的儿子被人家欺负,压在地上时,会不顾一切地将欺负她儿子的小范丢到了学校门口的水塘里,然后一脸漠然地走开了。这就是母爱。当儿子由于学习紧不能回家,又由于没有钱买不起学校的咸菜时,就是这位疯子要走 20 公里的羊肠山路,她竟然把这羊肠山路牢牢地记了下来,风雨无阻。20 公里的羊肠山路,来回就是 40 公里,80 里路。这 80 里路不是平坦、宽阔的马路,而是羊肠山路,正常人都可能会迷路,何况是个疯子呢?读到这些话,我仿佛看到这位疯子披星戴月走在这羊肠山路,我们不知她跌了多少跟头,不知她的脚下起了多少水泡,不知她挨了多少饿,不知她受了多少苦,只知道她把咸菜送给了她儿子,因此,这咸菜包含着浓浓的母爱。2003 年 4 月的一个星期天,疯娘又来了,不但为儿子送来了咸菜,还带来了十几个野鲜桃。儿子拿起一个,咬了一口,笑着问她:"挺甜的,哪来的?"疯娘说:"我……我摘的……"没想到疯娘还会摘野桃,儿子由衷地表扬她的疯娘。可以想象,疯娘从小到大没有买过一分钱的东西给儿子吃过,看到她儿子这样喜欢吃野鲜桃,而且儿子还表扬她,她肯定回头还要再给儿子摘些野鲜桃。要知道,这羊肠山路如果有野鲜桃,早被人家摘光了。如果还有,可能在那些悬崖峭壁上。儿子喜欢吃野鲜桃的样子,在疯娘心里挥之不去,最后,她冒着生命危险,到悬崖峭壁上摘儿子喜欢吃的野鲜桃。不幸的是,她从悬崖峭壁上摔了下去,摔死了。"娘静静地躺在谷底,周边是一些散落的桃子,她手里还紧紧攥着一个,身上的血早就凝固成了沉重的黑色。我悲痛得五脏俱裂,紧紧地抱住娘,说:'娘啊,我的苦命娘啊,儿悔不该说这桃子甜啊,是儿子要了你的命……'我将头贴在娘冰凉的脸上,哭得漫山遍野的石头都陪着落泪……"我们这里注意一个细节,她摔死的时候,手里还紧紧攥着一个桃子。这根本就不是桃子,是母爱,是以生命为代价的母爱。

Step 4:Reading with a focus on how to show parental love through what they thought
We'll look at showing parental love through what they thought. When you read, pay

attention to the signal word "think".

> And what makes my mother grieve right now, I think, is not simply that her mother will die in a day or two, but that once her mother dies, there will never again be someone to love her in quite such an unreserved and unquestioning way. No one else who believes that fifty years ago she could have put Shirley Temple out of a job, no one else who remembers the moment of her birth. She will only be a mother, then, not a daughter anymore. [From Text Ⅲ]

From this paragraph, we can see that maternal love is unreserved and unquestioning and that deep down in every mother's heart, her daughter is always the best. "No one else who believes that fifty years ago she could have put Shirley Temple out of a job" means "my grandmother believes that fifty years ago my mother could have put Shirley Temple out of a job", which is a good case in point.

Step 5: Reading with a focus on the most-used way and the least-used way to show parental love in the four texts

The whole class is divided into four groups. Each group reads one text with a focus on the most-used way to show parental love and the least-used way to show parental love. After 30 minutes, each group presents their products. The conclusion is naturally drawn from the four groups' presentations, that is, the most-used way to show parental love is through what they did and the least-used way to show parental love is through what they said with through what they thought in between.

Step 6: Summarization of parental love in the four texts

From the four texts we've just covered, we can see that whether you are a white-collar worker or a blue-collar worker, whether you are an American or a Chinese, whether you are sane or insane, the parental love remains the same, unreserved and unquestioning. Every time our parents tell us to get home safe, stay warm, have a good day, or sleep well, what they are really saying is that I love you. As children of our parents, we are so grateful to them that we shall never ask what our parents can do for us and we shall ask what we can do for our parents. In addition, we say to ourselves from the bottom of our hearts "*FAMILY*", which means "*F*ather *A*nd *M*other, *I L*ove *Y*ou!"

Step 7: Gratitude for parental love by singing the song *East or west*, *Mama is the best*

OK! Let's watch a video about "世上只有妈妈好" and sing along. I translate it into "East or west, Mama is the best". Most probably, you will think that this class is concerned with parental love, and ask where dad is in the song. "Ma" in Chinese can refer to both mum and dad. For instance,"皇阿玛"的"ma"是"爸爸"的意思。So, the first ma refers to mum and the second ma refers to dad.

Step 8：Assignment：Reading *Mother* with feelings

Mother

Those Childhood Days

When you came into the world, she held you in her arms.

You thanked her by weeping your eyes out.

When you were 1 year old, she fed you and bathed you.

You thanked her by crying all night long.

When you were 2 years old, she taught you to walk.

You thanked her by running away when she called.

When you were 3 years old, she made all your meals with love.

You thanked her by tossing your plate on the floor.

When you were 4 years old, she gave you some crayons.

You thanked her by coloring the dining room table.

When you were 5 years old, she dressed you for the holidays.

You thanked her by plopping into the nearest pile of mud.

When you were 6 years old, she walked you to school.

You thanked her by screaming, "I'm not going!"

When you were 7 years old, she bought you a baseball.

You thanked her by throwing it through the next-door-neighbor's window.

When you were 8 years old, she handed you an ice cream.

You thanked her by dripping it all over your lap.

When you were 9 years old, she paid for piano lessons.

You thanked her by never even bothering to practice.

When you were 10 years old, she drove you all day, from soccer to gymnastics to one birthday party after another.

You thanked her by jumping out of the car and never looking back.

When you were 11 years old, she took you and your friends to the movies.

You thanked her by asking to sit in a different row.

When you were 12 years old, she warned you not to watch certain TV shows.

You thanked her by waiting until she left the house.

Those Teenage Years

When you were 13, she suggested a haircut that was becoming.

You thanked her by telling her she had no taste.

When you were 14, she paid for a month away at summer camp.

You thanked her by forgetting to write a single letter.

When you were 15, she came home from work, looking for a hug.

You thanked her by having your bedroom door locked.

When you were 16, she taught you how to drive her car.

You thanked her by taking it every chance you could.

When you were 17, she was expecting an important call.

You thanked her by being on the phone all night.

When you were 18, she cried at your high school graduation.

You thanked her by staying out partying until dawn.

When you were 19, she paid your college tuition, drove you to campus, carried your bags.

You thanked her by saying good-bye outside the dorm so you wouldn't be embarrassed in front of your friends.

Growing Old and Gray

When you were 20, she asked whether you were seeing anyone.

You thanked her by saying, "It's none of your business. "

When you were 21, she suggested certain careers for your future.

You thanked her by saying, "I don't want to be like you. "

When you were 22, she hugged you at your college graduation.

You thanked her by asking whether she could pay for a trip to Europe.

When you were 23, she gave you furniture for your first apartment.

You thanked her by telling your friends it was ugly.

When you were 24, she met your fiancé and asked about your plans for the future.

You thanked her by glaring and growling, "Muuhh-ther, please!"

When you were 25, she helped to pay for your wedding, and she cried and told you how deeply she loved you.

You thanked her by moving halfway across the country.

When you were 30, she called with some advice on the baby.

You thanked her by telling her, "Things are different now. "

When you were 40, she called to remind you of a relative's birthday.

You thanked her by saying you were "really busy right now. "

When you were 50, she fell ill and needed you to take care of her.

You thanked her by reading about the burden parents become to their children.

And then one day she quietly died.

And everything you never did came crashing down like thunder.

"Rock me baby, rock me all night long. "

"The hand who rocks the cradle... may rock the world".

Let us take a moment of the time just to pay tribute and show appreciation to the person called MOM though some may not say it openly to their mother. There's no substitute for her. Cherish every single moment. Though at times she may not be the best of friends, may not agree to our thoughts, she is still your mother!

Your mother will be there for you; to listen to your woes, your brags, your frustrations, etc. Ask yourself "Have you put aside enough time for her, to listen to her 'blues' of working in the kitchen, her tiredness?"

Be tactful, loving and still show her due respect, though you may have a different view from hers. Once gone, only fond memories of the past and also regrets will be left.

Do not take for granted the things closest to your heart. Love her more than you love yourself. Life is meaningless without her.

Ⅱ. Analysis

在对本教学设计进行分析前,我们先来看两个小故事。

第一个故事

Eleanor's younger brother Freder was a simple youth. One day, Eleanor's husband, Babo, went to Africa in a hunting trip accompanied by Freder. About 3 weeks later, she received a telegram from her brother saying: "Babo died in hunting a lion."

In great sorrow, Eleanor sent an answer to her brother saying: "Send the dead body home."

Three weeks later, a parcel arrived from Africa in which was the corpse of a lion.

Eleanor sent an urgent telegram back to Freder: "Lion received. You are wrong. Wanted dead Babo." The next day she received a final telegram from Freder: "I'm not wrong. Babo and one of my legs are in the abdominal cavity of the lion."

第二个故事

大清乾隆朝王翰林为母亲做寿,请纪晓岚即席做个祝寿词助兴。老纪也不推辞,当着满堂宾客脱口而出:"这个婆娘不是人。"老夫人一听脸色大变,王翰林十分尴尬。老纪不慌不忙念出了第二句:"九天仙女下凡尘。"顿时全场活跃、交口称赞,老夫人也转怒为喜。老纪接着高声朗读第三句:"生的儿子都是贼。"满场宾客变成哑巴,欢悦变成难堪。老纪喊出第四句:"偷得仙桃献母亲。"大家立刻欢呼起来。

第一个故事是一篇在美国夺得大奖的超短篇小说,总共才116个词。然而,在这有限的篇幅里,作者的笔墨时而顺向,时而逆向,竟掀起了三次大的艺术波澜。巴布与其妻弟去非洲打猎度假,然而却"猎狮身死",此一波澜;妻子想见丈夫一面,今弟运尸回来,然而运回的却是"狮尸",此二波澜;妻子再复电说有误,弟弟再回电说"无误,巴布在狮腹内",此三波澜。这三次波澜,都是由顺向发展与逆向回答相结合而构成的,委婉曲折,错落有致,情节完整,变化多姿,给人以完美的艺术享受。

第二个故事同样也波澜起伏。纪晓岚在为大清乾隆朝王翰林母亲做寿时,做了四句诗,每句诗都是一个波澜。王翰林本来请纪晓岚即席做个祝寿词助兴,没想到纪晓岚出口就说了句:"这个婆娘不是人。"这使得老夫人一听脸色大变,王翰林十分尴尬。此为第一波澜。

纪晓岚不慌不忙念出了第二句:"九天仙女下凡尘。"顿时全场活跃、交口称赞,老夫人也转怒为喜。此为第二波澜。纪晓岚接着高声朗读第三句:"生的儿子都是贼。"满场宾客变成哑巴,欢悦变成难堪。此为第三波澜。纪晓岚喊出第四句:"偷得仙桃献母亲。"大家立刻欢呼起来。此为第四波澜。

事实上,优秀的教学设计和扣人心弦的故事一样,也应该波澜起伏。本教学设计最大特点也有三个波澜。第一个波澜在导入,学生在做问卷调查时,由于问卷上只是说"他"和"她",学生往往下意识地把他们看成情侣关系。因此,当"她"毁容和当"他"破产时,情侣关系会发生巨大的变化,甚至会分手。而当老师把他们的关系改为父母和孩子的关系时,即使女儿毁容,儿子破产,父母对他们的爱仍没有变化。这样,就引出这节课的主题:父母对孩子的爱。第二个波澜在第六步:对四篇课文的总结。由父母对孩子的爱变成孩子要对父母感恩,要爱父母。第三个波澜在第七步:唱《世上只有妈妈好》,老师把它翻译成了"East or west, Mama is the best"。因为本课的主题父母的爱,而这首歌里只有妈妈,没有爸爸。而清朝皇子和公主对父皇称"皇阿玛",这里的"ma"是"爸爸"的意思。这样,这首歌里既有妈妈也有爸爸。

此外,检验一个英语教学设计的标准是看它是否有效果(effective)、是否有效率(efficient)和是否激发学生的兴趣(appealing)。上完课后,曾有学生跑到我身边说:"这节课让我终身难忘""听老师一节课,胜读十年书",说明这节课有效果。四篇课文字数近 8 千,正常情况需要 6—7 节课上完。经过精心设计后,四篇课文只要两节课的时间,说明这节课有效率。在四篇课文的教学中,有学生竟然流下了眼泪,说明这节课激发了学生的兴趣。

Ⅲ. Full Texts

Text 1

The Law vs. the Piano

My father was a lawyer with no sons, so he decided that his older daughter, Susie, would follow his career and take over his business when he died. When Susie was in kindergarten, he began to work on her: "Susie," he would say, "you will never have to worry about a thing, for I have paved all the roads for you. I have done all the dirty work in establishing a good business in law, and all you will have to do is take it over."

By the time Susie could read and write, my father read law books to her at bedtime. The dull passages lulled her to sleep, but some of the legal terms became fixed in her mind. He enjoyed having her show off to visitors in his office and his business associates were amazed at her recitations of difficult passages.

Susie's brainwashing continued through her high school years, and when she finished high school, she obediently followed my father to the university where he guided her into the first-semester courses needed to enter Law School.

Everything went smoothly for a while, and no one in the family was aware of the slow change that came over Susie, although she did seem to show poor understanding of law sometimes.

One day, Susie announced that she would like to take piano lessons. Dad, a supporter of all forms of education, did not oppose her wishes. He just reminded her that one lesson a week would be enough considering the heavy schedule she kept at the university. Susie seemed pleased and did not argue.

A piano teacher was chosen, an old, semi-retired lady, who came every Friday afternoon for 45 minutes. We all suspected that Dad agreed to that hour because the piano would be heard in his office next door at an hour when few clients would be present. Soon we became accustomed to the do-re-mi's—up and down the scale, down and up the scale. The added noise was not disturbing at the beginning because Susie practiced only half an hour each day, but gradually the practicing increased. Slowly but surely it began to interrupt the conversations between Dad and his clients next door when Susie gradually extended her practicing to several hours per day. Finally my father realized that as the piano playing had increased, the study of Law had decreased. The following excitement threw the Law Office and the entire family into disorder. Such scenes were seen now and then: "Susie," my father would shout, "good lawyers make good money and enjoy the secure future I have set up for you." Weeping wildly, Susie would respond, "But I like piano. I want to be a concert pianist." My mother made many useless attempts to make peace between them, but the battle continued. "Su-u-u-san," my father would shout slowly but forcefully, "Law—will—give—you—a—secure—and—profitable—future. Be—practical. Be—reasonable." But Susie was happy only when she was absorbed in music and was utterly miserable among her law books. She continued to respond simply, "I do not like law; I like to play the piano." In the end, my father would thunder like an echoing drum: "Reason. That's what you should use. REASON," and end the argument by slamming the door as he went back to his office.

Many tears later—with my seventy-year-old grandmother's help—there was a compromise. Susie agreed to continue in Law School until she could complete her Law Certificate, which involved three years. She would, however, continue to take piano lessons and to practice as often as her energy and that of the listeners at home would permit.

Susie stuck to her part of the compromise, and she was twenty-two years old when she completed requirements for the degree in Law. My father was so proud that he organized a champagne party and invited all his friends. He was ready to stand by Susie's side, to greet well-meaning friends and relatives, and to receive the traditional compliments as he shook hands with those who sang praises to his wisdom in guiding his daughter toward a promising career in Law.

But Susie became quite ill and began vomiting before the guests arrived. Mother's medicine did not help. Grandmother's prayers did not help. Even Susie could not help, no matter how much she wanted to, for in her heart she knew she was not going to fulfill her father's dream: She intended to become a concert pianist.

And she did just that. Years later, after Susie became a concert pianist of some fame and a visiting lecturer at one of the best universities on the East Coast, Father was almost as proud of her as he would have been to see her a lawyer. But he never did admit that Susie is a reasonable woman.

Text 2

Bricklayer's Boy

My father and I were both at the same college back in the mid 1970s while I was in class at Columbia, he was on a bricklayer's scaffold not far from the street, working on a campus building.

Sometimes we'd took the subway home together, he with his tools, I with my books. We didn't chat much about what went on during the day. My father wasn't interested in Dante, I wasn't interested in buildings. We'd share a New York Post and talk about the baseball.

My dad has built lots of places in New York City he can't get into. It doesn't bother him, though. For him, earning the cash that paid for my entry into a good university was satisfaction enough. We didn't know it then, but those days were the start of a separation between us. Related by blood, we're separated by class. I am the white-collar son of a blue-collar man.

Despite the myth of mobility in America, the true rule, experts say, is rags to rags, riches to riches. According to Bucknell University economist and author Charles Sackrey, maybe 10 percent climb from the working to the professional class. My father has had a tough time accepting my decision to become a mere newspaper reporter, a field that pays just a little more than construction does. He wonders why I haven't taken a profitable job like a lawyer. After bricklaying for thirty years, my father promised himself I'd take a better job and earn more money with an education. He didn't want his son to break blue-collar rule No. 1 : Make as much money as you can, to pay for as good a life as you can get. He'd tell me about it when I was nineteen :"You better make a lot of money. "

In 1980, after college and graduate school, I was offered my first job, on a daily paper in Columbus, Ohio. I broke the news in the kitchen, where all the family business is discussed. My mother wept as if it were Vietnam. My father had a few questions :"Ohio? Where the hell is Ohio?"

I said it's somewhere west of New York City. I told him I wanted to write, and these were the only people who'd take me.

"Why can't you get a good job that pays something, like in advertising in the city, and write in your spare time?"

Advertising is lying," I said. "I wanna tell the truth. "

"The truth?" the old man exploded, his face reddening. "What's truth?" I said it's real life, and writing about it would make me happy. "You're happy with your family," my father said, stating blue-collar rule No. 2 "That's what makes you happy. After that, it all comes down to dollars and cents. What gives you comfort besides your family? Money, only money."

During the two weeks before I moved, he reminded me that newspaper journalism is a dying field, and I could do better. The he pressed advertising again, though neither of us really knew anything about it, except that you could work in Manhattan, the island polished clean by money. I could not explain myself, so I packed, unpopular and confused. No longer was I the good son who studied hard and did things as expected. However, after I said my good-byes, my father took me aside and pressed five $100 bills into my hands. "It's okay," he said over my weak protests. "Don't tell your mother."

When I broke the news about what the paper was paying me, my father suggested I get a part-time job to supplement my income. "Maybe you could drive a cab." Once, after I was blamed by the editor for something trivial, I made the mistake of telling my father during a visit home. "They pay you nothin', and they push you around too much in that business," he told me angrily. "Next time, you gotta grab the guy by the throat and tell him he's a big jerk."

"Dad, I can't talk to the boss like that."

"Tell him. You get results that way. Never take any shit." A few years before, a guy didn't like the wall my father and his partner had built. They tore it down and did it again, but the guy still complained. My father's partner pushed the guy onto the freshly laid bricks. "Pay me off," my father said, and he and his partner took the money and walked away. Eventually, I moved on to a job in Cleveland, on a paper my father has heard of. I think he looks on it as a sign of progress, because he hasn't mentioned advertising for a while.

When he was my age, my father was already married and had two sons and a house in a neighborhood in Brooklyn not far from where he was born. I live in a dormitory-like place in Cleveland suburb, in a student kind of unmarried and carefree way. I rent movies during the week and feed single women in restaurants on Saturday nights. My dad asks me about my dates, but goes crazy over the word "woman." "A girl," he corrects. "You went out with a girl. Don't say 'woman.' It sounds like you're taking out your grandmother."

I've often believed blue-collaring is the more genuine of lives. My father is provider and protector, concerned only with the basics: food and home, love and children. I live for my career, and frequently feel lost, lacking the blue-collar rules my father grew up with.

My father isn't crazy about this life. He wanted to be a singer and actor when he was young, but that was silly fancy to his Italian family, who expected him to live a steady life. My dad learned a trade, as he was supposed to, and settled into a life as expected of him.

My brother Chris has a lot more blue-collar in him than I do, despite his management-level career; for a short time, he wanted to be a construction worker, but my parents persuaded him to go to Columbia. It was Chris who helped my dad most when my father tried to change his life several months ago. My dad wanted a bricklayer foreman's job that wouldn't be so physically demanding. There was a written test that included essay questions about construction work. My father hadn't done anything like that in forty years, but he worked very hard on it. Every morning before sunrise, Chris would be ironing a shirt, and my father would sit at the kitchen table and read aloud his practice essays on how to wash down a wall, or how to build a corner. Chris would suggest words and approaches. It was hard for my dad. He had to take a prep course in a junior high school three nights a week after work for six weeks.

"Is this what finals felt like?" my father would ask me on the phone. "Were you always this nervous?" I told him yes. I told him writing is always difficult. He thanked Chris and me for coaching, for putting him through school this time. My father thinks he did okay, but he's still awaiting the test results. In the meantime, he lives his life in the usual way.

When we see each other these days, my father still asks how the money is. Sometimes he reads my stories; usually he likes them, although he recently criticized one piece as being a bit sentimental.

During one of my visits to Brooklyn not long ago, he and I were in the car, on our way to a supermarket, one of my father's weekly routines. "You know, you're not as successful as you could be," he began as usual. "You paid your dues in school. You deserve better restaurants, better clothes." Here we go, I thought, the same old stuff. I'm sure every family has five or six similar big issues that are replayed like well-worn videotapes. I wanted to change this topic when we stopped at a red light.

Just then my father turned to me, solemn and intense. "I envy you," he said quietly. "For a man to do something he likes and get paid for it—that's fantastic." He smiled at me before the light changed, and we drove on. To thank him for the understanding, I bought the deodorant and shampoo. For once, my father let me pay.

Text 3

Four Generations

My mother called to tell me that my grandmother was dying. She had refused an operation that would postpone, but not prevent, her death from pancreatic cancer. She could no longer eat, she had been hemorrhaging, and she had severe jaundice. "I always prided myself on being different," she told my mother. "Now I *am* different. I'm yellow."

My mother, telling me this news, began to cry. So I became the mother for a moment, reminding her, reasonably, that my grandmother was eighty-seven, she'd had a full life, she had all her faculties, and no one who knew her could wish that she live long enough to lose them. Lately my mother had begun finding notes in my grandmother's drawers at the nursing home, reminding her, "Joyce's husband's name is Steve. Their daughter is named Audrey." In the last few years, she hadn't had the strength to cook or garden, and she'd begun to say that she'd had enough of living.

My grandmother was born in Russia, in 1892, the oldest daughter of a large and prosperous Jewish family. But the prosperity didn't last. She used to tell stories of the pogroms and the

Cossacks who raped her when she was twelve. Soon after that her family emigrated to Canada, where she met my grandfather.

Their children were the center of their life. The story I loved best as a child was of my grandfather opening every box of Cracker Jacks in the general store he ran, in search of the particular toy my mother coveted. Though they never had much money, my grandmother saw to it that her daughter had elocution lessons and piano lessons, and assured her that she would go to college.

But while she was at college my mother met my father, who was blue-eyed and blond-haired and not Jewish. When my father sent love letters to my mother, my grandmother would open and hide them, and when my mother told her parents she was going to marry this man, my grandmother said if that happened, it would kill her.

Not likely, of course. My grandmother was a woman who used to crack Brazil nuts open with her teeth, a woman who once lifted a car off the ground when there was an accident and it had to be moved. She had been representing her death as imminent ever since I could remember, and had discussed, at length, the distribution of her possessions and her lamb coat. Every time we said goodbye, after our annual visit to Winnipeg, she'd weep and say she might never see us again. But in the meantime, while nearly every other relative of her generation, and a good many younger ones, had died (nursed usually by her) she kept making knishes, shopping for bargains, tending the healthiest plants I've ever seen.

After my grandfather died, my grandmother lived, more than ever, through her children. When she came to visit, I would hide my diary. She couldn't understand any desire for privacy. She couldn't bear it if my mother left the house without her.

This made my mother furious (and then guilt-ridden that she felt that way, when of course she owed so much to her mother). So I harbored the resentment that my mother, the dutiful daughter, would not allow herself. I, who had always performed specially well for my grandmother—danced and sung for her, presented her with kisses and good report cards—stopped writing to her, ceased to visit.

But when I heard she was dying I realized I wanted to go to Winnipeg to see her one more time. Mostly to make my mother happy, I told myself (certain patterns being hard to break). But also, I was offering up one more particularly successful accomplishment: my own dark-eyed, dark skinned, dark-haired daughter, whom my grandmother had never met.

I put my daughter's best dress on her for our visit to Winnipeg, the way the best dresses were always put on me. I filled my pockets with animal crackers in case Audrey started to cry. I scrubbed her face mercilessly. On the elevator going up to her room, I realized how much I was sweating.

Grandma was lying flat with an IV tube in her arm and her eyes shut, but she opened them when I leaned over to kiss her. "It's Fredelle's daughter, Joyce," I yelled, because she didn't hear well any more, but I could see that no explanation was necessary. "You came," she said. "You brought the baby."

Audrey was just one, but she had already seen enough of the world to know that people in beds are not meant to be still and yellow, and she looked frightened. I had never wanted more for her to smile.

Then Grandma waved at her—the same kind of slow, finger-flexing wave a baby makes— and Audrey waved back. I spread her toys out on my grandmother's bed and sat her down. There she stayed most of the afternoon, playing and humming and sipping on her bottle, taking a nap at one point, leaning against my grandmother's leg. When I cranked her Snoopy guitar, Audrey stood up on the bed and danced. Grandma couldn't talk much any more, though every once in a while she would say how sorry she was that she wasn't having a better day. "I'm not always like this," she said.

Mostly she just watched Audrey. Sometimes Audrey would get off the bed, inspect the get-well cards, totter down the hall. "Where is she?" Grandma kept asking. "Who's looking after her?" I had the feeling, even then, that if I'd said "Audrey's lighting matches," Grandma would have shot up to rescue her.

We were flying home that night, and I had dreaded telling her, remembering all those other tearful partings. But in the end, I was the one who cried. She said she was ready to die. But as I leaned over to stroke her forehead, what she said was, "I wish I had your hair," and, "I wish I was well."

On the plane flying home, with Audrey in my arms, I thought about mothers and daughters, and the four generations of the family that I know most intimately. Every one of those mothers loves and needs her daughter more than her daughter will love or need her some day, and we are, each of us, the only person on earth who is quite so consumingly interested in our child.

Sometimes, I kiss and hug Audrey so much she starts crying, which is in effect what my grandmother was doing to my mother all her life. And what makes my mother grieve right now, I think, is not simply that her mother will die in a day or two, but that once her mother dies, there will never again be someone to love her in quite such an unreserved and unquestioning way. No one else who believes that fifty years ago she could have put Shirley Temple out of a job, no one else who remembers the moment of her birth. She will only be a mother, then, not a daughter anymore. Audrey and I stopped over for a night in Toronto, where my mother lives. Tomorrow, she will go to a safe deposit box at the bank to take out the receipt for my grandmother's burial plot. Then she will fly back to Winnipeg, where, for the first time in anybody's memory, there was waist-high snow on April Fool's Day. But tonight, she is feeding me as she always does when I come, and I am eating more than I do anywhere else. I admire the wedding china (once my grandmother's) that my mother has set on the table. She said (the way

Grandma used to say to her of the lamb coat）, "Someday it will be yours. "

Text 4

疯　娘

23 年前,有个年轻的女子流落到我们村,蓬头垢面,见人就傻笑,且毫不避讳地当众小便。因此,村里的媳妇们常对着那女子吐口水,有的媳妇还上前踹几脚,叫她"滚远些"。可她就是不走,依然傻笑着在村里转悠。

那时,我父亲已有 35 岁。他曾在石料场干活被机器绞断了左手,又因家穷,一直没娶媳妇。奶奶见那女子还有几分姿色,就动了心思,决定收下她给我父亲做媳妇,给我家"续上香火"。父亲虽老大不情愿,但看着家里这番光景,咬咬牙还是答应了。结果,父亲一分未花,就当了新郎。

娘生下我的时候,奶奶抱着我,瘪着没剩几颗牙的嘴欣喜地说:"这疯婆娘,还给我生了个带把儿的孙子。"只是,我一生下来,奶奶就把我抱走了,而且从不让娘靠近。

娘一直想抱抱我,多次在奶奶面前吃力地喊:"给,给我……"奶奶没理她。我那么小,像个肉嘟嘟,万一娘失手把我掉在地上怎么办? 毕竟,娘是个疯子。每当娘有抱我的请求时,奶奶总瞪起眼睛训她:"你别想抱孩子,我不会给你的。要是我发现你偷抱了他,我就打死你。即使不打死,我也要把你撵走。"奶奶说这话时,没有半点儿含糊的意思。娘听懂了,满脸的惶恐,每次只是远远地看着我。尽管娘的奶胀得厉害,可我没能吃到娘的半口奶水,是奶奶一匙一匙把我喂大的。奶奶说娘的奶水里有"神经病",要是传染给我就麻烦了。

那时,我家依然在贫困的泥潭里挣扎。特别是添了娘和我后。奶奶决定把娘撵走,因为娘不但在家吃"闲饭",时不时还惹是生非。一天,奶奶煮了一大锅饭,亲手给娘添了一大碗,说:"媳妇儿,这个家太穷了,婆婆对不起你。你吃完这碗饭,就去找个富点儿的人家过日子,以后也不准来了,啊?"娘刚扒拉一大团饭在口里,听了奶奶下的"逐客令"。显得非常吃惊,一团饭就在嘴里凝滞了。娘望着奶奶怀中的我,口齿不清地哀叫:"不,不要……"奶奶猛地沉下脸,拿出威严的家长作风厉声吼道:"你这个疯婆娘,撵什么撵,撵下去没你的好果子吃。你本来就是到处流浪的,我收留了你两年了,你还要怎么样? 吃完饭就走,听到没有?"说完奶奶从门后拿出一柄锄,像佘太君的龙头杖似的往地上重重一磕,"咚"地发出一声响。娘吓了一大跳,怯怯地看着婆婆,又慢慢低下头去看面前的饭碗,有泪水落在白花花的米饭上。在奶奶逼视下,娘突然有个很奇怪的举动,她将碗中的饭分了一大半给另一只空碗,然后可怜巴巴地看着奶奶。

奶奶呆了,原来,娘是向奶奶表示,每餐只吃半碗饭,只求别赶她走。奶奶的心仿佛被人狠狠揪了几把,奶奶也是女人,她的强硬态度也是装出来的。奶奶别过头,生生地将热泪憋了回去,然后重新板起了脸说:"快吃快吃,吃了快走。"娘似乎绝望了,连那半碗饭也没吃,跟跟跄跄地出了门,却长时间站在门前不走。奶奶硬着心肠说:"你走,你走,不要回头。"娘反而走拢来,一双手伸向婆婆怀里,原来,娘想抱抱我。奶奶犹豫了一下,还是将襁褓中的我递给了娘。娘第一次将我搂在怀里,咧开嘴笑了,笑得春风满面。奶奶却如临大敌,两手在我身下接着,生怕娘的疯劲一上来,将我像扔垃圾一样丢掉。娘抱我的时间不足三分钟,奶奶便迫不及待地将我夺了过去,然后转身进屋关上了门。

当我懵懵懂懂地晓事时,我才发现,除了我,别的小伙伴都有娘。我找父亲要,找奶奶要,他们说,你娘死了。可小伙伴却告诉我:"你娘是疯子,被你奶奶赶走了。"我便找奶奶扯皮,要她还我娘,还骂她是"狼外婆",甚至将她端给我的饭菜泼了一地。那时我还没有"疯"的概念,只知道非常想念她,她长什么样?还活着吗?没想到,在我六岁那年,离家5年的娘居然回来了。那天,几个小伙伴飞也似的跑来报信:"小树,快去看,你娘回来了,你的疯娘回来了。"我喜得屁颠屁颠的,撒腿就往外跑,父亲奶奶随着我也追了出来。这是我有记忆后第一次看到娘。她还是破衣烂衫,头发上还有些枯黄的碎草末,天知道是在哪个草堆里过的夜。娘不敢进家门,却面对着我家,坐在村前稻场的石磙上,手里还拿着个脏兮兮的气球。当我和一群小伙伴站在她面前时,她急切地从我们中间搜寻她的儿子。娘终于盯住我,死死地盯住我,咧着嘴叫我:"小树……球……球"她站起来,不停地扬着手中的气球,讨好地往我怀里塞。我却一个劲儿地往后退。我大失所望,没想到我日思夜想的娘居然是这样一副形象。一个小伙伴在一旁起哄说:"小树,你现在知道疯子是什么样了吧?就是你娘这样的。"

我气愤地对小伙伴说:"她是你娘!你娘才是疯子,你娘才是这个样子。"我扭头就跑了。这个疯娘我不要了。奶奶和父亲却把娘领进了门。当年,奶奶撵走娘后,她的良心受到了拷问,随着一天天衰老,她的心再也硬不起来,所以主动留下了娘,而我老大不乐意,因为娘丢了我的面子。

我从没给娘好脸色看,从没跟她主动说过话,更没有喊她一声"娘",我们之间的交流是以我"吼"为主,娘是绝不敢顶嘴的。

家里不能白养着娘,奶奶决定训练娘做些杂活。下地劳动时,奶奶就带着娘出去"观摩",稍不听话就要挨打。

过了些日子,奶奶以为娘已被自己训练得差不多了,就叫娘单独出去割猪草。没想到,娘只用了半小时就割了两筐"猪草"。奶奶一看,又急又慌,娘割的是人家田里正生浆拔穗的稻谷。奶奶气急败坏地骂她"疯婆娘谷草不分……"奶奶正想着如何善后时,稻田的主人找来了,竟说是奶奶故意教唆的。奶奶火冒三丈,当着人家的面拿出根棒槌一下敲在娘的后腰上,说:"打死你这个疯婆娘,你给老娘些……"

娘虽疯,疼还是知道的,她一跳一跳地躲着奶奶的棒槌,口里不停地发出"别、别……"的哀号。最后,人家看不过眼,主动说"算了,我们不追究了。以后把她看严点就是……"这场风波平息后,娘歪在地上抽泣着。我鄙夷地对她说:"草和稻子都分不清,你真是个猪。"话音刚落,我的后脑勺挨了一巴掌,是奶奶打的。奶奶瞪着眼骂我:"小兔崽子,你怎么说话的?再怎么着,她也是你娘啊!"我不屑地嘴一撇:"我没有这样的傻疯娘!"

"嗬,你真是越来越不像话了。看我不打你!"奶奶又举起巴掌,这时只见娘像弹簧一样从地上跳起,横在我和奶奶中间,娘指着自己的头,"打我、打我"地叫着。

我懂了,娘是叫奶奶打她,别打我。奶奶举在半空中的手颓然垂下,嘴里喃喃地说道:"这个疯婆娘,心里也知道疼爱自己的孩子啊!"我上学不久,父亲被邻村一位养鱼专业户请去守鱼池,每月能赚50元。娘仍在奶奶带领下出门干活,主要是打猪草,她没再惹什么大的乱子。

记得我读小学三年级时一个冬日,天空突然下起了雨,奶奶让娘给我送雨伞。娘可能一路摔了好几跤,浑身像个泥猴似的,她站在教室的窗户旁望着我傻笑,口里还叫:"树……伞……"一些同学嘻嘻地笑。带头起哄的是小范,当他还在夸张地模仿时,我抓起面前的文具盒,猛地向他砸过去。他冲上前来掐住我的脖子,我俩厮打起来。我个子小,根本不是他的对手,被他轻易压在地上。这时,只听教室外传来"嗷"的一声长啸,娘像个大侠似的飞跑进来,一把抓起小范,拖到了屋外。都说疯子力气大,真是不假。娘双手将欺负我的小范举向半空,他吓得哭爹喊娘,一双胖乎乎的小腿在空中乱踢蹬。娘毫不理会,居然将他丢到了学校门口的水塘里,然后一脸漠然地走开了。

娘为我闯了大祸,她却像没事似的。在我面前,娘又恢复了一副怯怯的神态,讨好地看着我。我明白这就是母爱,即使神志不清,母爱也是清醒的,因为她的儿子遭到了别人的欺负。当时我情不自禁地叫了声:"娘!"这是我会说话以来第一次喊她。娘浑身一震,久久地看着我,然后像个孩子似的羞红了脸,咧了咧嘴,傻傻地笑了。那天,我们母子俩第一次共撑一把伞回家。我把这事跟奶奶说了,奶奶吓得跌倒在椅子上,连忙请人去把爸爸叫了回来。爸爸刚进屋,一群拿着刀棒的壮年男人闯进我家,不分青红皂白,先将锅碗瓢盆砸了个稀巴烂。这都是范家请来的人,范父恶狠狠地指着爸爸的鼻子说:"我儿子吓出了神经病,现在卫生院躺着。你家要不拿出1 000块钱的医药费,我一把火烧了你家的房子。"

1 000块?爸爸每月才50块钱啊!看着杀气腾腾的范家人,爸爸的眼睛慢慢烧红了,他用非常恐怖的目光盯着娘,一只手飞快地解下腰间的皮带,劈头盖脸地向娘打去。一下又一下,娘像只惶惶偷生的老鼠,无助地跳着、躲着,她发出的凄厉声以及皮带抽在她身上发出的那种清脆的声响,我一辈子都忘不了。最后还是派出所所长赶来制止了爸爸施暴的手。派出所的调解结果是,双方互有损失,两不亏欠。谁再闹就抓谁!一帮人走后,爸看看满屋狼藉的锅碗碎片,又看看伤痕累累的娘,他突然将娘搂在怀里痛哭起来,说:"疯婆娘,不是我硬要打你,我要不打你,这事下不了地,咱们没钱赔人家啊。"爸又看着我说:"树儿,你一定要争气。要不,咱们就这样被人欺负一辈子啊!"我懂事地点点头。

2000年夏,我以优异成绩考上了高中。积劳成疾的奶奶不幸去世,家里的日子更难了。民政局将我家列为特困家庭,每月补助40元钱,我所在的高中也适当减免了我的学杂费,我这才得以继续读下去。

由于是住读,学习又抓得紧,我很少回家。父亲依旧在为50元打工,为我送菜的担子就责无旁贷地落在娘身上。每次总是隔壁的婶婶帮忙为我炒好咸菜,然后交给娘送来。20公里的羊肠山路亏娘牢牢地记了下来,风雨无阻。也真是奇迹,凡是为儿子做的事,娘一点儿也不疯。除了母爱,我无法解释这种现象在医学上应该怎么破译。

2003年4月的一个星期天,娘来了,不但为我送来了菜,还带来了十几个野鲜桃。我拿起一个,咬了一口,笑着问她:"挺甜的,哪来的?"娘说:"我……我摘的……"没想到娘还会摘野桃,我由衷地表扬她:"娘,您真是越来越能干了。"娘嘿嘿地笑了。

娘临走前,我照例叮嘱她注意安全,娘"哦哦"地应着。送走娘,我又扎进了高考前最后的复习中。第二天,我正在上课,婶婶匆匆地赶到学校,问我娘送菜来没有,说我娘到现在还没回家。我心一紧,娘该不会走错道吧?婶婶问:"你娘没说什么?"我说没有,她给我带了十几个野鲜桃哩。婶婶两手一拍:"坏了坏了,可能就坏在这野鲜桃上。"婶婶替我请了假,我们沿着山路往回找,回家的路上确有几棵野桃树,桃树上稀稀拉拉地挂着几个桃子,因为长在峭壁上才得以保存下来。我们同时发现一棵桃树有枝丫折断的痕迹,树下是百丈深渊。婶婶看了看我说,"到峭壁底下去看看吧!"我说,"婶婶你别吓我……"婶婶不由分说,拉着我就往山谷里走……

娘静静地躺在谷底,周边是一些散落的桃子,她手里还紧紧攥着一个,身上的血早就凝固成了沉重的黑色。我悲痛得五脏俱裂,紧紧地抱住娘,说:"娘啊,我的苦命娘啊,儿悔不该说这桃子甜啊,是儿子要了你的命……"我将头贴在娘冰凉的脸上,哭得漫山遍野的石头都陪着落泪……

2003 年 8 月 7 日,在娘下葬后的第 100 天,大学烫金的录取通知书穿过娘所走过的路,穿过那几株野桃树,穿过村前的稻场,径直"飞"进了我的家门。我把这份迟到的书信插在娘冷寂的坟头:"娘,儿出息了,您听到了吗? 您可以含笑九泉了!"

Case 2 ## Instructional Design of *Storytellers* from the Perspective of Education and Analysis

I . Instructional Design of *Storytellers* from the Perspective of Education

Step 1: Lead-in with a discussion on the questions about a better education

Before we learn *Storytellers* by Mo Yan, I'd like to ask you some questions. Who received a better education, Mo Yan or Li Tianyi? Why do you think so? It is not surprising that almost all the students think that Li received a better education, because he went to one of the best schools in China, where they have very good teachers, very good facilities and very good environments. Mo had only less than five years of primary education without graduation. The school he attended was not good in terms of teachers, facilities and environments. But a good school does not mean a good education. Let's look at their names first. Mo Yan means "don't speak". His parents often cautioned him not to speak, for trouble comes out of mouth and whoever talks much is bound to have a slip of tongue. Li Tianyi means "I am No. 1 in the world". You can imagine that whoever thinks he is No. 1 in the world will look down upon others and will show no respect for them. Next, let's look at the result. Mo Yan received the Nobel Prize in Literature and Li received ten-year imprisonment. Their differences are poles apart. We will look at what kind of education Mo received.

Step 2: Close reading with a focus on Mo Yan's moral education

When he got the Nobel Prize in Literature, Mo Yan missed his mother most, because she influenced him most and everyone except her in his family shared the honor of winning this prize. So the first few stories he told in his speech were all about his mother.

The first story is about his breaking the only vacuum bottle when he went to fetch drinking water. Mo Yan had seven siblings: three brothers and four sisters, in other words, his parents had eight children altogether. In the age of extreme poverty, only half of them survived, that is, his two brothers and his sister and Mo Yan himself. At that time, there were at least six people in his family: his parents, his three siblings and himself. Maybe there were more than six people if his grandparents lived with them. Just imagine at least six people shared one vacuum bottle. We can see how poor they were. By the way, I once asked how many vacuum bottles the students at College of Foreign Studies, Yangzhou University had, about 60% had two, and two students even had three. Because of poverty, he did not have enough to eat, which resulted in his great weakness. He became so weak that he dropped the bottle and broke it. When he realized that he had made such a big trouble, he was scared witless, or simply to death or out of senses. He hid all day in a haystack, without eating anything at all, which increased his hunger intensely. Toward evening, he heard his mother calling his childhood name, which indicates that "I love you. Come back home". If his mother called his full name in an angry voice, most probably, he dared not crawl out of his hiding place. He was prepared to receive a beating or a scolding since he had made the biggest trouble. But his mother neither hit him nor even scolded him. She just rubbed his head and heaved a sigh. All these including calling his childhood name, not beating or scolding, and rubbing his head show Mo Yan was loved. So that's education of love.

Let's digress a little and look at a short story entitled *Used vs. Loved*.

> While a man was polishing his new car, his 4-year-old son picked up a stone and scratched lines on the side of the car. In anger, the man took the child's hand and hit it many times, not realizing he was using a wrench.
>
> At the hospital, the child lost all his fingers due to multiple fractures. When the child saw his father with painful eyes he asked, "Dad, when will my fingers grow back?" The man was so hurt and speechless; he went back to his car and kicked it a lot of times.
>
> Devastated by his own actions ... sitting in front of that car he looked at the scratches; the child had written "I LOVE YOU, DAD".
>
> The next day that man committed suicide....

Anger and Love have no limits; choose the latter to have a beautiful, lovely life.... Things are to be used and people are to be loved. But the problem in today's world is that people are used and things are loved.... Let's be careful to keep this thought in mind:

> Things are to be used, but People are to be loved.
> Watch your thoughts; they become words. Watch your words; they become actions. Watch your actions; they become habits. Watch your habits; they become character. Watch your character; it becomes your destiny.

By comparing Mo Yan's mother with the man, we can find some big differences between them.

The second story is about his going out in the collective's field with his mother to glean ears of wheat. And she was caught by the watchman, a hulk of a man because she had bound feet. She was slapped so hard that she fell to the ground with her lip bleeding. His mother wore a look of hopelessness he would never forget. Years later, when Mo Yan encountered the watchman, a gray-haired old man, in the marketplace, he thought of what had happened to them and wanted to avenge his mother by beating him or slapping him. His mother had to stop him from beating the old man black and blue or even beating him to death. She said evenly to him, "the man who hit me and this man are not the same person." That is, his mother forgave the man who had slapped her. If we'll look at Deuteronomy in the *Bible*, we will find that Moses tells his people that "the punishment is to be a life for a life, an eye for an eye, a tooth for a tooth, a hand for a hand and a foot for a foot". Since Moses actually speaks for God, we can regard these words as God's words. In a certain sense, Mo Yan's mother is greater than God, for she is forgiving. So that's education of forgiving.

The third story is about an aging beggar coming to Mo Yan's door for *jiaozi* on the Moon Festival. In those days, Mo Yan's family rarely ate *jiaozi*, one bowl apiece, just a couple of times a year. Can you guess why the beggar came to Mo Yan's door at the exact time when they were at table, neither too early nor too late? OK! In the times of extreme poverty and extreme hunger, if someone cooked meat at home, you could smell it from a far-away place. We can imagine that the smell of *jiaozi* floated in the air and reached the beggar, who traced it back to Mo Yan's home. Apparently, the beggar came for nothing but *jiaozi*. So when Mo Yan wanted to send him away with half a bowlful of dried sweet potatoes, the beggar, quite unexpectedly, reacted angrily by saying that they were heartless. Hearing this, Mo Yan was just as angry and asked him to get the hell out of their home if he did not want sweet potatoes. When his mother saw this, she reprimanded or scolded Mo Yan for treating an old man like this. Do you still remember that his mother did not hit or scold him when he broke the only vacuum bottle at home? In her eyes, treating an old man like this was more severe than breaking the only vacuum bottle at home. She dumped her half bowlful of *jiaozi* into the old man's bowl to show her kindness or goodness. So that's education of kindness or goodness.

The fourth story is about his overcharging an old villager one *jiao* at market when he helped his mother sell cabbages. Most probably, the old villager came back to Mo Yan's mother for overcharged money after Mo Yan headed off to school. And most probably, the old villager said something to Mo Yan's mother so insulting, so humiliating, so embarrassing that made her cry. Do you still remember that his mother did not cry when she was slapped so hard that she fell to the ground with her lip bleeding? So we can see that overcharging someone or being dishonest hurt her more than being slapped with her lip bleeding. His mother did not scold him and instead merely said something like "you made your mother lose face", which taught Mo Yan to be honest. So that's education of honesty.

The fifth story is about his great worry about his mother when she contracted a serious lung disease. He was so worried that his mother might take her own life or commit suicide. So every day, the first thing he did when he walked in the door after a day of hard labor was call out for his mother. One day, after searching everywhere without finding her, he sat down in the yard and cried like a baby, which made his mother unhappy with him. This suggests that his mother asked him to be strong-willed or strong-minded and be a real man who does not shed tears easily. That's education of strong-willedness or strong-mindedness. She assured him that she would not commit suicide even though there was no joy in her life. Let's imagine that Mo Yan's mother had 8 children, half of whom had died, with the mortality rate reaching 50%. Do you know what it means to a mother when her child dies? One child's death means that she is stabbed once in the heart. The death of her four children meant she was stabbed four times in the heart. Their only vacuum bottle at home was broken by Mo Yan. When she gleaned ears of wheat, she was slapped so hard that she fell to the ground, with her lip bleeding. When she was eating *jiaozi* at the table, an aging beggar came to their door. She dumped her half bowlful of *jiaozi* into the old man's bowl. When she sold cabbages at market, with Mo Yan overcharging an old villager one *jiao*, she was insulted, humiliated and embarrassed by the old man. Besides, she contracted a serious lung disease. She said, "I won't leave you till the God of the Underworld calls me." So that's education of life cherishing.

The sixth story is about his appearance. Many people thought Mo Yan was ugly. Some laughed at him either behind his back or even to his face; others even beat him up because of his ugliness. His mother, however, did not think so. She said, "You're not ugly, Son. You've got a nose and two eyes, and there's nothing wrong with your arms and legs, so how could you be ugly? If you have a good heart and always do the right thing, what is considered ugly becomes beautiful." So that's education of beauty.

Besides, his mother did not like lazy children and did not like those smooth-talking men in a dubious profession. These mean his mother gave him education of diligence, education of "minding your own mouth" and education of "engagement in a decent job".

Step 3: Close reading with a focus on Mo Yan's intellectual education

In terms of intellectual education, I'd like to share my experiences in the U. S. during my stay there, I visited seven or eight elementary schools in Richmond, Virginia. All these schools without exception offer a class or a subject called *Story Hour* from Grade One to Grade Four when a teacher tells them stories every day. The school kids listen to stories every day for four years. Two schools offer more story hour for the fifth-graders and sixth-graders every other day. Surely, these stories help nurture and nourish them very much, which paves the way for their future intellectual development.

Let's look at Mo Yan's intellectual education. One part of his intellectual education involved retelling stories. A storyteller once came to the marketplace, and Mo Yan sneaked off to listen to him. That night, while his mother was stitching padded clothes for them under the weak light of a kerosene lamp, Mo Yan couldn't keep from retelling stories he had heard that day. Slowly she was dragged into his retold stories and from that day on, she gave him unspoken permission to go to the marketplace on market day and listen to new stories. As repayment for his mother's kindness and a way to demonstrate his memory, he'd retell the stories for her in vivid detail . . . . It did not take long to find retelling someone else's stories unsatisfying, so he began embellishing his narration . . . . He'd say things that would please his mother, even changed the ending once in a while.

Mo Yan did more and better than American graders. Mo Yan sneaked off to listen to the stories at the market place, which suggests that he was an active listener and was interested in them while American graders listen to the stories passively; maybe they were not interested in them. Mo Yan listened to the stories for the purpose of retelling them, which involved his attention, comprehension, memory and expression. "As repayment for his mother's kindness and a way to demonstrate his memory, he'd retell the stories for her in vivid detail . . . . ", which involved the effectiveness of expression. "It did not take long to find retelling someone else's stories unsatisfying, so he began embellishing his narration . . . . He'd say things that would please his mother, even changed the ending once in a while. ", which involved some creativity.

After dropping out of elementary school, Mo Yan became a cattle-and-sheep-herder on a nearby grassy riverbank. He turned the animals loose on the riverbank to graze beneath the blue sky. There was no other person in sight, no human sounds, nothing but bird calls above him. He was all by himself and terribly lonely. Sometimes he lay in the grass and watched clouds float lazily by, which gave rise to all sorts of fanciful images. He would fantasize a fox-turned-beautiful girl coming to tend animals with him. Sometimes he'd crouch down beside the cows and gaze into their deep blue eyes, eyes that captured his reflection. At times he'd have a dialogue with birds in the sky, mimicking their cries, while at other times he'd divulge my hopes and desires to a tree. All these helped develop a rich imagination.

After leaving school, Mo Yan had an early start on reading the great book of life. When he tended cattle and sheep, he observed grass-carpeted land, towering old trees, cows' deep blue eyes, birds, clouds and sky. When he was in the world of adults, he observed different kinds of men and women, many of whom later became the characters of his stories. In this way, Mo Yan developed a keen observation.

Mo Yan mixed what he heard, seen and read with his imagination, mixed domestic traditions with foreign techniques, mixed fiction with art from other realms like local opera, fine art, music, even acrobatics and turned them into stories, which help develop his combination and creativity.

In a nutshell, his intellectual education involves interest, attention, comprehension, memory，expression，observation，imagination，combination and creativity.

Step 4：Close reading with a focus on Mo Yan's physical education

In a broad sense，Mo Yan got a good physical education，which includes walking to the public canteen for drinking water and walking to the marketplace to listen to stories；gleaning ears of wheat in the fields by bending up and down；selling cabbages at market by showing and weighing them with his hands；working the bellows for a blacksmith on a bridge site by pushing and pulling；tending sheep and cattle by waving the whip；later joining the army by more exercises. All these helped to lead to a good health.

Step 5：Extended reading with a focus on tranquility education

Having learned about Mo Yan's moral education，intellectual education and physical education，we should say that Mo Yan accidentally had a good education. In our present life，the world is full of temptations and distractions. Just as what *Daodejing* said in Chapter 12：Five colors dazzle the eyes；five sounds deafen the ears；five tastes baffle the palate；galloping to hunt drives one crazy；and rare goods reduce one to misconduct.（五色令人目盲,五音令人耳聋,五味令人口爽,驰骋畋猎令人心发狂,难得之货令人行妨。）What I'd like you to do is to be tranquil. We'll listen to what a mother said，what a father said and what a master said.

We'll listen to what a mother said first.

These Are My Wishes for You
by Sandra Sturtz Hauss

May you find serenity and tranquility in a world you may not always understand. May the pain you have known and the conflict you have experienced give you the strength to walk through life，facing each new situation with courage and optimism. Always know that there are those whose love and understanding will always be there，even when you feel most lonely. May you discover enough goodness in others to believe in a world of peace. May a kind word，a reassuring touch，and a warm smile be yours every day of your life. And may you give these gifts as well as receive them. Remember the sunshine when the storm seems unending. Teach love to those who know hate，and let that love embrace you as you go into the world. May the teachings of those you admire become part of you，so that you may call upon them. Remember，those whose lives you have touched and who have touched yours are always a part of you，even if the encounters were less than you would have wished. It is the content of the encounter that is more important than its form. May you not become too concerned with material matters，but instead place immeasurable value on the goodness in your heart. Find time in each day to see beauty and love in the world around you. Realize that each person has limitless abilities，but each of us is different in our own way. What you may feel you lack in one regard may be more than compensated for in another. What you feel you lack in the present may become one of your strengths in the future. May you see your future as one filled with promise and possibility. Learn to view everything as a worthwhile experience. May you find enough inner strength to determine your own worth by yourself, and not be dependent on another's judgment of your accomplishments. May you always feel loved.

Next, we'll listen to what a father said.

Letter from Zhuge Liang to His Son

A gentleman behaves himself as tranquility cultivates his character and frugality fosters his virtues. Only the eyes that seek no fame or wealth can see their lofty aspirations; only the minds that rest in peace and at ease can reach their distant ends. Learning, which requires tranquility, feeds talents. It is nothing but learning that increases talents; and it is nothing but aspiration that spurs learning. Morale slackens with negligence, while character cannot be built with impulsiveness. As time flies, the will fades away with age; and most likely, he becomes left out of the time, like a fallen leaf from the branch into the wind. Where will he drift to, being left with regretful loneliness, if not alone, under the shabby roof? (夫君子之行,静以修身,俭以养德;非澹泊无以明志,非宁静无以致远。夫学须静也,才须学也;非学无以广才,非志无以成学。淫慢则不能励精,险躁则不能治性。年与时驰,意与岁去,遂成枯落,多不接世。悲守穷庐,将复何及!)

Finally, we'll listen to what a master said.

Great Learning

The way of great learning consists in manifesting one's bright virtues, consists in loving/renovating the people, consists in stopping in perfect goodness. When you know where to stop, you have stability. When you have stability, you can be tranquil. When you are tranquil, you can be at ease. When you are at ease, you can deliberate. When you can deliberate you can attain your aims. Things have their roots and branches, affairs have their end and beginning. When you know what comes first and what comes last, then you are near the Way. The ancients who wanted to manifest their bright virtues to all in the world first governed well their own states. Wanting to govern well their states, they first harmonized their own clans. Wanting to harmonize their own clan, they first cultivated themselves. Wanting to cultivate themselves, they first corrected their minds. Wanting to correct their minds, they first made their wills sincere. Wanting to make their wills sincere, they first extended their knowledge. Extension of knowledge consists of the investigation of things. When things are investigated, knowledge is extended. When knowledge is extended, the will becomes sincere. When the will is sincere, the mind is correct. When the mind is correct, the self is cultivated. When the self is cultivated, the clan is harmonized. When the clan is harmonized, the country is well governed. When the country is well governed, there will be peace throughout the land. From the king down to the common people, all must regard the cultivation of the self as the most essential thing. It is impossible to have a situation wherein the essentials are in disorder, and the externals are well-managed. You simply cannot take the essential things as superficial, and the superficial things as essential. This is called "Knowing the root." This is called "The extension of knowledge."（大学之道,在明明德,在亲民,在止于至善。知止而后有定,定而后能静,静而后能安,安而后能虑,虑而后能得。物有本末,事有终始,知所先后,则近道矣。古之欲明明德于天下者,先治其国;欲治其国者,先齐其家;欲齐其家者,先修其身;欲修其身者,先正其心;欲正其心者,先诚其意;欲诚其意者,先致其知,致知在格物。物格而后知至,知至而后意诚,意诚而后心正,心正而后身修,身修而后家齐,家齐而后国治,国治而后天下平。自天子以至于庶人,壹是皆以修身为本。其本乱而末治者,否矣。其所厚者薄,而其所薄者厚,未之有也。此谓知本,此谓知之至也。）

These three pieces have something in common: tranquility is very important, for it can not only preserve our health, but also bring the sense to light; it can not only enlighten us, but also produce wisdom; it can not only reach the distant ends, but also even lead us to god.（静不仅能养生,还能明道;静不仅能开悟,还能生慧,静不仅能致远,还能通神。）

II. Analysis

《莫言诺贝尔文学奖获奖感言》可以进行多维解读,如:从社会、历史的纬度,我们可以读到那个时代的经济状况,物质极其贫乏,人们极端贫困、极端饥饿;从心理分析的纬度,我们可以读到莫言有很强的恋母情结;从莫言解剖自己的纬度,我们可以读到莫言是个强者,他敢于把自己缺点和错误拿出来示众。多维的解读方式构成了多维教学设计。这些多维教学设计就构成了同课异构。

本教学设计另辟蹊径,从教育的维度进行解读,进行教学设计。在解读过程中,我们有些意外的发现:莫言在德育方面受到的是爱的教育、恕的教育、真善美的教育、坚强的教育、珍爱生命的教育、勤劳的教育、管好嘴(祸从口出、言多必失)的教育、务正业的教育等;在智育方面是培养兴趣、注意力、理解力、记忆力、表达力、观察力、想象力、创造力等;在体育方面是走路、捡麦穗、帮忙搬运和卖白菜、放牛羊、拉风箱,还有参军后的各种锻炼,这些活动为莫言身体健康和强壮打下了一个良好的基础。在此解读基础上,又增加了一些关于"静心"的拓展性阅读,以帮助学生在这充满诱惑、比较浮躁的社会,静下心来,扎扎实实、踏踏实实、老老实实地读一点东西,走得远一些。

"有心栽花花不开,无心插柳柳成荫。"其意思是说:用心地栽花、施肥、灌溉,但花却总是不开,最后还是枯萎了;而随意折下来的一只柳条插在地里,从来没有照料它,几年过去,却成了郁郁葱葱的柳树。莫言无意中受到这么好的教育,且是润物细无声的教育,这些教育为莫言日后的文学创作打下一个坚实的基础。回想起我们小时候无意中吃最绿色的食品、呼吸最干净的空气、喝着无污染的水。看看今天,我们确实需要一些反思,需要一些回归。同样,我们今天在大力倡导素质教育的时候,可能我们的教育是应试教育最盛行的时候。也许莫言所受的教育,才是我们孜孜以求的理想的教育。那就是:"众里寻他千百度,蓦然回首,那人却在灯火阑珊处。"

Ⅲ. Full Text

Storytellers

Distinguished members of the Swedish Academy, Ladies and Gentlemen:

Through the mediums of television and the Internet, I imagine that everyone here has at least a nodding acquaintance with far-off Northeast Gaomi Township. You may have seen my ninety-year-old father, as well as my brothers, my sister, my wife and my daughter, even my granddaughter, now a year and four months old. But the person who is most on my mind at this moment, my mother, is someone you will never see. Many people have shared in the honor of winning this prize, everyone but her.

My mother was born in 1922 and died in 1994. We buried her in a peach orchard east of the village. Last year we were forced to move her grave farther away from the village in order to make room for a proposed rail line. When we dug up the grave, we saw that the coffin had rotted away and that her body had merged with the damp earth around it. So we dug up some of that soil, a symbolic act, and took it to the new gravesite. That was when I grasped the knowledge that my mother had become part of the earth, and that when I spoke to mother earth, I was really speaking to my mother.

I was my mother's youngest child.

My earliest memory was of taking our only vacuum bottle to the public canteen for drinking water. Weakened by hunger, I dropped the bottle and broke it. Scared witless, I hid all that day in a haystack. Toward evening, I heard my mother calling my childhood name, so I crawled out of my hiding place, prepared to receive a beating or a scolding. But Mother didn't hit me, didn't even scold me. She just rubbed my head and heaved a sigh.

My most painful memory involved going out in the collective's field with Mother to glean ears of wheat. The gleaners scattered when they spotted the watchman. But Mother, who had bound feet, could not run; she was caught and slapped so hard by the watchman, a hulk of a man, that she fell to the ground. The watchman confiscated the wheat we'd gleaned and walked off whistling. As she sat on the ground, her lip bleeding, Mother wore a look of hopelessness I'll never forget. Years later, when I encountered the watchman, now a gray-haired old man, in the marketplace, Mother had to stop me from going up to avenge her. "Son," she said evenly, "the man who hit me and this man are not the same person."

My clearest memory is of a Moon Festival day, at noontime, one of those rare occasions when we ate *jiaozi* at home, one bowl apiece. An aging beggar came to our door while we were at the table, and when I tried to send him away with half a bowlful of dried sweet potatoes, he reacted angrily:"I'm an old man," he said. "You people are eating *jiaozi*, but want to feed me sweet potatoes. How heartless can you be?" I reacted just as angrily:"We're lucky if we eat *jiaozi* a couple of times a year, one small bowlful apiece, barely enough to get a taste! You should be thankful we're giving you sweet potatoes, and if you don't want them, you can get the hell out of here!" After (dressing me down) reprimanding me, Mother dumped her half bowlful of *jiaozi* into the old man's bowl.

My most remorseful memory involves helping Mother sell cabbages at market, and me overcharging an old villager one *jiao*—intentionally or not, I can't recall—before heading off to school. When I came home that afternoon, I saw that Mother was crying, something she rarely did. Instead of scolding me, she merely said softly, "Son, you embarrassed your mother today."

Mother contracted a serious lung disease when I was still in my teens. Hunger, disease, and too much work made things extremely hard on our family. The road ahead looked especially bleak, and I had a bad feeling about the future, worried that Mother might take her own life. Every day, the first thing I did when I walked in the door after a day of hard labor was call out for Mother. Hearing her voice was like giving my heart a new lease on life. But not hearing her threw me into a panic. I'd go looking for her in the side building and in the mill. One day, after searching everywhere and not finding her, I sat down in the yard and cried like a baby. That is how she found me when she walked into the yard carrying a bundle of firewood on her back. She was very unhappy with me, but I could not tell her what I was afraid of. She knew anyway. "Son," she said, "don't worry, there may be no joy in my life, but I won't leave you till the God of the Underworld calls me."

I was born ugly. Villagers often laughed in my face, and school bullies sometimes beat me up because of it. I'd run home crying, where my mother would say, "You're not ugly, Son. You've got a nose and two eyes, and there's nothing wrong with your arms and legs, so how could you be ugly? If you have a good heart and always do the right thing, what is considered ugly becomes beautiful." Later on, when I moved to the city, there were educated people who laughed at me behind my back, some even to my face; but when I recalled what Mother had said, I just calmly offered my apologies.

My illiterate mother held people who could read in high regard. We were so poor we often did not know where our next meal was coming from, yet she never denied my request to buy a book or something to write with. By nature hard working, she had no use for lazy children, yet I could skip my chores as long as I had my nose in a book.

A storyteller once came to the marketplace, and I sneaked off to listen to him. She was unhappy with me for forgetting my chores. But that night, while she was stitching padded clothes for us under the weak light of a kerosene lamp, I couldn't keep from retelling stories I'd heard that day. She listened impatiently at first, since in her eyes professional storytellers were smooth-talking men in a dubious profession. Nothing good ever came out of their mouths. But slowly she was dragged into my retold stories, and from that day on, she never gave me chores on market day, unspoken permission to go to the marketplace and listen to new stories. As repayment for Mother's kindness and a way to demonstrate my memory, I'd retell the stories for her in vivid detail.

It did not take long to find retelling someone else's stories unsatisfying, so I began embellishing my narration. I'd say things I knew would please Mother, even changed the ending once in a while. And she wasn't the only member of my audience, which later included my older sisters, my aunts, even my maternal grandmother. Sometimes, after my mother had listened to one of my stories, she'd ask in a care-laden voice, almost as if to herself: "What will you be like when you grow up, son? Might you wind up prattling for a living one day?"

I knew why she was worried. Talkative kids are not well thought of in our village, for they can bring trouble to themselves and to their families. There is a bit of a young me in the talkative boy who falls afoul of villagers in my story *Bulls*. Mother habitually cautioned me not to talk so much, wanting me to be a taciturn, smooth and steady youngster. Instead I was possessed of a dangerous combination—remarkable speaking skills and the powerful desire that went with them. My ability to tell stories brought her joy, but that created a dilemma for her.

A popular saying goes "It is easier to change the course of a river than a person's nature." Despite my parents' tireless guidance, my natural desire to talk never went away, and that is what makes my name—Mo Yan, or "don't speak"—an ironic expression of self-mockery.

After dropping out of elementary school, I was too small for heavy labor, so I became a cattle-and-sheep-herder on a nearby grassy riverbank. The sight of my former schoolmates playing in the schoolyard when I drove my animals past the gate always saddened me and made me aware of how tough it is for anyone—even a child—to leave the group.

I turned the animals loose on the riverbank to graze beneath a sky as blue as the ocean and grass-carpeted land as far as the eye could see—not another person in sight, no human sounds, nothing but bird calls above me. I was all by myself and terribly lonely; my heart felt empty. Sometimes I lay in the grass and watched clouds float lazily by, which gave rise to all sorts of fanciful images. That part of the country is known for its tales of foxes in the form of beautiful young women, and I would fantasize a fox-turned-beautiful girl coming to tend animals with me. She never did come. Once, however, a fiery red fox bounded out of the brush in front of me, scaring my legs right out from under me. I was still sitting there trembling long after the fox had vanished. Sometimes I'd crouch down beside the cows and gaze into their deep blue eyes, eyes that captured my reflection. At times I'd have a dialogue with birds in the sky, mimicking their cries, while at other times I'd divulge my hopes and desires to a tree. But the birds ignored me, and so did the trees. Years later, after I'd become a novelist, I wrote some of those fantasies into my novels and stories. People frequently bombard me with compliments on my vivid imagination, and lovers of literature often ask me to divulge my secret to developing a rich imagination. My only response is a wan smile.

Our Taoist master Laozi said it best:"Fortune depends on misfortune. Misfortune is hidden in fortune." I left school as a child, often went hungry, was constantly lonely, and had no books to read. But for those reasons, like the writer of a previous generation, Shen Congwen, I had an early start on reading the great book of life. My experience of going to the marketplace to listen to a storyteller was but one page of that book.

After leaving school, I was thrown uncomfortably into the world of adults, where I embarked on the long journey of learning through listening. Two hundred years ago, one of the great storytellers of all time—Pu Songling—lived near where I grew up, and where many people, me included, carried on the tradition he had perfected. Wherever I happened to be—working the fields with the collective, in production team cowsheds or stables, on my grandparents' heated *kang*, even on oxcarts bouncing and swaying down the road, my ears filled with tales of the supernatural, historical romances, and strange and captivating stories, all tied to the natural environment and clan histories, and all of which created a powerful reality in my mind.

Even in my wildest dreams, I could not have envisioned a day when all this would be the stuff of my own fiction, for I was just a boy who loved stories, who was infatuated with the tales people around me were telling. Back then I was, without a doubt, a theist, believing that all living creatures were endowed with souls. I'd stop and pay my respects to a towering old tree; if I saw a bird, I was sure it could become human any time it wanted; and I suspected every stranger I met of being a transformed beast. At night, terrible fears accompanied me on my way home after my work points were tallied, so I'd sing at the top of my lungs as I ran to build up a bit of courage. My voice, which was changing at the time, produced scratchy, squeaky songs that grated on the ears of any villager who heard me.

I spent my first twenty-one years in that village, never traveling farther from home than to Qingdao, by train, where I nearly got lost amid the giant stacks of wood in a lumber mill. When my mother asked me what I'd seen in Qingdao, I reported sadly that all I'd seen were stacks of lumber. But that trip to Qingdao planted in me a powerful desire to leave my village and see the world.

In February 1976 I was recruited into the army and walked out of the Northeast Gaomi Township village I both loved and hated, entering a critical phase of my life, carrying in my backpack the four-volume *Brief History of China* my mother had bought by selling her wedding jewelry. Thus began the most important period of my life. I must admit that were it not for the thirty-odd years of tremendous development and progress in Chinese society, and the subsequent national reform and opening of her doors to the outside, I would not be a writer today.

In the midst of mind-numbing military life, I welcomed the ideological emancipation and literary fervor of the nineteen-eighties, and evolved from a boy who listened to stories and passed them on by word of mouth into someone who experimented with writing them down. It was a rocky road at first, a time when I had not yet discovered how rich a source of literary material my two decades of village life could be. I thought that literature was all about good people doing good things, stories of heroic deeds and model citizens, so that the few pieces of mine that were published had little literary value.

In the fall of 1984 I was accepted into the Literature Department of the PLA Art Academy, where, under the guidance of my revered mentor, the renowned writer Xu Huaizhong, I wrote a series of stories and novellas, including: *Autumn Floods*, *Dry River*, *The Transparent Carrot*, *and Red Sorghum*. Northeast Gaomi Township made its first appearance in *Autumn Floods*, and from that moment on, like a wandering peasant who finds his own piece of land, this literary vagabond found a place he could call his own. I must say that in the course of creating my literary domain, Northeast Gaomi Township, I was greatly inspired by the American novelist William Faulkner and the Columbian Gabriel García Márquez. I had not read either of them extensively, but was encouraged by the bold, unrestrained way they created new territory in writing, and learned from them that a writer must have a place that belongs to him alone. Humility and compromise are ideal in one's daily life, but in literary creation, supreme self-confidence and the need to follow one's own instincts are essential. For two years I followed in the footsteps of these two masters before realizing that I had to escape their influence; this is how I characterized that decision in an essay: They were a pair of blazing furnaces, I was a block of ice. If I got too close to them, I would dissolve into a cloud of steam. In my understanding, one writer influences another when they enjoy a profound spiritual kinship, what is often referred to as "hearts beating in unison". That explains why, though I had read little of their work, a few pages were sufficient for me to comprehend what they were doing and how they were doing it, which led to my understanding of what I should do and how I should do it.

What I should do was simplicity itself: Write my own stories in my own way. My way was that of the marketplace storyteller, with which I was so familiar, the way my grandfather and my grandmother and other village old-timers told stories. In all candor, I never gave a thought to audience when I was telling my stories; perhaps my audience was made up of people like my mother, and perhaps it was only me. The early stories were narrations of my personal experience: the boy who received a whipping in *Dry River*, for instance, or the boy who never spoke in *The Transparent Carrot*. I had actually done something bad enough to receive a whipping from my father, and I had actually worked the bellows for a blacksmith on a bridge site. Naturally, personal experience cannot be turned into fiction exactly as it happened, no matter how unique that might be. Fiction has to be fictional, has to be imaginative. To many of my friends, *The Transparent Carrot* is my very best story; I have no opinion one way or the other. What I can say is, *The Transparent Carrot* is more symbolic and more profoundly meaningful than any other story I've written. That dark-skinned boy with the superhuman ability to suffer and a superhuman degree of sensitivity represents the soul of my entire fictional output. Not one of all the fictional characters I've created since then is as close to my soul as he is. Or put a different way, among all the characters a writer creates, there is always one that stands above all the others. For me, that laconic boy is the one. Though he says nothing, he leads the way for all the others, in all their variety, performing freely on the Northeast Gaomi Township stage.

A person can experience only so much, and once you have exhausted your own stories, you must tell the stories of others. And so, out of the depths of my memories, like conscripted soldiers, rose stories of family members, of fellow villagers, and of long-dead ancestors I learned of from the mouths of old-timers. They waited expectantly for me to tell their stories. My grandfather and grandmother, my father and mother, my brothers and sisters, my aunts and uncles, my wife and my daughter have all appeared in my stories. Even unrelated residents of Northeast Gaomi Township have made cameo appearances. Of course they have undergone literary modification to transform them into larger-than-life fictional characters.

An aunt of mine is the central character of my latest novel, *Frogs*. The announcement of the Nobel Prize sent journalists swarming to her home with interview requests. At first, she was patiently accommodating, but she soon had to escape their attention by fleeing to her son's home in the provincial capital. I don't deny that she was my model in writing *Frogs*, but the differences between her and the fictional aunt are extensive. The fictional aunt is arrogant and domineering, in places virtually thuggish, while my real aunt is kind and gentle, the classic caring wife and loving mother. My real aunt's golden years have been happy and fulfilling; her fictional counterpart suffers insomnia in her late years as a result of spiritual torment, and walks the nights like a specter, wearing a dark robe. I am grateful to my real aunt for not being angry with me for how I changed her in the novel. I also greatly respect her wisdom in comprehending the complex relationship between fictional characters and real people.

After my mother died, in the midst of almost crippling grief, I decided to write a novel for her. *Big Breasts and Wide Hips* is that novel. Once my plan took shape, I was burning with such emotion that I completed a draft of half a million words in only eighty-three days.

In *Big Breasts and Wide Hips* I shamelessly used material associated with my mother's actual experience, but the fictional mother's emotional state is either a total fabrication or a composite of many of Northeast Gaomi Township's mothers. Though I wrote "To the spirit of my mother" on the dedication page, the novel was really written for all mothers everywhere, evidence, perhaps, of my overweening ambition, in much the same way as I hope to make tiny Northeast Gaomi Township a microcosm of China, even of the whole world.

The process of creation is unique to every writer. Each of my novels differs from the others in terms of plot and guiding inspiration. Some, such as *The Transparent Carrot*, were born in dreams, while others, like *The Garlic Ballads* have their origin in actual events. Whether the source of a work is a dream or real life, only if it is integrated with individual experience can it be imbued with individuality, be populated with typical characters molded by lively detail, employ richly evocative language, and boast a well crafted structure. Here I must point out that in *The Garlic Ballads* I introduced a real-life storyteller and singer in one of the novel's most important roles. I wish I hadn't used his real name, though his words and actions were made up. This is a recurring phenomenon with me. I'll start out using characters' real names in order to achieve a sense of intimacy, and after the work is finished, it will seem too late to change those names. This has led to people who see their names in my novels going to my father to vent their displeasure. He always apologizes in my place, but then urges them not to take such things so seriously. He'll say: "The first sentence in *Red Sorghum*, 'My father, a bandit's offspring,' didn't upset me, so why should you be unhappy?"

My greatest challenges come with writing novels that deal with social realities, such as *The Garlic Ballads*, not because I'm afraid of being openly critical of the darker aspects of society, but because heated emotions and anger allow politics to suppress literature and transform a novel into reportage of a social event. As a member of society, a novelist is entitled to his own stance and viewpoint; but when he is writing he must take a humanistic stance, and write accordingly. Only then can literature not just originate in events, but transcend them, not just show concern for politics but be greater than politics.

Possibly because I've lived so much of my life in difficult circumstances, I think I have a more profound understanding of life. I know what real courage is, and I understand true compassion. I know that nebulous terrain exists in the hearts and minds of every person, terrain that cannot be adequately characterized in simple terms of right and wrong or good and bad, and this vast territory is where a writer gives free rein to his talent. So long as the work correctly and vividly describes this nebulous, massively contradictory terrain, it will inevitably transcend politics and be endowed with literary excellence.

Prattling on and on about my own work must be annoying, but my life and works are inextricably linked, so if I don't talk about my work, I don't know what else to say. I hope you are in a forgiving mood.

I was a modern-day storyteller who hid in the background of his early work; but with the novel *Sandalwood Death* I jumped out of the shadows. My early work can be characterized as a series of soliloquies, with no reader in mind; starting with this novel, however, I visualized myself standing in a public square spiritedly telling my story to a crowd of listeners. This tradition is a worldwide phenomenon in fiction, but is especially so in China. At one time, I was a diligent student of Western modernist fiction, and I experimented with all sorts of narrative styles. But in the end I came back to my traditions. To be sure, this return was not without its modifications. *Sandalwood Death* and the novels that followed are inheritors of the Chinese classical novel tradition but enhanced by Western literary techniques. What is known as innovative fiction is, for the most part, a result of this mixture, which is not limited to domestic traditions with foreign techniques, but can include mixing fiction with art from other realms. *Sandalwood Death*, for instance, mixes fiction with local opera, while some of my early work was partly nurtured by fine art, music, even acrobatics.

Finally, I ask your indulgence to talk about my novel *Life and Death Are Wearing Me Out*. The Chinese title comes from Buddhist scripture, and I've been told that my translators have had fits trying to render it into their languages. I am not especially well versed in Buddhist scripture and have but a superficial understanding of the religion. I chose this title because I believe that the basic tenets of the Buddhist faith represent universal knowledge, and that mankind's many disputes are utterly without meaning in the Buddhist realm. In that lofty view of the universe, the world of man is to be pitied. My novel is not a religious tract; in it I wrote of man's fate and human emotions, of man's limitations and human generosity, and of people's search for happiness and the lengths to which they will go, the sacrifices they will make, to uphold their beliefs. Lan Lian, a character who takes a stand against contemporary trends, is, in my view, a true hero. A peasant in a neighboring village was the model for this character. As a youngster I often saw him pass by our door pushing a creaky, wooden-wheeled cart, with a lame donkey up front, led by his bound-foot wife. Given the collective nature of society back then, this strange labor group presented a bizarre sight that kept them out of step with the times. In the eyes of us children, they were clowns marching against historical trends, provoking in us such indignation that we threw stones at them as they passed us on the street. Years later, after I had begun writing, that peasant and the tableau he presented floated into my mind, and I knew that one day I would write a novel about him, that sooner or later I would tell his story to the world. But it wasn't until the year 2005, when I viewed the Buddhist mural "The Six Stages of Samsara" on a temple wall that I knew exactly how to go about telling his story.

The announcement of my Nobel Prize has led to controversy. At first I thought I was the target of the disputes, but over time I've come to realize that the real target was a person who had nothing to do with me. Like someone watching a play in a theater, I observed the performances around me. I saw the winner of the prize both garlanded with flowers and besieged by stone-throwers and mudslingers. I was afraid he would succumb to the assault, but he emerged from the garlands of flowers and the stones, a smile on his face; he wiped away mud and grime, stood calmly off to the side, and said to the crowd:

For a writer, the best way to speak is by writing. You will find everything I need to say in my works. Speech is carried off by the wind; the written word can never be obliterated. I would like you to find the patience to read my books. I cannot force you to do that, and even if you do, I do not expect your opinion of me to change. No writer has yet appeared, anywhere in the world, who is liked by all his readers; that is especially true during times like these.

Even though I would prefer to say nothing, since it is something I must do on this occasion, let me just say this:

I am a storyteller, so I am going to tell you some stories.

When I was a third-grade student in the 1960s, my school organized a field trip to an exhibit of suffering, where, under the direction of our teacher, we cried bitter tears. I let my tears stay on my cheeks for the benefit of our teacher, and watched as some of my classmates spat in their hands and rubbed it on their faces as pretended tears. I saw one student among all those wailing children—some real, some phony—whose face was dry and who remained silent without covering his face with his hands. He just looked at us, eyes wide open in an expression of surprise or confusion. After the visit I reported him to the teacher, and he was given a disciplinary warning. Years later, when I expressed my remorse over informing on the boy, the teacher said that at least ten students had done what I did. The boy himself had died a decade or more earlier, and my conscience was deeply troubled when I thought of him. But I learned something important from this incident, and that is: When everyone around you is crying, you deserve to be allowed not to cry, and when the tears are all for show, your right not to cry is greater still.

Here is another story: More than thirty years ago, when I was in the army, I was in my office reading one evening when an elderly officer opened the door and came in. He glanced down at the seat in front of me and muttered, "Hm, where is everyone?" I stood up and said in a loud voice, "Are you saying I'm no one?" The old fellow's ears turned red from embarrassment, and he walked out. For a long time after that I was proud about what I consider a gutsy performance. Years later, that pride turned to intense qualms of conscience.

Bear with me, please, for one last story, one my grandfather told me many years ago: A group of eight out-of-town bricklayers took refuge from a storm in a rundown temple. Thunder rumbled outside, sending fireballs their way. They even heard what sounded like dragon shrieks. The men were terrified, their faces ashen. "Among the eight of us," one of them said, "is someone who must have offended the heavens with a terrible deed. The guilty person ought to volunteer to step outside to accept his punishment and spare the innocent from suffering. Naturally, there were no volunteers. So one of the others came up with a proposal: Since no one is willing to go outside, let's all fling our straw hats toward the door. Whoever's hat flies out through the temple door is the guilty party, and we'll ask him to go out and accept his punishment. " So they flung their hats toward the door. Seven hats were blown back inside; one went out the door. They pressured the eighth man to go out and accept his punishment, and when he balked, they picked him up and flung him out the door. I'll bet you all know how the story ends: They had no sooner flung him out the door than the temple collapsed around them.

I am a storyteller.

Telling stories earned me the Nobel Prize for Literature.

Many interesting things have happened to me in the wake of winning the prize, and they have convinced me that truth and justice are alive and well.

So I will continue telling my stories in the days to come.

Thank you all.

Case 3 Instructional Design of *The Bible Stories* Based on 3R and Analysis

I . Instructional Design of *The Bible Stories* Based on 3R

Step 1: Lead-in with a brief introduction to the *Bible*

The *Bible*, also called the book of books, is an encyclopedia or even a library of different literary types rather than a single book. It is a collection of sacred texts or scriptures that Jews and Christians consider to be a product of divine inspiration and a record of the relationship between God and humans. It consists of two sections: Old Testament and New Testament. There are 39 books in the Old Testament and 27 books in the New Testament. Altogether, it has 66 books. Testament has two basic meanings. One is covenant or contract or agreement and the other is strong evidence. The Old Testament is concerned with the covenant or contract or agreement between God and Israelites. The New Testament is concerned with the covenant or contract or agreement between Jesus and Christians. There is strong evidence to show whether humans obey or disobey the testament or covenant or contract or agreement. 3R in the instructional design refers to reading the lines, reading between the lines and reading beyond the lines. Step by step, we will go into the Bible stories and experience one of the sources of western civilization.

Step 2: Reading the lines with a focus on factual questions

Reading the lines refers to the idea that students read what they are assigned to read and can directly find the answers to the questions in the reading materials with the aid of dictionaries. In this part, ten questions are designed, of which three questions are:

1) On what day did God create man?

2) How did God create Eve?

3) What are the Ten Commandments?

If students read assigned reading materials, they can easily find the answers to these questions. They are:

1) God created man on the sixth day.

2) God made the Adam fall into a deep sleep, and while he was sleeping, he took out one

of his ribs and closed up the flesh. He formed Eve out of the rib and brought her to him.

3) The Ten Commandments are:

(1) I am the Lord your God, who brought you out of the land of Egypt, out of the house of slavery; you shall not have any other gods before me. (2) You shall not make for yourself an idol, whether in the form of anything that is in heaven above, or that is on the earth beneath, or that is in the water under the earth. You shall not bow down to them or worship them; for I the Lord your God am a jealous God, punishing children for the iniquity of parents, to the third and the fourth generation of those who reject me, but showing steadfast love to the thousandth generation of those who love me and keep my commandments. (3) You shall not make wrongful use of the name of the Lord your God, for the Lord will not acquit anyone who misuses his name. (4) Remember the Sabbath day and keep it holy. For six days you shall labor and do all your work. But the seventh day is a Sabbath to the Lord your God; you shall not do any work—you, your son or your daughter, your male or female slave, your livestock, or the alien resident in your towns. For in six days the LORD made heaven and earth, the sea, and all that is in them, but rested the seventh day; therefore the Lord blessed the Sabbath day and consecrated it. (5) Honor your father and your mother, so that your days may be long in the land that the Lord your God is giving you. (6) You shall not murder. (7) You shall not commit adultery. (8) You shall not steal. (9) You shall not bear false witness against your neighbor. (10) You shall not covet your neighbor's house; you shall not covet your neighbor's wife, or male or female slave, or ox, or donkey, or anything that belongs to your neighbor.

The purpose for which the teacher designs these questions is to encourage students to read. This is the basis of *English Reading*, with which students can discuss, think, ask questions and associate what they read with their prior knowledge; without which they can do nothing.

Step 3: Reading between the lines with a focus on inference questions

Reading between the lines means that students read closely, think about what they read, infer or understand the real or hidden meaning by something that is not written explicitly or openly and draw conclusions by themselves. One thing worth mentioning is that their inference or conclusion must be logical, reasonable and well-grounded on the reading materials. In order to encourage students to read actively and use their imagination, the teacher repeatedly emphasizes "There are no right or wrong answers in this class. That is your opinion. We respect everyone's opinion". Therefore the atmosphere is very relaxed in class and everyone can voice their own opinions. In this part, three of the questions designed by the teacher are:

1) What can you dig out of the first paragraph in the *Genesis*?

2) How do you interpret the Ten Commandments?

3) What do you think of God?

After their careful reading, active thinking and heated discussion, together with the teacher's guidance, the students may have the possible answers as follows.

In terms of the first question, the possible answers are:

Dichotomy. There are at least five pairs of dichotomy: time vs. space, heavens vs. earth, light vs. darkness, day vs. night, and evening vs. morning. The dichotomy is well illustrated by the opening paragraph in the *A Tale of Two Cities* by Charles Dickens: "It was the best of times, it was the worst of times; it was the age of wisdom, it was the age of foolishness; it was the epoch of belief, it was the epoch of incredulity; it was the season of Light, it was the season of Darkness; it was the spring of hope, it was the winter of despair; we had everything before us, we had nothing before us; we were all going direct to Heaven, we were all going direct the other way." They are best vs. worst, wisdom vs. foolishness, belief vs. incredulity, light vs. darkness, hope vs. despair, everything vs. nothing, and Heaven vs. Hell.

Trinity. Trinity holds that God is three consubstantial persons: the Father, the Son and the Holy Spirit or one God in three divine persons. The three persons are distinct, yet they are one substance, essence or nature. Trinity can be compared to water in three states: liquid, solid and gas. The three states are distinct, yet they are one substance, essence or nature. Liquid is something like the Father, solid is something like the Son and gas is something like the Holy Spirit.

Heavens. Heavens refer to three heavens: the sky, the outer space and the paradise where God and angels dwell. By the way, we Chinese have nine heavens which are called "九霄".

Creation. We do not know exactly how many types of creation God has, but one thing is sure: there is more than one type of creation—verbal creation, that is, use language to create, like creating light by saying "let there be light" and there was light. Maybe God also has physical creation.

Day calculation. There are two things about day calculation. One is that their way of calculation is from evening to morning, which is very different from ours: from morning to evening; and the other is how long one day lasts. Is it twenty-four hours or a hundred years? It is really hard to say.

With regard to the second question, the possible answers are:

The Ten Commandments is a list of religious and moral imperatives that were given by God to the Israelites. God wrote an inscription on two stone tablets and gave them to Moses on Mount Sinai.

There is an explicit and implicit cause-and-effect relationship in the Ten Commandments. One reason why God gave Israelites the Ten Commandments is that God knows what is the best for them and how they can live a happy, long, and holy life. The other reason is that they were disobedient to God. Let us suppose that you are a parent, what is the most important thing you want your children to do? Most probably, you ask them to obey what you said. Why? Because we have been where they are now going and we have learned what is good and what is bad. We want only what is good for our children, so that is why we want them to obey what we tell them. God is no different from us. He just wants his children to do the same.

The Ten Commandments is divided into two parts: the first part, including the first four commandments, is concerned with the love of God; the second part, consisting of the next six commandments, with the love of one's neighbors. The first part is the cause and the second part is the effect, that is, because you love God, you must love your neighbors.

There is an explicit cause-and-effect relationship in the first five commandments. The first commandment is that "you shall have no other God before me". The reasons why God asked them to have no other gods before him are that one is that God is the Lord, who created them and created everything they had; another is that God brought them out of the land of Egypt, out of the house of slavery; the other is that God will save them. God just wants to remind them never to forget who He is. For these reasons, they must only worship or glorify God. They must not give worship and glory to any other God. The second commandment is that "You shall not make for yourself an idol, whether in the form of anything that is in heaven above, or that is on the earth beneath, or that is in the water under the earth. You shall not bow down to them or worship them; for I the Lord your God am a jealous God, punishing children for the iniquity of parents, to the third and the fourth generation of those who reject me, but showing steadfast love to the thousandth generation of those who love me and keep my commandments". This commandment is the longest, which is divided into three sections. The first section deals with the effect: the distinction between creator and creature. God reminds them that He created everything and they are just the creatures and anything they make into an idol is just taken from something He created and is no more important than they themselves are. So they must not worship them. In a modern sense, they must not worship money, power, fame or sex, either. The second and third sections deal with cause: punishment and rewards. If they reject God and make an idol, God will punish them, their children, their grandchildren and their great grandchildren. If they love God and keep his commandments, they will have a thousand generations of blessings from God. Therefore, they must weigh and consider those two: four generations of punishment versus a thousand generations of blessing. The third commandment enjoins that those who make false oaths in the name of God, specifically the ones which are pointless, insincere and or never carried out, will commit a crime; and those who participate in occult practices and blaspheme against places or people that are holy to God, will commit a crime. The fourth commandment requires that they shall keep the Sabbath day without any omission or careless performance of the religious duties, or using the day for idleness or doing something that is sinful, because in six days the LORD made heavens and earth, the sea, and all that is in them, but rested on the seventh day. The fifth commandment is about honouring their parents, which is the greatest inter-generation obligation. If they do, their days may be long, otherwise their days may be short. The sixth commandment is about murder: the greatest injury to others, which enjoins that they shall not murder physically, orally or even mentally like hating or cursing. The seventh commandment is about adultery, the greatest injury to family, which is likely to result in their loss of fame or dignity or decency or money or health (like sexually transmitted diseases, heart disease or high blood pressure) or even life. The eighth commandment is about theft, which is the greatest injury to movable property. It requires that they shall be honest and fair in our dealings; and that they shall seek justice, freedom, and the necessities of life for all people. The ninth commandment is about false witness or dishonesty, which is the greatest injury to law and commerce. It requires the maintaining and promoting of the truth between people and of our neighbor's good name and our own especially in witness-bearing. The tenth commandment enjoins that they shall resist temptations to envy, greed, and jealousy; that they shall rejoice in other people's gifts and graces.

As for the third question, the possible answers are:

God is creative. On the first day, God created light; on the second day, God created sky; on the third day, God created dry land and seas; on the fourth day, God created the sun, the moon and the stars; on the fifth day, God created birds and sea creatures; on the sixth day, God created animals, creeping things and humans. God is like magician, saying "let there be something" and there was something.

God is "fooling" for the reason that He did not allow Adam and Eve to eat the fruit from the Tree of Knowledge or even touch it and that if they ate it, they would be like God and know what is good and what is evil.

God is very "vindictive" for the following reasons. One is that because Satan tricked Eve into eating the apple, he was punished like this: his feet were removed and he would crawl on his belly; and he would have to eat dust as long as lived; Eve and he would hate each other, her offspring and his would always be enemies; her offspring would crush his head and he would bite their heel. Another reason is that because Eve took some of the apple and ate it, she got the following punishments: God would increase her trouble in pregnancy and her pain in giving birth. In spite of this, she would still have the desire for her husband, yet she would be subject to him. A third reason is that because Adam listened to his wife and ate the fruit, he would have to work all his life and sweat to make the soil produce anything until he went back to the soil from which he was formed. In order to prevent Adam and Eve from eating the fruit from the Tree of Life, God drove them out of the Garden of Eden. The last reason is that God confused human language and scattered them abroad over the face of all the earth in order to stop the people from building a tower in the heavens and make a name for themselves.

God is "immoral", because God made Mary pregnant with child. In fact, God knew that Mary had been engaged to Joseph and made her pregnant before they lived together. From God's point of view, He wanted to save his people from their sins. But from modern perspective, He should not have had an affair with somebody else's fiancée, which is immoral.

God is "jealous", because He made it clear in the second commandment, "You shall not make for yourself an idol, whether in the form of anything that is in heaven above, or that is on the earth beneath, or that is in the water under the earth. You shall not bow down to them or worship them; for I the Lord your God am a jealous God, punishing children for the iniquity of parents, to the third and the fourth generation of those who reject me, but showing steadfast love to the thousandth generation of those who love me and keep my commandments. "

God is illogical. On the first day, God created light. On the fourth day, God created the sun. It is known that the light we have on the earth comes from the sun. Without the sun, there would be no light. If there were no sun, light still existed, which means God carried coal to Newcastle or sold snow to Eskimos. Furthermore, after the God created light, there was day and night. As a matter of fact, in our daily life, when we face the sun, we have day. When we turn away from the sun, we have night.

God is unjust. When Cain murdered his brother Abel out of jealousy, God made him a fugitive and a wanderer on the earth. But when anyone killed Cain, he would suffer a sevenfold vengeance.

God is not omniscient, because if He had known that Satan was wicked, He would not have created him; or because if He had known that Satan was wicked, He would have killed him before he tricked Eve into eating the apple; or because if He had known that Satan tricked Eve into eating the apple, He would have stopped it. When God was walking in the Garden of Eden at the time of the evening breeze, Adam and Eve hid themselves from the presence of God. God called to the man and said to him, "Where are you?" If God had been omniscient, he would not have asked where he was.

God is not omnipresent. If God had been omnipresent, it would not have been necessary for him to tell Adam and Eve not to eat from the Tree of Knowledge, because whenever they ate, he could appear and stop them. It was because God was not omnipresent that they were driven out of the Garden of Eden.

God is not omnipotent. For one thing, he rested on the seventh day from all the work he had done, which means he was tired. If he had not been tired, he would not have needed a rest. For another, after Eve ate the forbidden fruit, if he had been really omnipotent, he could have let her disgorge the fruit to restore her innocence, ignorance and naivety. Besides, there is a dilemma question: "Can God make a rock so heavy that even He can't lift it?" If He could make a rock so heavy that even He couldn't lift it, He is not omnipotent, because He can't lift it. If He can't make a rock so heavy that even He can't lift it, He is not omnipotent, either, because He can't make a rock. Finally, God cannot lie or break his promise.

The purpose for which the researcher designs this kind of questions is to stimulate or provoke students' thinking. Just as Confucius said, "learning without thinking leads to confusion and thinking without learning ends in danger." If students read without thinking, they won't amount to anything.

Step 4 : Reading beyond the lines with a focus on association questions

Reading beyond the lines indicates that students associate what they read with something else while reading so as to foster students' ability to draw inferences about other cases from one instance. In the teaching of *the Bible Stories*, the researcher designed another three questions corresponding to the three questions in reading the lines. They go like this :

1) What associations do you have with the creation of man by God?

2) What associations do you have with the creation of Eve by God?

3) What associations do you have with the Ten Commandments?

On the basis of the creation of man by God, students use their associations. Some think of a Chinese legend *Nǚ Wa Created Men*. Like God, she also created men out of clay. Since the men created in this way were easy to break, she decided to make them strong by putting them in the oven and baking them. Because it was for the first time that she did not have much experience, she baked them so long that they turned black. That was where the black men came from. For the second time, she was extremely cautious, perhaps too cautious, that she did not bake them long enough and took them out. In this case, they were underdone and became white. That was where the white men came from. For the third time, she became so careful and so alert that she baked them neither too long nor too short. They were properly done and became yellow. That was where the yellow men came from. Others think of *Pan Gu Created Heaven and Earth*. Before creation, Pan Gu spent 18,000 years sleeping in an egg-shaped, chaotic universe. One day, he woke up and stretched himself, shattering the universe into pieces. The pure lighter elements gradually rose up to become heaven and impure heavier parts slowly sank down to form the earth. Another 18,000 years later, Pan Gu died. After his death, great transformations occurred in him. His breath turned into winds and clouds; his voice became clapping thunder. His left eye turned into the sun and his right eye became the moon. His four limbs and his trunk turned into four cardinal directions and mountains. His blood became rivers and his veins the roads and paths. His flesh turned into fields and soil. The hair on his head turned into stars in heaven; his skin and the hair on his body became grass, trees and flowers. His teeth and bones turned into metals and rocks, his marrow into pearls and jade, and his perspiration became dew and rain. The various bugs on his body changed into many peoples of the world.

Talking about the association about the creation of Eve by God, one student thinks of what rib God took from Adam. She said, "Woman was taken out of man, not out of his head to top him, nor out of his feet to be trampled underfoot; but out of his side to be equal to him, from under his arm to be protected and from near his heart to be loved."

The last discussion question about the Ten Commandments remind some students of The Ten Precepts in Buddhism, that is, people refrain from: (1) taking life; (2) taking what is not given; (3) sexual misconduct; (4) lying and deception; (5) drinking liquor; (6) eating after noon; (7) observing dancing, singing, and other entertainments; (8) wearing garlands, scents, unguents, or ornaments; (9) the use of high beds; (10) accepting gold and silver. Some students think of *Ten Commandments for a College Freshman* by an American father. They are (1) you shall plan to succeed; (2) you shall handle freedom responsibly; (3) you shall spread the joy of learning; (4) you shall play down those reports on sex and liquor; (5) you shall plan to have fun—and often; (6) you shall know at least one professor or one dean personally; (7) you shall be concerned or keep informed; (8) you shall be selective; (9) you shall strive to keep healthy; and (10) you shall forget and remember. Others think of ten don'ts in their studies, to be more specific, (1) don't start well, but end poorly; (2) don't be impractical; (3) don't enjoy undeserved fame; (4) don't work casually and carelessly; (5) don't have a little learning; (6) don't copy something mechanically; (7) don't be absent-minded; (8) don't profit yourself in a confused environment; (9) don't give yourself up; and (10) don't be anxious for success.

The purpose for which the researcher designed this type of questions is to encourage students use their imagination and associate what they read with their prior knowledge. In this way, they can form a network of knowledge, which will help to internalize their knowledge, to expand their horizons, to enrich their experiences and to result in their creativity.

Step 5: Assignment: Reading more *Bible* stories after class

We have just had a taste of the *Bible* stories. More needs to be read, dug and explored. For instance, the two trees in the Garden of Eden symbolize the two issues we humans cannot resolve: morality and mortality. In our real life, power politics is still rampant. We cannot decide which is right and which is wrong. Every one wants to be immortal by regular life style, balanced diet and proper exercise, and yet every day, people die of hunger, diseases, wars, earthquake, tsunami and famine. By more in-depth reading after class, you will have a better understanding of the world and expand your horizon. Keep your eyes open and you can see different things; keep your ears open and you can hear different voices; keep your minds open and you can accept different opinions and keep your hearts open and you can understand different emotions. Choose whatever stories you are interested in, just read, read and read.

II. Analysis

文有文脉,课有课脉。这篇教学设计的第一个特点是课脉非常清晰,且层层递进。这篇教学设计的第二个特点是以学生为中心。Reading the lines 是这节课的基础和根本所在。只有读了,才有可能让学生讨论、让学生思考、让学生提问、让学生联想。没有这个基础,一切都无从谈起。Reading between the lines 就是要让学生思考,培养他们细读文本的能力和逻辑思维能力。孔子说得好:"学而不思则罔,思而不学则殆。"学生读书时若不思考,其结果也只能是如入宝山,徒手而归。Reading beyond the lines 就是让学生展开想象的翅膀,让学生在已有的知识和新获得的知识之间架起一座桥梁。通过联想使学生所学知识形成纵横捭阖的网络,最终培养他们的想象力和创造力。

III. Full Texts

The Bible Stories

1. Six Days of Creation and the Sabbath

In the beginning when God created the heavens and the earth, the earth was a formless void and darkness covered the face of the deep, while a wind from God swept over the face of the waters. Then God said, "Let there be light"; and there was light. And God saw that the light was good; and God separated the light from the darkness. God called the light Day, and the darkness he called Night. And there was evening and there was morning, the first day.

And God said, "Let there be a dome in the midst of the waters, and let it separate the waters from the waters." So God made the dome and separated the waters that were under the dome from the waters that were above the dome. And it was so. God called the dome Sky. And there was evening and there was morning, the second day.

And God said, "Let the waters under the sky be gathered together into one place, and let the dry land appear." And it was so. God called the dry land Earth, and the waters that were gathered together he called Seas. And God saw that it was good. Then God said, "Let the earth put forth vegetation: plants yielding seed, and fruit trees of every kind on earth that bear fruit with the seed in it." And it was so. The earth brought forth vegetation: plants yielding seed of every kind, and trees of every kind bearing fruit with the seed in it. And God saw that it was good. And there was evening and there was morning, the third day.

And God said, "Let there be lights in the dome of the sky to separate the day from the night; and let them be for signs and for seasons and for days and years, and let them be lights in the dome of the sky to give light upon the earth." And it was so. God made the two great lights—the greater light to rule the day and the lesser light to rule the night—and the stars. God set them in the dome of the sky to give light upon the earth, to rule over the day and over the night, and to separate the light from the darkness. And God saw that it was good. And there was evening and there was morning, the fourth day.

And God said, "Let the waters bring forth swarms of living creatures, and let birds fly above the earth across the dome of the sky." So God created the great sea monsters and every living creature that moves, of every kind, with which the waters swarm, and every winged bird of every kind. And God saw that it was good. God blessed them, saying, "Be fruitful and multiply and fill the waters in the seas, and let birds multiply on the earth." And there was evening and there was morning, the fifth day.

And God said, "Let the earth bring forth living creatures of every kind: cattle and creeping things and wild animals of the earth of every kind. " And it was so. God made the wild animals of the earth of every kind, and the cattle of every kind, and everything that creeps upon the ground of every kind. And God saw that it was good.

Then God said, "Let us make humankind in our image, according to our likeness; and let them have dominion over the fish of the sea, and over the birds of the air, and over the cattle, and over all the wild animals of the earth, and over every creeping thing that creeps upon the earth. " So God created humankind in his image, in the image of God he created them; male and female he created them. God blessed them, and God said to them, "Be fruitful and multiply, and fill the earth and subdue it; and have dominion over the fish of the sea and over the birds of the air and over every living thing that moves upon the earth. " God said, "See, I have given you every plant yielding seed that is upon the face of all the earth, and every tree with seed in its fruit; you shall have them for food. And to every beast of the earth, and to every bird of the air, and to everything that creeps on the earth, everything that has the breath of life, I have given every green plant for food. " And it was so. God saw everything that he had made, and indeed, it was very good. And there was evening and there was morning, the sixth day.

Thus the heavens and the earth were finished, and all their multitude. And on the seventh day God finished the work that he had done, and he rested on the seventh day from all the work that he had done. So God blessed the seventh day and hallowed it, because on it God rested from all the work that he had done in creation.

These are the generations of the heavens and the earth when they were created.

2. Another Account of the Creation

In the day that the LORD God made the earth and the heavens, when no plant of the field was yet in the earth and no herb of the field had yet sprung up—for the LORD God had not caused it to rain upon the earth, and there was no one to till the ground; but a stream would rise from the earth, and water the whole face of the ground—then the LORD God formed man from the dust of the ground, and breathed into his nostrils the breath of life; and the man became a living being. And the LORD God planted a garden in Eden, in the east; and there he put the man whom he had formed. Out of the ground the LORD God made to grow every tree that is pleasant to the sight and good for food, the tree of life also in the midst of the garden, and the tree of the knowledge of good and evil.

The LORD God took the man and put him in the garden of Eden to till it and keep it. And the LORD God commanded the man, "You may freely eat of every tree of the garden; but of the tree of the knowledge of good and evil you shall not eat, for in the day that you eat of it you shall die. "

Then the LORD God said, "It is not good that the man should be alone; I will make him a helper as his partner. " So out of the ground the LORD God formed every animal of the field and every bird of the air, and brought them to the man to see what he would call them; and whatever the man called every living creature, that was its name. The man gave names to all cattle, and to the birds of the air, and to every animal of the field; but for the man there was not found a helper as his partner. So the LORD God caused a deep sleep to fall upon the man, and he slept; then he took one of his ribs and closed up its place with flesh. And the rib that the LORD God had taken from the man he made into a woman and brought her to the man. [23] Then the man said,

"This at last is bone of my bones and flesh of my flesh; this one shall be called Woman, for out of Man this one was taken. "

Therefore a man leaves his father and his mother and clings to his wife, and they become one flesh. And the man and his wife were both naked, and were not ashamed.

3. The First Sin and Its Punishment

Now the serpent was more crafty than any other wild animal that the LORD God had made. He said to the woman, "Did God say, 'You shall not eat from any tree in the garden'?" The woman said to the serpent, "We may eat of the fruit of the trees in the garden; but God said, 'You shall not eat of the fruit of the tree that is in the middle of the garden, nor shall you touch it, or you shall die. ' " But the serpent said to the woman, "You will not die; for God knows that when you eat of it your eyes will be opened, and you will be like God, knowing good and evil. " So when the woman saw that the tree was good for food, and that it was a delight to the eyes, and that the tree was to be desired to make one wise, she took of its fruit and ate; and she also gave some to her husband, who was with her, and he ate. Then the eyes of both were opened, and they knew that they were naked; and they sewed fig leaves together and made loincloths for themselves.

They heard the sound of the LORD God walking in the garden at the time of the evening breeze, and the man and his wife hid themselves from the presence of the LORD God among the trees of the garden. But the LORD God called to the man, and said to him, "Where are you?" He said, "I heard the sound of you in the garden, and I was afraid, because I was naked; and I hid myself. " He said, "Who told you that you were naked? Have you eaten from the tree of which I commanded you not to eat?" The man said, "The woman whom you gave to be with me, she gave me fruit from the tree, and I ate. " Then the LORD God said to the woman, "What is this that you have done?" The woman said, "The serpent tricked me, and I ate. " The LORD God said to the serpent,

"Because you have done this, cursed are you among all animals and among all wild creatures; upon your belly you shall go, and dust you shall eat all the days of your life. I will put enmity between you and the woman, and between your offspring and hers; he will strike your head, and you will strike his heel. "

To the woman he said,

"I will greatly increase your pangs in childbearing; in pain you shall bring forth children, yet your desire shall be for your husband, and he shall rule over you."

And to the man he said,

"Because you have listened to the voice of your wife, and have eaten of the tree about which I commanded you, 'You shall not eat of it,' cursed is the ground because of you; in toil you shall eat of it all the days of your life; thorns and thistles it shall bring forth for you; and you shall eat the plants of the field. By the sweat of your face you shall eat bread until you return to the ground, for out of it you were taken; you are dust, and to dust you shall return."

The man named his wife Eve, because she was the mother of all living. And the LORD God made garments of skins for the man and for his wife, and clothed them.

Then the LORD God said, "See, the man has become like one of us, knowing good and evil; and now, he might reach out his hand and take also from the tree of life, and eat, and live forever"—therefore the LORD God sent him forth from the garden of Eden, to till the ground from which he was taken. He drove out the man; and at the east of the garden of Eden he placed the cherubim, and a sword flaming and turning to guard the way to the tree of life.

4. Cain Murders Abel

Now the man knew his wife Eve, and she conceived and bore Cain, saying, "I have produced a man with the help of the LORD." Next she bore his brother Abel. Now Abel was a keeper of sheep, and Cain a tiller of the ground. In the course of time Cain brought to the LORD an offering of the fruit of the ground, and Abel for his part brought of the firstlings of his flock, their fat portions. And the LORD had regard for Abel and his offering, but for Cain and his offering he had no regard. So Cain was very angry, and his countenance fell. The LORD said to Cain, "Why are you angry, and why has your countenance fallen? If you do well, will you not be accepted? And if you do not do well, sin is lurking at the door; its desire is for you, but you must master it."

Cain said to his brother Abel, "Let us go out to the field." And when they were in the field, Cain rose up against his brother Abel, and killed him. Then the LORD said to Cain, "Where is your brother Abel?" He said, "I do not know; am I my brother's keeper?" And the LORD said, "What have you done? Listen; your brother's blood is crying out to me from the ground! And now you are cursed from the ground, which has opened its mouth to receive your brother's blood from your hand. When you till the ground, it will no longer yield to you its strength; you will be a fugitive and a wanderer on the earth." Cain said to the LORD, "My punishment is greater than I can bear! Today you have driven me away from the soil, and I shall be hidden from your face; I shall be a fugitive and a wanderer on the earth, and anyone who meets me may kill me." Then the LORD said to him, "Not so! Whoever kills Cain will suffer a sevenfold vengeance." And the LORD put a mark on Cain, so that no one who came upon him would kill him. Then Cain went away from the presence of the LORD, and settled in the land of

Nod, east of Eden.

5. The Tower of Babel

Now the whole earth had one language and the same words. And as they migrated from the east, they came upon a plain in the land of Shinar and settled there. And they said to one another, "Come, let us make bricks, and burn them thoroughly." And they had brick for stone, and bitumen for mortar. Then they said, "Come, let us build ourselves a city, and a tower with its top in the heavens, and let us make a name for ourselves; otherwise we shall be scattered abroad upon the face of the whole earth." The LORD came down to see the city and the tower, which mortals had built. And the LORD said, "Look, they are one people, and they have all one language; and this is only the beginning of what they will do; nothing that they propose to do will now be impossible for them. Come, let us go down, and confuse their language there, so that they will not understand one another's speech." So the LORD scattered them abroad from there over the face of all the earth, and they left off building the city. Therefore it was called Babel, because there the LORD confused the language of all the earth; and from there the LORD scattered them abroad over the face of all the earth.

6. The Ten Commandments

Then God spoke all these words:

I am the LORD your God, who brought you out of the land of Egypt, out of the house of slavery; you shall have no other gods before me.

You shall not make for yourself an idol, whether in the form of anything that is in heaven above, or that is on the earth beneath, or that is in the water under the earth. You shall not bow down to them or worship them; for I the LORD your God am a jealous God, punishing children for the iniquity of parents, to the third and the fourth generation of those who reject me, but showing steadfast love to the thousandth generation of those who love me and keep my commandments.

You shall not make wrongful use of the name of the LORD your God, for the LORD will not acquit anyone who misuses his name.

Remember the Sabbath day, and keep it holy. Six days you shall labor and do all your work. But the seventh day is a Sabbath to the LORD your God; you shall not do any work—you, your son or your daughter, your male or female slave, your livestock, or the alien resident in your towns. For in six days the LORD made heaven and earth, the sea, and all that is in them, but rested the seventh day; therefore the LORD blessed the Sabbath day and consecrated it.

Honor your father and your mother, so that your days may be long in the land that the LORD your God is giving you.

You shall not murder.

You shall not commit adultery.

You shall not steal.

You shall not bear false witness against your neighbor.

You shall not covet your neighbor's house; you shall not covet your neighbor's wife, or male or female slave, or ox, or donkey, or anything that belongs to your neighbor.

When all the people witnessed the thunder and lightning, the sound of the trumpet, and the mountain smoking, they were afraid and trembled and stood at a distance, and said to Moses, "You speak to us, and we will listen; but do not let God speak to us, or we will die." Moses said to the people, "Do not be afraid; for God has come only to test you and to put the fear of him upon you so that you do not sin." Then the people stood at a distance, while Moses drew near to the thick darkness where God was.

7. The Birth of Jesus the Messiah

Now the birth of Jesus the Messiah took place in this way. When his mother Mary had been engaged to Joseph, but before they lived together, she was found to be with child from the Holy Spirit. Her husband Joseph, being a righteous man and unwilling to expose her to public disgrace, planned to dismiss her quietly. But just when he had resolved to do this, an angel of the LORD appeared to him in a dream and said, "Joseph, son of David, do not be afraid to take Mary as your wife, for the child conceived in her is from the Holy Spirit. She will bear a son, and you are to name him Jesus, for he will save his people from their sins." All this took place to fulfill what had been spoken by the LORD through the prophet:

"Look, the virgin shall conceive and bear a son, and they shall name him Emmanuel," which means, "God is with us." When Joseph awoke from sleep, he did as the angel of the LORD commanded him; he took her as his wife, but had no marital relations with her until she had borne a son; and he named him Jesus.

8. The Visit of the Wise Men

In the time of King Herod, after Jesus was born in Bethlehem of Judea, wise men from the East came to Jerusalem, asking, "Where is the child who has been born king of the Jews? For we observed his star at its rising, and have come to pay him homage." When King Herod heard this, he was frightened, and all Jerusalem with him; and calling together all the chief priests and scribes of the people, he inquired of them where the Messiah was to be born. They told him, "In Bethlehem of Judea; for so it has been written by the prophet:

'And you, Bethlehem, in the land of Judah, are by no means least among the rulers of Judah; for from you shall come a ruler who is to shepherd my people Israel.' "

Then Herod secretly called for the wise men and learned from them the exact time when the star had appeared. Then he sent them to Bethlehem, saying, "Go and search diligently for the child; and when you have found him, bring me word so that I may also go and pay him homage." When they had heard the king, they set out; and there, ahead of them, went the star that they had seen at its rising, until it stopped over the place where the child was. When they saw that the star had stopped, they were overwhelmed with joy. On entering the house, they saw the child with Mary his mother; and they knelt down and paid him homage. Then, opening their treasure chests, they offered him gifts of gold, frankincense, and myrrh. And having been warned in a dream not to return to Herod, they left for their own country by another road.

9. The Escape to Egypt

Now after they had left, an angel of the LORD appeared to Joseph in a dream and said, "Get up, take the child and his mother, and flee to Egypt, and remain there until I tell you; for Herod is about to search for the child, to destroy him." Then Joseph got up, took the child and his mother by night, and went to Egypt, and remained there until the death of Herod. This was to fulfill what had been spoken by the LORD through the prophet, "Out of Egypt I have called my son."

10. The Massacre of the Infants

When Herod saw that he had been tricked by the wise men, he was infuriated, and he sent and killed all the children in and around Bethlehem who were two years old or under, according to the time that he had learned from the wise men. Then was fulfilled what had been spoken through the prophet Jeremiah:

"A voice was heard in Ramah, wailing and loud lamentation, Rachel weeping for her children; she refused to be consoled, because they are no more."

11. The Return from Egypt

When Herod died, an angel of the LORD suddenly appeared in a dream to Joseph in Egypt and said, "Get up, take the child and his mother, and go to the land of Israel, for those who were seeking the child's life are dead." Then Joseph got up, took the child and his mother, and went to the land of Israel. But when he heard that Archelaus was ruling over Judea in place of his father Herod, he was afraid to go there. And after being warned in a dream, he went away to the district of Galilee. There he made his home in a town called Nazareth, so that what had been spoken through the prophets might be fulfilled, "He will be called a Nazorean."

12. The Proclamation of John the Baptist

In those days John the Baptist appeared in the wilderness of Judea, proclaiming, "Repent, for the kingdom of heaven has come near." This is the one of whom the prophet Isaiah spoke when he said,

"The voice of one crying out in the wilderness: 'Prepare the way of the LORD, make his paths straight.'"

Now John wore clothing of camel's hair with a leather belt around his waist, and his food was locusts and wild honey. Then the people of Jerusalem and all Judea were going out to him, and all the region along the Jordan, and they were baptized by him in the river Jordan, confessing their sins.

But when he saw many Pharisees and Sadducees coming for baptism, he said to them,

"You brood of vipers! Who warned you to flee from the wrath to come? Bear fruit worthy of repentance. Do not presume to say to yourselves, 'We have Abraham as our ancestor'; for I tell you, God is able from these stones to raise up children to Abraham. Even now the ax is lying at the root of the trees; every tree therefore that does not bear good fruit is cut down and thrown into the fire.

"I baptize you with water for repentance, but one who is more powerful than I is coming after me; I am not worthy to carry his sandals. He will baptize you with the Holy Spirit and fire. His winnowing fork is in his hand, and he will clear his threshing floor and will gather his wheat into the granary; but the chaff he will burn with unquenchable fire."

13. The Baptism of Jesus

Then Jesus came from Galilee to John at the Jordan, to be baptized by him. John would have prevented him, saying, "I need to be baptized by you, and do you come to me?" But Jesus answered him, "Let it be so now; for it is proper for us in this way to fulfill all righteousness." Then he consented. And when Jesus had been baptized, just as he came up from the water, suddenly the heavens were opened to him and he saw the Spirit of God descending like a dove and alighting on him. And a voice from heaven said, "This is my Son, the Beloved, with whom I am well pleased."

Case 4　Instructional Design of *Getting the Best Value for Time* under Question-based Approach and Analysis

Ⅰ. Instructional Design of *Getting the Best Value for Time* under Question-based Approach

Step 1：Brief introduction to this course and course requirements

1. 本课程的教学理念：得法于课堂,得益于课外。

2. 本课程的教学内容：课堂教学以王守仁等编写的《泛读教程》一到四册为主,在此基础上,适度补充和增加一些内容。课后以阅读为主,既可以阅读我们推荐的阅读书目,其中以英美文学经典的一些简写本为主,如：*Pride and Prejudice*、*The Adventures of Tom Sawyer*；也可以阅读我们推荐的英语杂志、英文报纸、英文网站,如：《英语世界》、*Beijing Review*、*China Daily*、*21st Century*、asia. wsj. com、www. xinhuanet. com 等；还可以让他们阅读他们自己感兴趣的材料。

3. 本课程的教学要求：第一,课堂要积极参与,具体表现为上课要专心致志,积极思考,大胆质疑,积极参与小组和班级讨论和敢于发言,同时学会倾听其他同学的发言。课后要认真阅读。各人根据自己的实际情况,每天坚持读 1 000 ~ 1 500 个单词不等,贵在坚持。不仅要读,而且要做笔记,把自己认为有用的单词、短语、句子,甚至好的段落记下来；每周至少写一篇 summary；每两周至少写一篇读后感。此外,记下阅读过程中的问题,以便向教师或同学请教。

4. 本课程的考核：本课程的成绩由两部分组成，平时成绩占 30%，其中课堂参与占 10%，课后读书笔记占 20%；期终成绩占 70%。

Step 2：Lead-in with the question about the differences between learning at high school and learning at college or university

教师以问题形式导入课文。具体问题是：Does anyone know the differences between learning at high school and learning at college or university?

经过思考后，学生们肯定会发现中学学习与大学学习有许多差别。不管学生回答得怎么样，教师都要给予充分肯定，尽可能保护和调动他们的积极性，尤其对踊跃发言的学生更应如此，因为学生积极参与是上好课的第一步。没有学生的参与，课堂上气氛沉闷、死水一潭，就激发不了学生的学习动机，树立不起学生的学习信心，培养不了学生的学习兴趣。由此看来，营造一个轻松、活泼的课堂气氛，让学生敢说、想说、最终能说，比什么都重要。同时，这也要求教师要全身心地投入，举手投足、眼神体态应充满鼓励、欣赏和期待。在课堂上，每个人都是平等的，每个人的观点只有不同，没有对错，都应得到充分地尊重。这为以后课堂上问题的讨论、良好气氛的形成奠定了一个基础。

接下来，教师应因势利导，特别强调其中的一个差别，那就是：中学学习受制于教师、教材和教室，目的是为了高考，将来进入大学；而大学学习就是要冲破教师、教材和教室制约，目的是为了培养能力，学会思考，将来进入社会。那么，如何冲破呢？这就引出"unlearn"，即要去除以前一些不好或不对观念、思维方式和习惯。例如：以前我们一直认为教师总是对的，教材总是对的，教室里学的总是对的。其实不然，教师可能出错，教材可能出错，教室里所学的可能出错。道理很简单，那就是"金无足赤，人无完人"。既然如此，教师是人，而且不是完人，不是完人的教师可能要出错，而且肯定会出错。同样，教材也是由不是完人的人写出来或编出来的，不是完人的人写出来或编出来的教材可能要出错，而且肯定会出错。既然教师和教材有可能出错，那在教室里所学的东西也可能会出错。因此，我们在课堂上不要轻信教师，也不要轻信教材。要学会用自己的大脑去思考，用自己的心灵去感受，用自己的眼睛去观察，用自己的耳朵去聆听，用自己的鼻子去嗅闻，用自己的舌头去品尝，用自己的双手去体验。如果我们认为教师说的或教材写的是对的或是有道理的，我们就接受；如果我们认为教师说的或教材写的是不对的或是没有道理的，我们就不接受。

Step 3：Skimming with a focus on the questions about the organization of the text

教师要求学生浏览这篇课文并讨论下面的问题：What do you think of the organization of the text? /Is this text well-organized? Why or why not?

既然是浏览，只要求学生从宏观上了解这篇课文。这篇课文的题目是 Getting the best value for time。整个课文由三个部分组成：第一部分是 Effective learning，第二部分是 Practical steps，第三部分是 Planning time。

针对上面的问题，学生的回答可能有两种：这篇课文的结构很好或这篇课文的结构不好。不管学生怎么回答，都要鼓励积极思考，给出相应的理由。然后在学生讨论的基础上，教师可以进行小结，也可以与学生分享自己的看法。从逻辑的角度看，这篇课文的结构不尽合理,三个组成部分的顺序不够自然,即先是讲有效学习(Effective learning),接下来讲采取的具体步骤(Practical steps),最后讲计划时间(Planning time)。较为合理的顺序为先Planning time,然后采取 Practical steps,最好的结果是 Effective learning。

Step 4:Close reading with a focus on the question about the writing quality of each part

教师要求学生仔细地阅读课文,并讨论下面两个问题。

1. Which part do you think is best written? Why?

2. Which part do you think is worst written? Why?

本课文分为三部分。第一部分是有效学习,它包括六点:(1)课后及时复习课堂笔记;(2)准确记住老师的要求,尽早完成课程论文与作业;(3)有规律地复习;(4)复习时,要把时间分散开来;(5)一次学习时间不要超过两小时;(6)找到你学习的最佳时间。第二部分是具体步骤,它包括五点:(1)制订一个各种活动较为平衡的计划;(2)制订如何使用学习时间的计划;(3)在固定的时间、地点学习;(4)如果偶发事件占用了学习时间,事后要立即补起来;(5)完成学习任务后,要稍微犒赏自己一下。第三部分是计划时间,它包括三点:(1)制订学期计划表;(2)制订周计划表;(3)制订日计划表。

这时,应抓住时机,趁热打铁,继续鼓励学生思考。在学生发言前,老师使用得较多的是:"Try"、"Who would like to have a try?"、"Will you try?";在学生发言时,老师使用较多的应是点头、微笑和鼓励的目光。在学生发言后,老师使用得较多的应是:"Good"、"A good job"、"Not so bad"。如果学生回答得不够好,老师使用得较多的应是:"That's your opinion or idea."、"Any different opinions or ideas?"和"Anything else to add?"

在学生讨论的基础上,教师可以进行小结,也可以与学生分享自己的看法。这篇课文第三部分计划时间写得最好。这一部分在论述计划时间时,按照从大到小,从宏观到微观的顺序,即从学期计划到周计划再到日计划,比较有逻辑性和连贯性。第一部分和第二部分都写得不太理想。第一部分的六点中,有三点跟复习有关,它们分别是:(1)课后及时复习课堂笔记;(3)有规律地复习;(4)复习时,要把时间分散开来。其他三点与时间有关,它们分别是:(2)尽早完成课程论文与作业;(5)一次学习时间不要超过两小时;(6)找到你学习的最佳时间。第二部分的五点中,有两点与计划有关,有三点与时间有关。这两部分各点之间均缺乏内在的逻辑联系,给人以零乱、随意之感。

Step 5:Close reading with a focus on the question about reorganization and recombination of the text

教师要求学生不要受原文结构的限制,把三个部分的内容重新归类、整合,并讨论下面三个问题。

1. Can you move some of Part I into Part II or some of Part II into Part I?

2. Can you move some of Part II into Part III or some of Part III into Part II?

3. Can you move some of Part III into Part I or some of Part I into Part III?

前面已经谈到,较为合理的顺序为 Planning time、Practical steps 和 Effective learning。这样,可以把 Practical steps 中有关"计划"的两点移到 Planning time 当中去。具体做法是,把 Plan a program of balanced activities 和 Plan how you will use your study time 分别纳入 Make out a master timetable for the term 和 Make a daily "shopping list" 当中去,然后再进行整合。可以把 Effective learning 的六点移到 Practical steps 当中来,与其中的三点进行重新整合。在重新整合时,首先要找到关键词,然后再以关键词为中心进行调整、归类和合并。在学生讨论的基础上,教师可以进行小结,也可以与学生分享自己的看法。把 Effective learning 中的第五、六两点与 Practical steps 中的第三、四两点进行重新整合,形成(1)Study regularly(at a regular time, for a regular period of time and in a regular place);把 Effective learning 中的第二点与 Practical steps 中的第五点进行重新整合,形成(2)Finish your work immediately and rewardingly;把 Effective learning 中的第一、三、四点移到 Practical steps 中进行重新整合,形成(3)Review immediately, regularly and separately。经过重新整合后,现在 Effective learning 下面没有任何具体内容了,换句话说,这篇课文只有两个部分:Planning time 和 Practical steps。

Step 6:Discussion of the questions about the title

教师要求学生认真思考这篇课文的题目,并讨论下面的问题。What do you think of the title of the text? Is it still proper? Why or why not?

经过重新整合后,现在再来看题目,讨论一下 Getting the best value for time 是否合适。如果合适,给出理由。如果不合适,能否给出比这更好的题目。再次鼓励学生思考和讨论。在学生讨论的基础上,教师可以进行小结,也可以与学生分享自己的看法。应该说 Getting the best value for time 还是基本合适的,它可以统领 Planning time 和 Practical steps。但 Practical steps 中的具体内容更多与 Effective learning 有关。因此如果把题目改为 How to learn effectively,可能会更好些。那就是:如何进行有效学习? 首先计划时间,然后采取一些具体步骤。

Step 7:Discussion of the questions about the text substantiation

教师要求学生认真思考已经修改的课文,看看能否对课文内容进行充实,并讨论下面的问题。

1. Can you add something more to *Part I Planning time*?

2. Can you add something more to *Part II Practical steps*?

应该说,这两方面的内容,都可以进行充实。就第一个问题,学生可能会增加 yearly plan(年度计划)或 a four-year plan at university(大学四年计划)等。就第二个问题,学生可能会增加 preview(预习)、concentrate while you learn(学习时要专心)、think while you learn(学习时要思考)、take notes while you learn(学习时要记笔记)等。

Ⅱ. Analysis

首先,"问题教学法"不是为了问问题而问问题,而是通过这些问题,学生不仅能比较容易掌握所学内容,而且能学会思考、学会讨论、学会参与。由于问题贯穿在这节课的始终,学生始终处于思考、讨论和参与的状态。其次,教师的鼓励、欣赏和期待会对学生起到潜移默化、润物无声的效果,从而激发他们的积极情感。最后,一切都变了。不仅课文的内容变了、课文的小标题变了,而且课文的题目也变了。更为重要的是,那些习惯依赖教师、依赖课本新生的思想可能也悄悄随之变了。顺便说一下,本教学案例评为扬州大学优秀教学案例。

III. Full Text

Getting the Best Value for Time

Are you satisfied with what you achieve in the hours spent studying, or do you wonder where all the time has gone, without much to show for it? How hard are you really working? Here are some hints to help you make the most of your study time.

I. Effective learning

1. Review lecture notes as soon after a lecture as possible. Half an hour spent while the lecture is still fresh in your mind will do more to help you to develop an understanding of what you have heard and remember it than twice the time later on. It can be helpful to go over new work with other students to check that you have grasped all the points.

2. If you have been given an essay or assignment to do, note accurately what is required and start it when your memory of it is clear.

3. Revise and review regularly. Set regular weekly times to review the work in each course. This revision should be cumulative—adding a bit to the total at a time, covering briefly all the work done so far in the term. This way, you will consolidate the groundwork and avoid panic before exams.

4. When you revise, space out the time devoted to any one topic. You will learn more in six one hour periods spread over one week than in one six hour period.

5. Limit your blocks of study to two hours on any one topic or type of work. After one and half to two hours of intensive study, you begin to tire and concentration weakens. Take a break at some "achievement point" (end of a chapter, solving a problem, etc.) and then change to another part of the course or another type of work (e. g. from reading to writing). It will provide the change necessary to keep up your efficiency.

6. Find out the best times for working for yourself. Some periods may be better than others for different types of work and also for your own biological clock. If you tend to feel sleepy in the afternoon, this may not be the best time to try to read history or work out math problems. You may think that working into the early hours suits you, but does it fit in with an early class next morning? You are likely to feel tired next day and so gain nothing!

II. Practical steps

1. Plan a program of balanced activities. University life has many aspects which are important for getting full benefit from your time here. Some activities have fixed time requirements (e. g. classes, meetings, and sport), others are more flexible (e. g. recreation, relaxation, study time, personal matters, eating and sleeping).

2. Plan how you will use your study time. Knowing what you are going to do and when saves a lot of time spent on making decisions, false starts, retracing your steps to get the books you need, etc. Commit yourself to studying a particular assignment at a particular time.

3. Study at a regular time and in a regular place. You will learn to associate that time and place with working. This is after all what the world's workers have to do.

4. Trade time and don't steal it. When something unexpected happens and takes up time you have planned for study, decide immediately how you can make up the study missed.

5. Give yourself rewards for work completed on time (e. g. two-hour solid work = a cup of tea or coffee; essay completed = one-hour TV). After a strenuous evening finishing an essay or a set of problems, allow yourself "unwinding time" before bed.

III. Planning time

Working out a timetable will not turn you into a perfectly efficient person, but having a plan and sticking to it for a few weeks can help you to form better study habits and actually to save time, so that in the end you have more free time than before. Here is a way to plan your time which is flexible and practical.

1. Make out a master timetable for the term, marking your fixed commitments only: classes, society meetings, sports, etc. Make it clear and attractive, as you will have to look at it for a long time.

2. Draw up a weekly work program based on your present work assignments and study commitments: take a blank postcard or file card and divide it up, and then list:

a. your work assignments and study commitment for the week;

b. estimated amount of time needed for each of these;

c. dates when the work is due or when it is to be done. Include routine reading and revising as well as set work. Put it in a prominent, or noticeable, place in your room, or carry it with you. A good time to prepare this might be Sunday evening as you plan the week ahead.

3. Make a daily "shopping list" of things you have to do next day and when you will do them. Use a small card which can be put into a pocket where it is easily found. The best time to prepare this is before going to bed. Include everything you have to do next day, not just work but posting a friend's birthday card, going to the launderette, etc. Having prepared your cards and planned out your work, stick to your program. Cross out each item as you deal with it. If you give study hours top priority, the remaining hours will be really free.

Case 5 Instructional Design of *Steve Jobs' Speech at Stanford Commencement* Based on Annotative Response Writing and Analysis

I. Instructional Design of *Steve Jobs' Speech at Stanford Commencement* Based on Annotative Response Writing

Step 1: Lead-in with a brief introduction to annotative response writing

Annotative response writing, also called "write-between-the-lines" reading, is a kind of active, effective and efficient way of reading. When you read, you've got to write whatever occurs to you, like your understanding, your interpretation, your imagination, your association, your questions, your comments, etc., which helps you to develop your divergent thinking, convergent thinking, critical thinking, and individualize and internalize your reading.

Step 2: Annotative response writing with a focus on association

I am honored to be with you today at your commencement [In English, commencement means the beginning of something as well as the end of something. In Chinese, 毕业 means the end of something rather than the beginning of something. Another word that occurs to me is "school", which comes from Greek "schole", meaning "leisure", "spare time" or "time from work". In ancient Greece, the people thought that it was rough and tough to engage in military and political affairs. Only those who were free from work or wars could have the "leisure" to pursue learning.] from one of the finest universities [Stanford is famous for business like Google and Gmail by Sergey Brin & Larry Page, Yahoo by Jerry Yang and David Filo, and Nike by Phil Knight; for politics, like Herbert Hoover thirty-first US president, Alejandro Toledo former president of Peru (2001~2006), Taro Aso (麻生太郎) and Yukio Hatoyama (鸠山由纪夫) former prime ministers of Japan, and Ehud Barak (埃胡德·巴拉克), former prime minister of Israel; for literature, like John Steinbeck, Nobel Prize winner. The university was founded by the former governor of California Leland Stanford when his son died of typhoid fever at the age of 15. When he and his wife found that they could no longer do anything for their son, they decided that "the children of California shall be our children".] in the world. I never graduated from college [Bill Gates did not graduate from college, either. Nor did Sam Walton, founder of Wal-Mart.]. **Truth be told, this is the closest I've ever gotten to a college graduation. Today I want to tell you three stories from my life. That's it. No big deal. Just three stories.**

Step 3: Annotative response writing with a focus on comments

None of this had even a hope of any practical application in my life. [It seems to me that we Chinese are a bit too utilitarian. The first thing that we think about is whether what we learn is useful or not. If it is useful, we learn it. If it is useless, we don't learn it. Actually it is really hard to say what is useful and what is not. Everything is always changing. What used to be useful turns out to be useless and what is useless will turn out to be useful in the future. Besides, there is no absolute usefulness or uselessness in this world, which varies from time to time, from place to place, from person to person, from degree to degree. My idea about education is that we must be a bit idealistic, romantic and poetic rather than too materialistic, realistic and utilitarian.] But ten years later, when we were designing the first Macintosh computer, it all came back to me. And we designed it all into the Mac. It was the first computer with beautiful typography. [In this sense, Jobs is a both a scientist and an artist.] If I had never dropped in on that single course in college, the Mac would have never had multiple typefaces or proportionally spaced fonts. And since Windows just copied the Mac, it's likely that no personal computer would have them. If I had never dropped out, I would have never dropped in on this calligraphy class, and personal computers might not have the wonderful typography that they do. 〔Here, we see what had been useless turned out to be useful and what had been foolish turned out to be intelligent.〕 Of course it was impossible to connect the dots looking forward when I was in college. But it was very, very clear looking backwards ten years later.

Step 4: Annotative response writing with a focus on understanding

It wasn't all romantic. I didn't have a dorm room, so I slept on the floor in friends' rooms, I returned coke bottles for the 5 ¢ deposits to buy food with, and I would walk the 7 miles across town every Sunday night to get one good meal a week at the Hare Krishna temple. I loved it. 〔My understanding of this part is about Jobs' basic necessities in his daily life: food, shelter and transportation. In terms of food, most probably, he did not have enough to eat and often went hungry, for he bought food with coke bottle deposits. Besides, if he had had enough to eat, he could not have walked 7 miles across town every Sunday night to get one good meal a week. Let's calculate that a mile is equal to 1.6 kilometers and 7 miles is about 11 kilometers. If he walked back and forth, that would be about 22 kilometers, which is a long distance for a good meal. In terms of shelter, he did not have a dorm room and slept on the floor in friends' rooms. In terms of transportation, he did not have a bike, for he would walk 7 miles across the town every Sunday night to get a good meal a week.〕

Step 5: Annotative response writing with a focus on interpretation

Stay Hungry. 〔When you are hungry, most probably you are quite inquisitive, like looking for food everywhere. When you are hungry, most probably you are quite imaginative, like the little match girl who saw her kind and loving grandmother, the warm stove, and the roast goose. When you are hungry, most probably you are highly motivated to learn or something so that you change your current situation as soon as possible.〕 Stay Foolish. 〔It was foolish of a poor boy like Jobs to choose an expensive college; it was foolish of him to drop out of college in six months with all his parents' money spent; it was foolish of him to drop in on calligraphy class, which seemed interesting to him; it was foolish of him to get fired from his own company. It was all the follies that led to his great success, which confirms the idea that a man of great wisdom appears foolish.〕

Step 6: Assignment with a focus on choice and voice of favorite sentences

You are supposed to pick out three or four sentences from the speech you like most and make comments on them.

Ⅱ. Analysis

俗话说"不动笔墨不读书",现在能做到"不动笔墨不读书"的学生越来越少了。其阅读效果可想而知,肯定不尽如人意。学生在阅读中要么不思考,要么浅层思考。许多人常常人云亦云,不能或不敢提出自己的独特见解,最后造成了"千篇一律,千人一面"的现象。基于"Annotative response writing"的教学设计就是针对上述问题,倡导一种积极、主动的阅读方式,即阅读者是边读、边思、边写。只有在积极的读和深层的思基础上,写才是水到渠成的。当然,写东西时,有话则长,无话则短。写的内容是包罗万象的,可以是理解的,也可以是解释的;可以是想象的,也可以是联想的;可以是质疑的,也可以是评论的。这样的阅读方式有助于阅读的内化和个性化。本教学设计的最大的亮点是言传身教、率先垂范、身体力行。

III. Full Text with Annotative Response Writing

Steve Jobs' Speech at Stanford Commencement

[Steve Jobs was the founder and CEO of Apple. From the two quotations, we can see he was more than that. One is from the former American president Barack Obama, "Steve was among the greatest of American innovators—brave enough to think differently, bold enough to believe he could change the world, and talented enough to do it". The other is from Bill Gates, "The world rarely sees someone who has had the profound impact Steve has had, the effects of which will be felt for many generations to come. For those of us lucky enough to get to work with him, it's been an insanely great honor. "]

I am honored to be with you today at your commencement [In English, commencement means the beginning of something as well as the end of something while in Chinese, 毕业 means the end of something rather than the beginning of something. Another word that occurs to me is "school", which comes from Greek "schole", meaning "leisure", "spare time" or "time free from work". In ancient Greece, the people thought that it was rough and tough to engage in military and political affairs. Only those who were free from work or wars could have the "leisure" to pursue learning. As we all know, school is an institution where young people receive education and where we have a leisurely frame of mind, a leisurely mood and a leisurely talk.] from one of the finest universities in the world [Stanford is among the top ten universities in the world, famous for business like Google and Gmail by Sergey Brin & Larry Page, Yahoo by Jerry Yang and David Filo, and Nike by Phil Knight; for politics, like Herbert Hoover thirty-first US president, Alejandro Toledo former president of Peru(2001 ~ 2006), Taro Aso (麻生太郎) and Yukio Hatoyama (鸠山由纪夫) former prime ministers of Japan, and Ehud Barak(埃胡德・巴拉克), former prime minister of Israel; for literature, like John Steinbeck, Nobel Prize winner. The university was founded by the former governor of California Leland Stanford when his son died of typhoid fever at the age of 15. When he and his wife found that they could no longer do anything for their son, they decided that "the children of California shall be our children", thus founding Stanford University for "their children".]. I never graduated from college. [Bill Gates did not graduate from college, either. Nor did Sam Walton, founder of Wal-Mart.] Truth be told, this is the closest I've ever gotten to a college graduation. Today I want to tell you three stories from my life. That's it. No big deal. Just three stories. [In this sense, Jobs is a story teller just like Mo Yan, the Nobel Prize winner for literature. Besides, if you want to be a good teacher, you must be a good story teller.]

The first story is about connecting the dots.

I dropped out of Reed College [It is a co-educational, independent liberal arts and sciences college with a 9 : 1 student-to-faculty ratio. Every student is required to take a yearlong interdisciplinary humanities course.] after the first 6 months, but then stayed around as a drop-in for another 18 months or so before I really quit. [American colleges are sort of liberal and open, otherwise Jobs could not drop in on any class. In China, that is different. You can't drop in on any class when you've dropped out.] So why did I drop out?

It started before I was born. My biological mother was a young, unwed college graduate student, [Jobs is an illegitimate child with mixed blood, who is considered exceptionally intelligent. I don't know who his biological father is. After surfing on the internet, we find that he is a Syrian, who is a workaholic. Because of strong opposition from her family, especially from her father, they didn't get married.] and she decided to put me up for adoption. She felt very strongly that I should be adopted by college graduates, so everything was all set for me to be adopted at birth by a lawyer and his wife. Except that when I popped out they decided at the last minute that they really wanted a girl. [Traditionally, we Chinese value boys more than girls. Some people even think boys are superior to girls. In western countries, that is a different story. They choose or adopt a child according to their preference. This reminds me of the comments William Golding, a Nobel Prize winner, made on women: "I think women are foolish to pretend they are equal to men, they are far superior and always have been. Whatever you give a woman, she will make greater. If you give her sperm, she'll give you a baby. If you give her a house, she'll give you a home. If you give her groceries, she'll give you a meal. If you give her a smile, she'll give you her heart. She multiplies and enlarges what is given to her. So, if you give her any crap, be ready to receive a ton of shit!"] So my parents, [Jobs thinks highly of his parents, regarding them as "1,000% parents" while he does not think much of his biological parents, regarding them as his "sperm and egg bank".] who were on a waiting list, got a call in the middle of the night asking: "We have an unexpected baby boy; do you want him?" They said: "Of course." My biological mother later found out that my mother had never graduated from college and that my father had never graduated from high school. She refused to sign the final adoption papers. She only relented a few months later when my parents promised that I would someday go to college. [Promise is debt that you've got to pay. So if you make a promise, you must keep it. That is why his biological mother relented.]

And 17 years later I did go to college. [His parents kept their promise. I admire them from the bottom of my heart, for it was not easy for them to send Jobs to college.] But I naively chose a college that was almost as expensive as Stanford, [My understanding of "naively" is "foolishly", so this was the first foolish choice that he had made. We know that his family was not rich enough to send him to such a good private college. If I were Jobs, I might have chosen an inexpensive state university or a community college so that I could easily afford it.] and all of my working-class parents' savings were being spent on my college tuition. [From this, we can see why Jobs regards his parents them as "1,000% parents".] After six months, I couldn't see the value in it. I had no idea what I wanted to do with my life and no idea how college was going to help me figure it out. [From these sentences above, we can see that he was completely at sea.] And here I was spending all of the money my parents had saved their entire life. So I decided to drop out [It seems to me that this was the second foolish choice that he had made. It was very bold.] and trust that it would all work out OK. [If I were Jobs, I couldn't do the same way as he did. His experience and success can't be replicated.] It was pretty scary at the time, but looking back it was one of the best decisions I ever made. The minute I dropped out I could stop taking the required classes that didn't interest me, and begin dropping in on the ones that looked interesting. [From the paragraphs below, we know that he is interested in calligraphy. Besides, he is also very interested in reading books and listening to music. Here are some of his favorite books: *The Innovators' Dilemma* by Cleyton Christensen, *Secrets of the Little Blue Box* by Ron Rosenbaum, *Zen Mind, Beginner's Mind* by Shunryu Suzuki, *Autobiography of a Yogi* by Paramahansa Yogananda, *King Lear* by William Shakespeare, *Be Here Now* by Ram Dass *and Moby Dick* by Herman Melville. And here are some of his favorite musical works: *Imagine* by John Lennon, *Hard Headed Woman* by Cat Stevens, *Highway 61 Revisited & Blowing in the Wind* by Bob Dylan, *Won't Get Fooled Again* by The Who. Interest is a strong motivator, a great driving force and the best teacher. As long as you have interest, everything will become easy. So we must try everything possible to arouse students' interest.]

It wasn't all romantic. I didn't have a dorm room, so I slept on the floor in friends' rooms, I returned coke bottles for the 5 ¢ deposits to buy food with, and I would walk the 7 miles across town every Sunday night to get one good meal a week at the Hare Krishna temple. I loved it. [My understanding of this part is about Jobs' basic necessities in his daily life: food, shelter and transportation. In terms of food, most probably, he did not have enough to eat and often went hungry, for he bought food with coke bottle deposits. Besides, if he had had enough to eat, he could not have walked 7 miles across town every Sunday night to get one good meal a week. Let's calculate that a mile is equal to 1.6 kilometers and 7 miles is about 11 kilometers. If he walked back and forth, that would be about 22 kilometers, which is a long distance for a good meal. In terms of shelter, he did not have a dorm room and slept on the floor in friends' rooms. In terms of transportation, he did not have a bike, for he would walk 7 miles across the town every Sunday night to get a good meal a week.] And much of what I stumbled into by following my curiosity and intuition [Jobs looks upon curiosity as "a beginner's mind". By the way, he is a firm believer in Zen Buddhism. One of his famous sayings is "it is wonderful to have a beginner's mind." A beginner's mind refers to a small child's mind, which is full of curiosity, wonder and amazement, and which is innocent of pretence, preconceptions and prejudices. It is a great pity that we Chinese students can't follow our curiosity and intuition. We are forced to learn what is so-called utilitarian, which turns out to be uninteresting and worthless.] turned out to be priceless later on. Let me give you one example：

Reed College at that time offered perhaps the best calligraphy instruction in the country. Throughout the campus every poster, every label on every drawer, was beautifully hand calligraphed. Because I had dropped out and didn't have to take the normal classes, I decided to take a calligraphy class to learn how to do this. [This was the third foolish choice that he had made. Calligraphy like poetry and philosophy seemed useless.] I learned about serif and sans serif typefaces, about varying the amount of space between different letter combinations, about what makes great typography great. [Form the perspective of language, I don't think that "what makes great typography great" is a good sentence. Maybe Jobs wanted to emphasize the greatness of typography, I am not sure. In my view, we can omit one of the two "greats", namely, "what makes great typography" or "what makes typography great".] It was beautiful, historical, artistically subtle in a way that science can't capture, and I found it fascinating.

None of this had even a hope of any practical application in my life. [It seems to me that we Chinese are a bit too utilitarian. The first thing that we think about is whether what we learn is useful or not. If it is useful, we learn it. If it is useless, we don't learn it. Actually it is really hard to say what is useful and what is not. Everything is always changing. What used to be useful turns out to be useless and what is useless will turn out to be useful in the future. Besides, there is no absolute usefulness or uselessness in this world, which varies from time to time, from place to place, from person to person, from degree to degree. My idea about education is that we must be a bit idealistic, romantic and poetic rather than too materialistic, realistic and utilitarian.] But ten years later, when we were designing the first Macintosh computer, it all came back to me. And we designed it all into the Mac. It was the first computer with beautiful typography. [In this sense, Jobs is a both a scientist and an artist.] If I had never dropped in on that single course in college, the Mac would have never had multiple typefaces or proportionally spaced fonts. And since Windows just copied the Mac, it's likely that no personal computer would have them. If I had never dropped out, I would have never dropped in on this calligraphy class, and personal computers might not have the wonderful typography that they do. [Here, we see what had been useless turned out to be useful and what had been foolish turned out to be intelligent.] Of course it was impossible to connect the dots looking forward when I was in college. But it was very, very clear looking backwards ten years later.

Again, you can't connect the dots looking forward; you can only connect them looking backwards. [Yes, the same is true of English learning. When you first read a text, most probably, you find a dot here and a dot there. Then, you read and read and read the text to find more dots; and gradually, you connect these dots in the text and form a thread, that is, the author's train of thought. You can't stop here. You can connect this text with what you have learned before in terms of author, theme, or style. You can connect this text with what you will learn in the future.

In this case, you must be far-sighted. Here is an example of connecting dots, which tells a story by connecting the titles of the old films in China. 我叫《小铃铛》，家住《槐树庄》，左邻《白毛女》，右邻《李双双》，屋前《分水岭》，屋后《沙家浜》，东望《龙须沟》，西看《汾水长流》。我出生在《革命家庭》，爸爸《县委书记》，妈妈《党的女儿》，哥哥《铁道卫士》，姐姐《赵一曼》，弟弟《小兵张嘎》，妹妹《女飞行员》。《今天我休息》，正在思考《家庭问题》，突然来了《七十二家房客》，他们都是《冰山上的来客》，据说丢了《秘密图纸》，让我《跟踪追击》。我带上《鸡毛信》和《神秘的旅伴》，《快马加鞭》以《一日千里》的速度追了《七天七夜》，冒着《暴风骤雨》，穿过《上甘岭》和《青松岭》的《边寨烽火》，走过《风雪大别山》、《寂静的山林》和《林海雪原》，渡过《金沙江畔》和《金银滩》的《岸边激浪》，《逆风千里》，《飞越天险》，途经《万水千山》，来到《箭杆河边》，听到了《红石钟声》和《古刹钟声》，遇见了《我们村里的年轻人》、《大李小李和老李》。我们先后加入到《延安游击队》、《平原游击队》、《独立大队》、《回民之队》、《洪湖赤卫队》、《铁道游击队》和《红色娘子军》等革命队伍中，分别参加了《和平保卫战》、《地道战》、《地雷战》、《南征北战》和《黑山狙击战》，曾经《智取华山》和《奇袭》《无名岛》，在《沙漠里的战斗》和《湖上的斗争》中，经历了《雾海夜航》和《渡江探险》，终于在《激战前夜》布下《天罗地网》，《斩断魔爪》，《冲破黎明前的黑暗》，迎来了《江山多娇》。《为了和平》，《人民的战士》：《董存瑞》、《英雄坦克手》、《狼牙山五壮士》、《吕梁英雄》、《暴风雨中的雄鹰》、《海上神鹰》和《地下尖兵》等战友都表现出了《英雄虎胆》，《他们在战斗》中谱写了壮丽的《英雄诗篇》和《青春之歌》。在《葡萄熟了的时候》，《太阳照亮红石沟》，我和《患难之交》的《三个战友》《胜利重逢》于《战斗的山村》。我们在战斗中结下了《永恒的友谊》使我们永远《心连心》，继续迈着《青春的脚步》，《乘风破浪》，《高歌猛进》，续写《战火中的青春》和《生命交响曲》。请您《千万不能忘记》，我一直在《战斗里成长》，我《以革命的名义》将我们《年青的一代》在《大风浪里的小故事》讲述与您，不知您听后《满意不满意》。] So you have to trust that the dots will somehow connect in your future. You have to trust in something—your gut, destiny, life, karma, [Karma is a term in Buddhism, which means the effects of a person's actions that determine his destiny in his next incarnation. This reminds me of another term in Buddhism, samsara, which means the continual repetitive cycle of birth, death and rebirth within six realms of existence: the realms of the gods, demi-gods, humans, animals, hungry ghosts and hell beings.] whatever. This approach has never let me down, and it has made all the difference in my life.

My second story is about love and loss. [Rhetorically, alliteration is used, which refers to the repetition of initial consonant or cluster in two or more words. Similarly, poetry and prose, part and parcel, safe and sound, now or never, and from top to toe, etc. We'll look at one more sentence with alliteration which is well translated. It was a splendid population—for all the slow, sleepy, sluggish-brained sloths stayed at home. (这帮人个个出类拔萃——因为凡是呆板、呆滞、呆头呆脑的呆子都待在了家里。)]

I was lucky—I found what I loved to do early in life. [Jobs found what he loved to do early in life. Think about it. We usually do not know what we love to do. Everything seems dull and uninteresting.] Woz and I started Apple [There are different versions about why he named the company Apple. The best-known version is that Jobs used to work summers on a California apple farm and was fond of the crisp, round fruit. Another version is that Jobs admired the Beatles' Apple Records, which the Fab Four formed in the late 1960s. The other version is that apple comes from the Garden of Eden in the Bible, which represents knowledge.] in my parents' garage when I was 20. We worked hard, and in 10 years Apple had grown from just the two of us in a garage into a ＄2 billion company with over 4000 employees. [That is fantastic! That company has more employees than Yangzhou University. You can hardly imagine how fast the company develops.] We had just released our finest creation—the Macintosh—a year earlier, and I had just turned 30. And then I got fired. How can you get fired from a company you started? [That's the first loss Jobs mentioned: loss of his company and his job. It's unbelievable! Too unbelievable!] Well, as Apple grew we hired someone who I thought was very talented to run the company with me, and for the first year or so things went well. But then our visions of the future began to diverge and eventually we had a falling out. When we did, our Board of Directors sided with him. [There is no question of who is right or who is wrong, but there is a big difference in their vision of the future.] So at 30 I was out. And very publicly out [That means loss of his face!]. What had been the focus of my entire adult life was gone, and it was devastating. [Jobs lost more than his company, his job and his face. He also lost honor, lost courage, lost confidence and lost hope. Loss of all these was such a crushing blow that no one else could endure it.]

I really didn't know what to do for a few months. I felt that I had let the previous generation of entrepreneurs down—that I had dropped the baton as it was being passed to me. [He had strong self-reproach.] I met with David Packard and Bob Noyce and tried to apologize for screwing up so badly. I was a very public failure, and I even thought about running away from the valley [It refers to the Silicon Valley, the area in California known for its high-tech industry]. But something slowly began to dawn on me—I still loved what I did. [It's wonderful to love what you do and do what you love.] The turn of events at Apple had not changed that one bit. I had been rejected, but I was still in love. And so I decided to start over.

I didn't see it then, but it turned out that getting fired from Apple was the best thing that could have ever happened to me. [You will never know what happens. A Chinese saying goes, "A loss may turn out to be a gain." or "Misfortune may be an actual blessing".] The heaviness of being successful was replaced by the lightness of being a beginner again, less sure about everything. It freed me to enter one of the most creative periods of my life.

During the next five years, I started a company named NeXT [When I first came across the word NeXT, I had two questions: Why did Jobs name his company NeXT after he was fired from Apple? Why was NeXT spelt in this way? In terms of the first question, most probably that was the "next" goal he set up. In terms of the second question, most probably Jobs thinks that a combination of capitals and lower case letter can make the lower case e different so as to provide a focal point and visual contrast among the capital letters which otherwise, consist only of straight lines. In his opinion, the e could stand for "education, excellence, expertise, exceptional, excitement, e$=$mc^2, etc.". In my opinion, the e stands for "English enthusiasts eagerly envision enhanced emotional elevation, exceeding even existing examples' elicited elation, encountering each ensuing eccentric exercise, ergo everyone's esteemed enlisted essayist ensures each exquisite excerpt exhibits explosive expressive efficacy evincing excruciating editing effort, extreme endurance, engineering excellence, etc." By the way, capitalized or lower case letter(s) can convey meaning. For instance, the blast was big, Big, BIG. Another example, a modern American poet is called e. e. cummings, whose name suggests he and other animals or plants like dog, elephant, tree or celery are equal.] another company named Pixar, and fell in love with an amazing woman who would become my wife. Pixar went on to create the world's first computer animated feature film, Toy Story, and is now the most successful animation studio in the world. In a remarkable turn of events, Apple bought NeXT, I retuned to Apple, and the technology we developed at NeXT is at the heart of Apple's current renaissance. [When he returned to Apple, Jobs produced his well-known advertisement: Think different! Here's to the crazy ones. The misfits. The rebels. The troublemakers. The round pegs in the square holes. The ones who see things differently. They're not fond of rules. And they have no respect for the status quo. You can quote them, disagree with them, glorify or vilify them. But the only thing that you can't do is ignore them, because they change things. They push the human race forward. While some may see them as the crazy ones, we see genius, because the people who are crazy enough to think that they can change the world, are the ones who do. (不同凡想! 这里向一群疯狂的人致敬: 他们不合时宜、桀骜不驯, 惹是生非、格格不入; 他们眼光独特; 他们既不墨守成规, 也不安于现状。你可以引用他们, 也可以反对他们; 你可以赞美他们, 也可以诽谤他们, 但你唯一不能做的就是漠视他们。因为他们改变了世界, 推动了人类前进。或许他们在别人眼里是疯子; 但在我们的眼里, 他们是天才。因为只有那些疯狂到认为能够改变世界的人才能改变世界。)] And Laurene and I have a wonderful family together.

I'm pretty sure none of this would have happened if I hadn't been fired from Apple. It was awful tasting medicine, but I guess the patient needed it. Sometimes life hits you in the head with a brick. Don't lose faith. [It's easy to say, but it's hard to do. When you really get a deadly blow, which makes you lose courage, lose confidence and lose hope, it is very hard to cheer up. In this sense, Jobs is wonderful.] I'm convinced that the only thing that kept me going was that I loved what I did. You've got to find what you love. And that is as true for your work as it is for your lovers. Your work is going to fill a large part of your life, and the only way to be truly satisfied is to do what you believe is great work. And the only way to do great work is to love what you do. If you haven't found it yet, keep looking. Don't settle. [Having a sense of purpose and striving towards goals gives life meaning, direction and satisfaction. It not only contributes to health and longevity, but also makes you feel better in difficult times.] As with all matters of the heart, you'll know when you find it. [Here is another grammatical problem: the word "matters" is not in agreement with the following "it". It would be better either to change "all matters" into "the matter" or to change "it" into them. 〕And, like any great relationship, it just gets better and better as the years roll on. So keep looking until you find it. Don't settle.

My third story is about death.

When I was 17, I read a quote that went something like: "If you live each day as if it was your last, someday you'll most certainly be right." 〔Live as if you were to die tomorrow and you will treasure every second of your life. Learn as if you were to live forever and you will make the best use of learning opportunity and maximize its learning effectiveness. 〕It made an impression on me, and since then, for the past 33 years, 〔From these two sentences above, we can guess that Jobs was 50 when he made his speech. 〕I have looked in the mirror every morning and asked myself: "If today were the last day of my life, would I want to do what I am about to do today?" And whenever the answer has been "No" for too many days in a row, I know I need to change something.

Remembering that I'll be dead soon is the most important tool I've ever encountered to help me make the big choices in life. 〔What is life? It is from b to d, from birth to death. What is between b and d? It is c, choices. Yes, life is choices. When you say yes to a goal or an objective, you say no to many more. Every prize has its price. The prize is the yes and the price is the no. 〕Because almost everything—all external expectations, all pride, all fear of embarrassment or failure—these things just fall away in the face of death, 〔Yes, everything falls away in the face of death, including your fame, your wealth and your power. 〕leaving only what is truly important. 〔What is truly important is to follow your heart, your curiosity and your intuition. 〕Remembering that you are going to die is the best way I know to avoid the trap of thinking you have something to lose. You are already naked. 〔When you are born, you are naked without bringing anything to this world; when you die, you are naked without taking anything away from this world. This reminds me of a story which goes like this. A man died. . . . When he realized it, he saw God coming closer with a suitcase in his hand. (Conversation between God and Dead Man)

God: Alright, son, it's time to go!

Man: So soon? I had a lot of plans . . .

God: I am sorry, but it's time to go.

Man: What do you have in that suitcase?

God: Your belongings.

Man: My belongings? You mean my things . . . clothes . . . money . . .

God: Those things were never yours, they belong to the Earth.

Man: Is it my memories?

God: No. They belong to Time.

Man: Is it my talent?

God: No. They belong to Circumstance.

Man: Is it my friends and family?

God: No, son. They belong to the Path you traveled.

Man: Is it my wife and children?

God: No. they belong to your Heart.

Man: Then it must be my body.

God: No, no . . . It belongs to Dust.

Man: Then surely it must be my Soul!

God: You are sadly mistaken, son. Your Soul belongs to me.

With tears in his eyes and full of fear, the man took the suitcase from the God's hand and opened it . . . EMPTY!! With heart broken and tears down his cheek he asked God . . .

Man: I never owned anything?

God: That's right. You never owned anything.

Man: Then? What was mine?

God: Your MOMENTS.

Every moment you lived was yours. Life is just a Moment. LIVE IT. LOVE IT. ENJOY IT.] There is no reason not to follow your heart.

About a year ago I was diagnosed with cancer. I had a scan at 7:30 in the morning, and it clearly showed a tumor on my pancreas [It is said that when one is too hungry or too full, he/she is most likely to suffer from pancreatic disease. Just imagine that in his college days, every Sunday night, Jobs was too hungry first, for he had to walk seven miles; and then he was too full, for there was no food limit so long as he could eat.]. I didn't even know what a pancreas was. The doctors told me this was almost certainly a type of cancer that is incurable, and that I should expect to live no longer than three to six months. My doctor advised me to go home and get my affairs in order, which is doctor's code for preparing to die. It means to try to tell your kids everything you thought you'd have the next 10 years to tell them in just a few months. It means to make sure everything is buttoned up so that it will be as easy as possible for your family. It means to say your goodbyes. [Go to visit a hospital and you will cherish your health; go to visit a prison and you will treasure your freedom; go to visit a graveyard and you will value your life. Health is 1 and all the others like money, beautiful houses, fashionable cars, fame, status, power, etc. are 0. Without health, there will be nothing.]

I lived with that diagnosis all day. Later that evening I had a biopsy, where they stuck an endoscope down my throat, through my stomach and into my intestines, put a needle into my pancreas and got a few cells from the tumor. I was sedated, but my wife, who was there, told me that when they viewed the cells under a microscope the doctors started crying because it turned out to be a very rare form of pancreatic cancer that is curable with surgery. I had the surgery and I'm fine now.

This was the closest I've been to facing death, and I hope it's the closest I get for a few more decades. Having lived through it, I can now say this to you with a bit more certainty than when death was a useful but purely intellectual concept. No one wants to die. Even people who want to go to heaven don't want to die to get there. [Yes, I quite agree with him. In Chinese, we say that even a good death is not better than a wretched existence.] And yet death is the destination we all share. [Yes, we share the same destination: death, but it is more than that. According to the traveling theory, we share the same departure: birth and the same process: growth.] No one has ever escaped it. And that is as it should be, because Death is very likely the single best invention of Life. It is Life's change agent. [Death is an active and efficient cause that changes life.] It clears out the old to make way for the new. [Just as the waves behind drive those before in the Yangtze River, so the young replace the old in the world.] Right now the new is you, but someday not too long from now, you will gradually become the old and be cleared away. Sorry to be so dramatic, [How time flies! This reminds me of Chairman Mao's saying that 38 years has passed like a mere snap of fingers.] but it is quite true.

Your time is limited, so don't waste it living someone else's life. Don't be trapped by dogma—which is living with the results of other people's thinking. Don't let the noise of other's opinions drown out your own inner voice. And most important, have the courage to follow your heart and intuition. [Following your heart and intuition is primary.] They ["They" refers to your heart and intuition] somehow already know what you truly want to become. Everything else is secondary. [Live your own life. Be yourself and be your own boss. The life is yours and you have every right and every reason to spend it in your own way without any hurdles or barriers from others. Give yourself a chance to nurture your creative qualities in a care-free, fear-free and pressure-free climate.]

When I was young, there was an amazing publication called *The Whole Earth Catalog*, which was one of the bibles of my generation. It was created by a fellow named Stewart Brand not far from here in Menlo Park, and he brought it to life with his poetic touch. This was in the late 1960's, before personal computers and desktop publishing, so it was all made with typewriters, scissors, and polaroid cameras. It was sort of like Google in paperback form, 35 years before Google came along: it was idealistic, and overflowing with neat tools and great notions.

Stewart and his team put out several issues of *The Whole Earth Catalog*, and then when it had run its course, they put out a final issue. It was the mid-1970s, and I was your age. On the back cover of their final issue was a photograph of an early morning country road, [This reminds me of John Denver's classic country song: *Take Me Home, Country Road*. I like it so much that I listen to it hundreds of times without getting tired of it.] the kind you might find yourself hitchhiking on if you were so adventurous. Beneath it were the words: "Stay Hungry. Stay Foolish." It was their farewell message as they signed off. Stay Hungry. Stay Foolish. And I have always wished that for myself. And now, as you graduate to begin anew, I wish that for you.

Stay Hungry. 〔When you are hungry, most probably you are quite inquisitive, like looking for food everywhere. When you are hungry, most probably you are quite imaginative, like the little match girl who saw her kind and loving grandmother, the warm stove, and the roast goose. When you are hungry, most probably you are highly motivated to learn or something so that you change your current situation as soon as possible. 〕 Stay Foolish. 〔It was foolish of a poor boy like Jobs to choose an expensive college; it was foolish of him to drop out of college in six months with all his parents' money spent; it was foolish of him to drop in on calligraphy class, which seemed interesting to him; it was foolish of him to get fired from his own company. It was all the follies that led to his great success, which confirms the idea that a man of great wisdom appears foolish. In addition, it reminds me of two things. One is Zhen Banqiao's famous saying, "It is difficult to be clever. It is difficult to be foolish or muddle-headed. It is more difficult to graduate from being clever into being foolish or muddle-headed. The other is Su Shi's poem to his son, which goes like this: 人皆养子望聪明,我被聪明误一生;唯愿孩儿愚且鲁,无灾无难到公卿。〕

Thank you all very much.

Case 6　Interaction-based Instructional Design of *Horoscopes* and Analysis

Ⅰ. Interaction-based Instructional Design of *Horoscopes*

Step 1: Lead-in with a video about the *Chinese Zodiac*

The class begins with a video about the Chinese Zodiac, which is based on a 12-year cycle related to animal signs: rat, ox, tiger, rabbit, dragon, snake, horse, sheep, monkey, rooster, dog, and pig. The rat ranks first on the Chinese zodiac signs. People born in the Year of Rat have characteristics of an animal with spirit, wit, alertness, delicacy, flexibility and vitality. People born in the Year of Ox are probably tardy in action, but industrious and cautious. Most of them are conservative and hold their faith firmly. Tigers, considered to be brave, cruel, forceful, stately and terrifying, are the symbol of power and LORDliness. People with Rabbit as Chinese zodiac sign are not aggressive but approachable. They have a decent, noble and elegant manner. Dragons have characteristics of authority, dignity, honor, success, luck, and capacity. Snake carries the meanings of malevolence, cattiness and mystery, as well as acumen and divination. Horse symbolizes enthusiasm, energy, independence and integrity. Sheep is gentle and calm, which reminds people of beautiful things. Monkey is a clever and smart animal, with an auspicious meaning. Rooster is almost the epitome of fidelity and punctuality. Dog is man's good friend who can understand the human's spirit and obey its master, whether he is wealthy or not. Pig is not thought to be a smart animal in China. It likes sleeping and eating and becomes fat, which usually features laziness and clumsiness. On the positive side, it behaves itself, has no calculation to harm others, and can bring affluence to people.

What is your Chinese Zodiac? Do you think that it accurately describes your characters? But in western countries, they have horoscopes, which are different from Chinese Zodiac.

Step 2: Reading with a focus on the interaction between students and the text about horoscopes

Reading with a focus on the interaction between students and the text about horoscopes involves three steps. The first step is that the students are asked to read the whole text to get a general idea about horoscopes; the second step is that the students are asked to read their own horoscopes to see to what degree the description of their horoscopes is correct; and the third step is that the students are asked to read other horoscopes to see to what degree the description of other horoscopes is correct.

The first step is that the students are asked to read the whole text to get a general idea about horoscopes. After students read the text, they summarize the character of each horoscope as follows:

Horoscopes	Birth dates	Description of characters
Aries	from March 21st to April 20th	enthusiastic, not afraid of difficult situation, impulsive, selfish
Taurus	from April 21st to May 21st	strong, hard-working, stubborn, humorous, not serious
Gemini	from May 22nd to June 21st	clever, energetic, good at dealing with people, loving to talk, liking to be new different
Cancer	from June 22nd to July 22nd	very sensitive, changeable, loving home and family, interested in history and ancient objects, imaginative
Leo	from July 23rd to August 22nd	born to command, proud, self-concerned, selfish, generous, and understanding
Virgo	from August 23rd to September 22nd	clear-thinking, careful, and hard-working, highly skilled, willing to help others
Libra	from September 23rd to October 23rd	character-balanced, kind, gentle, good at art and music
Scorpio	from October 24th to November 22nd	independent, energetic, self-controlling
Sagittarius	from November 23rd to December 21st	curious, interested, impatient, loving sports
Capricorn	from December 22nd to January 19th	steady, ambitious, successful, serious, understanding

（续表）

Horoscopes	Birth dates	Description of characters
Aquarius	from January 20th to February 18th	open-minded, honest, friendly, popular, a bit eccentric, patient
Pisces	from February 19th to March 20th	quiet, gentle, loyal, cold, distant, sensitive

The second step is that the students are asked to read their own horoscopes to see to what degree the description of their horoscopes is correct. Students read their own horoscopes and then share theirs with the whole class. It starts with the description of character which is completely consistent with their character, then what is largely consistent, followed by what is half consistent and little consistent, finally completely inconsistent.

At least five students volunteer or are asked to participate in this activity. It can be predicted there is no complete consistency or complete inconsistency between the description of character and one's real character. Most of them probably fall somewhere between largely consistent and little consistent, which is a matter of degree. There is some flexibility in responding to their description depending on the circumstances.

The third step is that the students are asked to read other horoscopes to see to what degree the description of character is correct.

Students read the other horoscopes and try to find out which description is completely in line with their characters, which description is largely in line with their characters, which description is half in line with their characters, which description is hardly in line with their characters, and which description is in no line with their characters.

By looking at their horoscopes and looking for the horoscopes that fit their character, the students learn and gradually grasp the horoscopes.

Step 3: Reading with a focus on the interaction between students and students about horoscopes

Reading with a focus on the interaction between students and students about horoscopes is made up of three steps. The first step is pair work to guess your deskmate's horoscope based on your reading about horoscope and your observation. The same is applied to the second step, which is group work to guess your classmate's horoscope. The third step is class work to guess the celebrities' horoscopes.

The first step is pair work to guess deskmate's horoscope. One can keep guessing the other's horoscope by referring to the text until he is right. When he guesses, he must give reasons why the other is such a horoscope. Attention must be paid to one thing: he must not guess more than three times. If he guesses three times without hitting the target, that means he fails. Then another round starts with their roles reversed and they will do the same thing again.

The second step is group work to guess classmate's horoscope and then explain the reasons.

The whole class is divided into six groups. In each group, one student is asked to stand up and the other members in the group to guess his horoscope by describing his characters. Their guesses may differ from person to person. When the last person finishes his or her guess, the standing student will reveal his horoscope to see who guesses right.

The third step is class work to guess the celebrities' horoscopes. A student proposes a celebrity and then the whole class will guess. The celebrities can be a movie star, a popular singer, a Nobel Prize winner, an entrepreneur, a famous writer, etc. After their guesses, they can search for relevant information with their cellar phones to confirm or disconfirm them.

Step 4: Reading with a focus on the interaction between students and teacher about horoscopes

Reading with a focus on the interaction between students and teacher about horoscopes consists of three steps. The first step is that students guess their *Reading* teacher's horoscope. The second step is that teacher guesses students' horoscopes and explains the reasons. The third step is that teacher and students guess *Basic English* teacher's and *Oral English* teacher's horoscopes together.

The first step is that students guess their reading teacher's horoscope. Since he has already taught English reading for nearly one semester, they have some vague idea about his horoscope, but not exactly. After several guesses, the teacher finally reveals his horoscope.

It is the teacher's turn to guess his students' horoscopes, which is the funniest and the most exciting part of this class. When the teacher guesses right, he will be given some applause of encouragement. When the teacher guesses wrong, he will be given some scream or outburst or ranting.

The last step is for the teacher and students to guess the two teachers' horoscopes together. And all the guesses are kept open. Based on these guesses, the conclusions can be drawn about their horoscopes if possible. The students will ask the two teachers for answers after class.

Step 5: Assignment with a focus on your opinions about *Horoscopes*

An assignment is made for the students to give their opinions about horoscopes. Before the end of class, the teacher shares a short story with the class, which goes like this:

> Once upon a time, three scholars went to the capital for imperial examination. Before they left, they went to a fortune-teller to see what would happen to them. The fortune-teller showed the index finger to them and then said, "Just go! When your examination results are announced, I'll show you how right I am in predicting your results." The fortune-teller's wife was puzzled and asked "Why do you say that?" "You see, the index finger means one, which can be interpreted in four ways: the first is that every one can pass the examination, which means that three can pass the examination; the second is that one can't pass the examination, which means that two can pass the examination; the third is that one can pass

the examination; the fourth is that no one can pass the examination, which means that nobody can pass the examination. The three scholars who take examination only have four possibilities, which I have already exhausted. So I am always right."

Though horoscopes are considered to be a pseudoscience, many people still believe them. One reason is that human characters are many-sided and there is always one or two aspects that matches the horoscopes. In a certain sense, horoscopes, just like the fortune-teller, are always right.

II. Analysis

互动式教学是一种民主、自由、平等、开放式的教学。它有两个最大的特点：一是"互"即"双方"，而不是"单方"；二是"动"，而不是"静"。本教学设计的特点就是"互动"，互动的中心是学生。第一次互动是学生与课文的互动，通过互动，学生了解自己的星座和性格特征。与此同时，从其他星座中寻找与自己的性格相吻合的地方。第二次互动是学生与学生的互动，通过配对互动和小组互动，学生了解彼此的星座与性格；通过班级互动，根据名人的性格，猜测他们的星座。第三次互动是学生与教师的互动，共分为三步。第一步，学生根据教师的性格，猜老师的星座；第二步，老师根据学生的性格，猜学生的星座；第三步，老师和学生共同猜《基础英语》老师和《英语口语》老师的星座。学生经过三次互动，不知不觉中了解并掌握了所学内容，并能学以致用。

III. Full Text

Horoscopes

For thousands of years, people have believed that the position of the stars affects our lives. This may or may not be true, but there is no doubt that astrology itself does affect our lives. Most newspapers print horoscopes, and in the United States about fifty million people read them every day. Many young people plan to marry at a time when their horoscopes will be favorable, while others decide not to marry because their signs are not harmonious. Some companies have hired astrologers to advise them, and one well-known businessman prefers to do his most important work at 3 a. m. because he was told that it is his most favorable hour. Perhaps, the most well-known acknowledgement of astrological influence occurred after an assassination attempted on United States President Ronald Reagan on March 30, 1981. For the next seven years his wife, Nancy, consulted a Californian astrologer about the most favorable times and dates for major events in the president's life: the takeoff and landing of Air Force One, State of the Union addresses, surgery, the signing of treaties, presidential debates, even press conference.

Of course, there are people who are skeptical about horoscopes which are said to be based on the movements of the planets in the sky. Some of them put horoscopes on trial. For example,

The Consumers' Association in London test many kinds of products to see whether they give value for money. In its magazine *Which*? It published a report on horoscopes. It began by quoting forecasts for Gemini people on the very same day of March in four different newspapers.

Daily Express: "Good day for any kind of desk work. "

Sun: "A period full of activities. "

Daily Mirror: "You can relax. "

Daily Mail: "This is an unusual day. "

The investigators asked 200 people to read their horoscopes every day for a month. Afterwards, 83 per cent reported that the advice was of very little help at all and 87 per cent said that the predictions were not really accurate.

Most revealing of all was a test in which people born under one sign of the Zodiac were sent predictions for completely different sign. *Which*? Reported.

Of course, if there was anything in them, predictions for their own sign should have been conspicuously more accurate. Unfortunately, the results proved otherwise. There was absolutely no difference in accuracy between your horoscope and reading any other one.

But even skeptics can't be sure that they are not affected by what the stars say. How do you know, for example, that your employer, your best friend, or perhaps even your husband or wife is not secretly following the direction of a horoscope?

Here is a set of horoscopes. Test it yourself and draw a conclusion on your own.

- Aries (sheep) March 21 to April 20

Persons born under the sign of the sheep tend to be enthusiastic and not afraid of difficult situations. They are natural leaders who like to bring about changes in the world, and they may do so as general or politicians. Often impulsive, they welcome hard work and get things done without wasting time, but they are sometimes thought as selfish because of this.

Harmonious signs: Sagittarius and Leo

- Taurus (bull) April 21 to May 21

The sign of the bull is a fitting one for Taurus, who is strong and known for working hard. They understand the importance of order and try to establish a system for their lives. Many are found in government work. Although sometimes stubborn, Taureans are not always serious, and usually have a good sense of humor.

Harmonious signs: Capricorn, Virgo, and Cancer

- Gemini (twin) May 22 to June 21

Clever and full of energy, Geminis are experts at dealing with other people. Because of their ability to use their minds well and their desire to express themselves, they make good inventors, scientists, and magicians. They are excited by the new and the different, and need a lot of variety in both their personal and professional lives.

Harmonious signs: Aquarius and Libra

- Cancer (crab) June 22 to July 22

Those born under the sign of crab are very sensitive, so they laugh and cry easily. They change their minds often, but when they decide they really want something, they don't let go of that desire. Cancers love their homes and families, and are interested in history and ancient objects. They have strong imaginations so that they make good teachers, public speakers, and writers.

Harmonious signs: Pisces, Scorpio and Taurus

- Leo (lion) July 23 to August 23

The lion is the sign of those who are born to command. They are proud people who may appear to be self-concerned and selfish, but they are frequently generous and understanding. It is not surprising to find that they are often politicians or the directors of large companies.

Harmonious signs: Sagittarius and Aries

- Virgo (virgin) August 24 to September 23

Virgoes are clear-thinking, careful, and hard workers. Although they have the ability to organize, they are often not very good in positions of authority. Virgoes often choose professions in which they can work alone, and they are highly skilled in all kinds of handicrafts. They are willing to give much of their time to helping others.

Harmonious signs: Capricorn and Taurus

- Libra (scale) September 24 to October 23

The sign of Libra is the scale, another fitting sign, since the strength of these people lies in their balanced character. Libras particularly dislike anything that is unfair, and they try to do everything as perfectly as possible. They are kind and gentle with others and never rigid—they know when to work and when to play. They are often good at art and music.

Harmonious signs: Aquarius and Gemini

- Scorpio (scorpion) October 24 to November 22

Scorpios are independent people with strong likes and dislikes. They are full of energy, yet they are able to maintain a complete control over themselves. Nothing seems impossible to Scorpio. They often choose to work in professions such as doctor or detective—jobs that require overcoming unusual difficulties.

Harmonious signs: Cancer and Pisces

- Sagittarius (archer) November 23 to December 21

People born under the sign of Sagittarius are noted for their extreme curiosity. Everything interests them and although they are impatient, they will make a great effort to learn. They love the outdoors and do well at all kinds of sports. Sagittarians often make good lawyers and journalists.

Harmonious signs: Aries, Leo and Sagittarius

- Capricorn (goat) December 22 to January 20

Capricornia's are people who move toward what they want on a sure and steady way. They are ambitious and usually succeed in doing whatever they decide to do. Capricornians take life seriously and defend tradition and authority. And because they understand the needs of others, they make good community leaders or diplomats.

Harmonious signs: Taurus, Virgo and Libra

- Aquarius (water-carrier) January 21 to February 19

Typical Aquarius are extremely open-minded about all things. They try not to judge other people, believing that everyone has the right to lead his or her own life. Their honesty and friendliness make them very popular, although some people think of them as being a bit eccentric. Because they are patient and pay attention to detail, they make good lawyers and scientists.

Harmonious signs: Libra, Gemini and Aries

- Pisces (fish) February 20 to March 20

People born under the sign of the fish are usually quiet and gentle. They give the impression of being cold and distant, but they are really sensitive and loyal to their friends. The Piscarian is usually a dreamer who is little interested in ambitions or money. While some find success in acting, most tend toward more solitary work, often in the other arts.

Harmonious signs: Cancer, Scorpio and Virgo

Case 7　Instructional Design of *l* (*a* Based on "From-Within-the-Text-to-Beyond-the-Text Reading" and Analysis

Ⅰ. Instructional Design of *l* (*a* Based on "From-Within-the-Text-to-Beyond-the-Text Reading"

Step 1: Lead-in with a brief introduction to e. e. cummings

When you first come across the name e. e. cummings, you are sure to find it a little bit unconventional or strange, because we usually have our names in upper case or capitalized rather than in lower case. It is said that one of reasons why he wrote his name in lower case is to show his humility. By the way, in his poems, he often wrote the first person singular "I" in lower case to get rid of self-importance and self-centeredness so that everybody is equal, because all the other pronouns begin with lower case letters.

e. e. cummings (1894 ~ 1962) was a famous American poet and painter. During his life time, he produced about 2,900 poems and more than 1,600 paintings. He regarded himself first as a painter and second as a poet, because he often spent the afternoon painting and the evening writing poetry. He not merely wrote a poem but painted it. So one of the characteristics of his poetry is that there is painting in his poetry. Because of this, he is known as a painter poet.

He is very controversial as "a radical experimenter and avant-garde poet" in the history of American poetry. The center of controversy is his dramatic and eccentric use of language, the subversion of conventional grammar and syntax and above all the ability to create exceptional visual effects in his poetry. Some critics admire and praise his unique poetic styles and skills and think he is the second greatest poet in the 20th century, next to Robert Frost while others condemn the total absurdity of his poetic language, which is meaningless and difficult for common readers to understand. Personally, I like his poetry. If you read his poetry for the first time, you will have a hard time in understanding it. After you read between the lines over and over again, you will gradually unfold it like a decoded enigma, revealing the charm of his poetry. We can see that from the poem 1(a.

Step 2: Within-the-text reading with a focus on the images

1 (a

1 (a

le

af

fa

ll

s)

one

l

iness

As I have just mentioned, when you read this poem for the first time, it may look like gibberish and you don't understand it at all. But please be patient! When you put these letters horizontally, you will have "1(a le af fa ll s) one l iness". Four words appear, that is, "a, leaf, falls and loneliness". e. e. cummings put "a leaf falls" within the surrounding word "loneliness". This poem is meant to be seen rather than be heard, which combines simplicity with complexity.

The whole poem seems constructed to resemble the very action of a leaf in descent. In the first line, "1" looks like a tree branch; the left half parenthesis, like breaking or splitting; "a", like a leaf; which means "a leaf" splits from the branch. "le" in the second line means that the leaf slowly moves downward, a little bit tilted. The pairs of letters: "af" and "fa" in the third and fourth lines reverse themselves and flit downwards, just as a leaf would flutter, twist and turn. This flip-flop is quickly followed by the "ll" in the fifth line which signifies a quicker drop, the leaf itself being perpendicular to the ground. "s)" in the sixth line indicates that a wind rises from the ground and holds the leaf in the air for a while. "one" in the seventh line means that the leaf flattens out. "1" in the eighth line means that the leaf glides downwards again, with one more swoop and then into the wider "iness" in the ninth line of the poem, as though it were joining other leaves that have previously fallen. The phrase "to join the majority" means "to die", so the last image suggests he or she dies.

Someone translated the poem "1 (a" into Chinese in terms of images online as follows:

孤独

孤 (一
片
树
叶
落
下
了)
独

On the whole, the Chinese translation is good, which resembles the very action of a leaf in descent. On second thought, I find that some images are missing, which accounts for untranslatability. A case in point is that "af" and "fa" in the third and fourth lines reverse themselves and flit downwards, just as a leaf would flutter, twist and turn, but there is no such image in the translation.

Step 3: Within-the-text reading with a focus on the theme

The theme of the poem l(a is "one-ness" and "loneliness.", which is intensified and highlighted by 4 languages: English, French, Hindu and Latin and 7 types of expression: "1", "a", "la", "le", "one", "i" and "soli".

Starting with the first line, we see that the letter "l" is the same character on the keyboard as the number "1", which means "loneliness". We know that 1 is an Arabic numeral, which originates from Hindu. The next letter "a" in the first line, which is a typical English word, is the indefinite article, whose singularity at the same time supports the concept of "one-ness" and "loneliness". When we put "1" and "a" together, we have "la" and move into another field of representation, French. We all know that "la" is the French definite article that is put before a feminine noun in its singularity. "le" in the second line is also the French definite article that is put before a masculine noun in its singularity. These two French definite articles suggest that both man and woman are lonely, or that humans are lonely. The fifth line has "ll" which is really two ones, intensifying loneliness. "One" in the seventh line is the only entire English word presented horizontally in the poem, which again indicates loneliness. This is followed by yet another "l" or 1, that is, one loneliness after another. "i-ness" in the last line is a pun, denoting "me-ness": loneliness, my state of mind and "one-ness": also loneliness. "i" is Roman numeral in lower case, standing for one, which belongs to Latin.

Acrostic is employed in the last four lines. The first letter in sixth, seventh, eighth and ninth lines form a word "soli", which is a Latin word, meaning "loneliness".

I tentatively translated the poem "l(a" into Chinese in terms of theme as follows:

孤独啊！孤独！

孤独啊！孤独！

一个男人的孤独！

孤独的心，

在翻腾！

孤独的心，

在坠落！

一阵轻风起，

托起孤独心！

孤独啊！

孤独！

我心孤独！

孤独我心！

Personally, I am not very satisfied with my translation. For one thing, the original has a richness of expression: seven ways to denote loneliness while my translation is a little monotonous, simply using "孤独". For another, "i-ness" in the last line is a pun, denoting "me-ness": loneliness, my state of mind and "one-ness": also loneliness, for "i" is Roman numeral in lower case, standing for one. Though I tried to convey the meaning by translating it into "我心孤独！孤独我心！" for emphasis, it is not as effective or powerful as the pun in the original.

Step 4: Beyond-the-text reading with a focus on the image

From the above, we know that there is painting in e. e. cummings' poetry. This is also true of Chinese poetry. Wang Wei, the famous poet in Tang Dynasty is a typical example. He wrote the one of his poems entitled *Painting* which goes like this:

When you look afar, the mountains are green and clear,

But no sound of stream is heard when you listen near.

The flowers remain in full bloom when spring's away,

And a human being's approaching but the bird doesn't fly.

（远看山有色,近听水无声。春去花还在,人来鸟不惊。）

This poem basically has four distinct images: mountains, stream, flowers and bird. These four images in this poem are sort of paradoxical, which are not in harmony with our human experience. When you look at the mountains in the distance, they usually appear dim or blurred, but they are green and clear. When you listen near a stream, you can hear the sound of stream, but you cannot hear any sound. When spring is away, the flowers usually fade and wither, but they remain in full bloom. When a person approaches, the bird will fly away, but it doesn't fly. Only these images in a painting can achieve this effect.

We are going to have two more poems with a focus on the image. One is an English poem *A Christmas Tree* written by William Burford; and the other is a Chinese poem *The Monument to the People's Heroes* written by Zhou Zhenzhong.

A Christmas Tree

Star

If you are

A love compassionate

You will walk with us this year.

We face a glacial distance, who are here

Huddld

At Your feet.

圣诞树

星啊

如果你那

爱中满含怜悯

来年就和我们同行

面对冰河距离的我们正

拥挤

在你脚底

The poem *A Christmas Tree* is designed in the shape of a Christmas tree. The first five lines have one, three, six, seven, and ten syllables respectively, standing for the top and body of the tree; the sixth line is reduced to one syllable, for the trunk; the last line is gradually increased to three syllables, for the root. The words "star" and "at your feet" appear in the proper places, at the top and at the bottom. The image "star", a symbol of God, is loving and compassionate, will bring us good fortune or blessings. The image "at your feet" shows our humility and piety. The image "huddld" with one letter "e" missing shows our crowdedness or our eagerness for His love and compassion. By the way, the image "glacial" suggests cold and remoteness, and image "glacial distance" means that we are poles apart from God and are not favored by God.

人民英雄纪念碑

一

尊
巨
大
的
磨
刀
石
砥砺着
民族的意志

The Monument to the People's Heroes

A
H
U
G
E
G
R
I
N
D
S
T
O
N
E
TEMPERS
NATIONALWILL

In the same way, the poem *The Monument to the People's Heroes* is arranged in the shape of a monument to pay respect to the people's heroes. Again, I tentatively translated it into English by using two devices: capitalization and shape of a monument.

Step 5: Beyond-the-text reading with a focus on the theme

Loneliness in an eternal theme. e. e. cummings was lonely. So was Robert Frost, for his father died in his childhood; his wife died when he was in his middle age; his daughter died in his old age.

The common people in New York were lonely for they suffered the most kinds of loneliness which are depicted by Richard Yates, an American writer in his collection of short stories called

Eleven Kinds of Loneliness.

The longest loneliness is the one the seven-generation Buendias suffered in *One Hundred Years of Solitude* written by Colombian Nobel winner Gabriel Garcia Márquez, which includes personal solitude, family solitude and national solitude.

Qu Yuan was lonely for "I keep clean while the whole world is dirty; I keep awake while everybody is drunk."(举世皆浊我独清,众人皆醉我独醒。)

Chen Zi'ang was lonely for his *Ode to Mounting Youzhou Tower*(《登幽州台歌》)revealed his loneliness.

> Where are the great men of the past?
>
> And where are those of future years?
>
> The heaven and earth forever last;
>
> Here and now I alone shed tears.

(前不见古人,后不见来者,念天地之悠悠,独怆然而涕下。)

Liu Zongyuan was lonely for his poem *Fishing in Snow*(《江雪》)expresses his extreme loneliness.

> From hill to hill no bird in flight;
>
> From path to path no man in sight.
>
> A lonely fisherman afloat,
>
> Is fishing snow in lonely boat.

(千山鸟飞绝,万径人踪灭。孤舟蓑笠翁,独钓寒江雪。)

By the way, acrostic is employed in this poem. The first letter in each line forms a phrase: 千万孤独, which means extreme loneliness.

Cao Xueqin was lonely, too, for he conveyed his loneliness in his masterpiece *Dream of Red Mansion* by saying,

> Pages full of fantastic talk
>
> Penned with bitter tears;
>
> All men called the author fool,
>
> None his message hears.

(满纸荒唐言,一把辛酸泪!都云作者痴,谁解其中味?)

Finally, I must add, God is lonely. If God is not lonely, why does he create humans? His purpose of creating humans is to have company. Unfortunately, Adam and Eve were not obedient and ate the forbidden fruit. God drove them out of the Garden of Eden. God is lonely, again.

注:除了文中说明是我本人翻译的,其他译文均来自网上,有些译文我做了些修改。

Ⅱ. Analysis

本教学设计以"源于课文到高于课文的阅读"为理念,紧紧围绕 e. e. cummings 的诗 *l(a*

展开。在源于课文方面,了解作者是个 painter poet(画家诗人),他的诗的最大特点就是诗中有画;了解诗的形象,整首诗像一片树叶慢慢地落到地上;了解诗的主题是孤独,在反映该主题时,e. e. cummings 运用了四种语言和七种表达方式,反复强化孤独。在高于课文的阅读方面,了解中国著名"诗中有画"的诗人——王维。在诗的形象方面,增加美国著名诗人 William Burford 的 *A Christmas Tree* 和现代诗人周振中的《人民英雄纪念碑》,加深了对象形诗的了解。在诗的主题方面,对孤独这一主题进行了适度的拓展。不仅 e. e. cummings 是孤独的,Robert Frost 也是孤独的。不仅诗人是孤独的,小说家也是孤独的,美国当代作家 Richard Yates 写下著名短篇小说集《十一种孤独》(*Eleven Kinds of Loneliness*);哥伦比亚著名作家,诺贝尔文学奖获得者 Gabriel Garcia Márquez 的长篇小说写下了《百年孤独》(*One Hundred Years of Solitude*)。不仅外国诗人和作家是孤独的,中国诗人和作家也是孤独的。屈原是孤独的,陈子昂是孤独的,柳宗元是孤独的,曹雪芹是孤独的。就连上帝也是孤独的。

Case 8   Instructional Design of *Genealogy of Deities in Greek Mythology* Based on Mind Map and Ananlysis

I. Instructional Design of *Genealogy of Deities in Greek Mythology* Based on Mind Map

Step 1: Lead-in with a focus on the characteristics of Greek mythology

Today, I am going to talk about the genealogy (神谱) of gods in Greek mythology or the family tree of Greek gods. There are many versions or inconsistencies (前后矛盾) concerning the genealogy of gods in Greek mythology.

OK! Before I talk about the genealogy of gods in Greek mythology, I'd like to say a few words about the characteristics of Greek mythology. The first one is nature worshipping (自然崇拜), which means that ancient Greeks personify natural forces and natural phenomena as gods or goddesses, like sun god, moon goddess or thunder god. The second one is polytheism (多神论), that is, they don't believe in just one god, but many gods. The third one is anthropomorphism (神人同形同性), in other words, gods have the same forms and traits as humans. For example, gods have the same physical beauty; the same emotions like happiness, joy, anger, sorrow and jealousy, etc; and the same desires. The fourth one is incest (乱伦), which is sexual intercourse between family members and close relatives, like sexual intercourse between brother and sister, between father and daughter, between mother and son, between aunt and nephew, between uncle and niece, and so on. The fifth one is different names for the same deity in different generations like Hyperion in the second generation, Helios in the third generation and Apollo in the fourth generation.

Step 2: Learning with a focus on Chaos: primeval state of existence

OK! Now let's talk about the genealogy of gods in Greek mythology. According to Greek mythology, in the very beginning was Chaos and nothing more. Chaos was not a god, but a primeval (原始的, 最初的) state of existence: void (bottomless), dark (lightless), silent (soundless), formless, directionless and lifeless. By the way, the word chaotic comes from chaos. Chaos was a she who gave birth to Gaea (earth), Tartarus (underworld), Eros (love), Erebus (dark silence) and Nyx (night). Gaea was self-fertilized and gave birth to Uranus (heaven), Pontus (sea) and Ourea (mountains) without any male help. Gaea was incestuous and productive. Gaea had affairs with her brother Tartarus, and gave birth to Typhon: father of Sphinx (狮身人面的怪兽); with her son Uranus, which I'll talk about later; with her grandson Oceanus; with her great grandson Zeus; and even her great, great grandson Hephaestus.

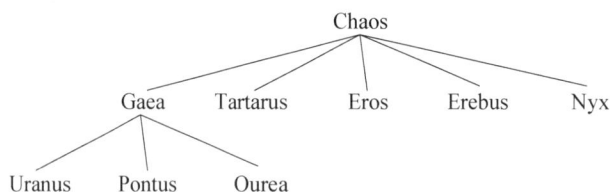

Step 3: Learning with a focus on Uranus-Gaea: the first-generation deities

Uranus (heaven) was Gaea's son and Gaea (earth) was his mother. Uranus was up above and Gaea was down below. Uranus's task was to surround and cover Gaea with his starry coat. Soon, a union came between Gaea and Uranus and they became the first divine couple of the world or the first-generation god and goddess. With Uranus, Gaea gave birth to 18 children: 12 Titans, 3 Cyclopes (one-eyed creatures) and 3 Centimani (hundred-handed creatures).

OK! Does anyone remember the word "titanic"? "Titanic" comes from titan, and which means a very, very big or gigantic creature. The twelve Titans were made up of six males and six females. Six male titans were Cronus (the ruling titan, father of Zeus), Coeus (titan of intelligence, father of Leto, who was mother of Apollo and Artemis), Crius (titan of growth), Iapetus (titan of death, father of Prometheus, Epimetheus and Atlas), Hyperion (titan of light, father of sun, moon and dawn) and Oceanus (titan of water or ocean, father of Metis, who was mother of Athena). Six female titans were Rhea (mother of Zeus), Phoebe (mother of Leto, who was mother of Apollo and Artemis), Themis (goddess of divine law and justice), Tethys (wife of Oceanus), Mnemosyne (mother of nine Muses), and Theia (wife of Hyperion, mother of sun, moon and dawn). Three Cyclopes were Brontes, Steropes and Arges. Three Centimani were Cottus, Gyes and Briareus.

Uranus was afraid that his gigantic children might usurp his throne and overthrow him, so he pushed his children back one by one into the womb of Gaea. His wife Gaea was in deep grief and sorrow over the loss of her own children, so in the end she decided to hand a sickle to her youngest, weakest but smartest son Cronus in order to castrate (阉割) his father. Cronus castrated his father and threw his genitals into the sea, which became Aphrodite, goddess of love and beauty.

```
                              Uranus-Gaea
        _____|_____
       |                           |                          |
   12 Titans                   3 Cyclops                  3 Centimani
```

Cronus   Coeus   Crius   Iapetus   Hyperion   Oceanus   Brontes Steropes   Arges   Cottus   Gyes   Briareus

Rhea   Phoebe   Themis   Tethys   Mnemosyne   Theia

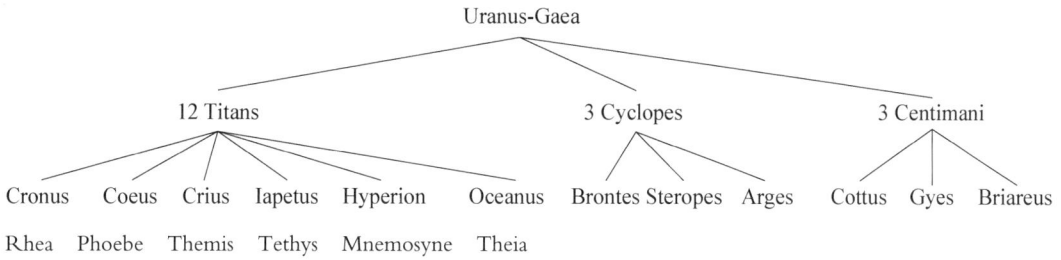

Step 4: Learning with a focus on Cronus-Rhea: the second-generation deities

Cronus took over as supreme ruler of the universe. Soon afterwards, Cronus rescued his brothers and sisters and shared the universe with them. Then, Cronus married his sister Rhea. Because Cronus had betrayed his father, he was afraid that his children would do the same, and so each time Rhea gave birth, he snatched up the child and swallowed it. Cronus swallowed five of his children, who were Hestia（女灶神）, Demeter（谷物女神）, Hera（天后）, Poseidon（海神）and Hades（冥王）. When Rhea bore the last child, Zeus, Cronus wanted to get rid of him in the same fashion. Rhea tricked him by hiding Zeus and wrapping a stone in a baby's blanket, which Cronus swallowed. Thus, Zeus was saved and sent to Mount Ida in Crete（克里特岛）, where the mountain nymphs did all in their power to protect him. By the time Cronus realized the deception, it was too late, for the young Zeus was fully grown. Zeus first used a drugged drink to make his father disgorge（吐出）his five brothers and sisters. Then Zeus challenged Cronus to war for kingship of gods. At last, with the help of his siblings and the Cyclopes, Zeus defeated his father Cronus and became the king of gods.

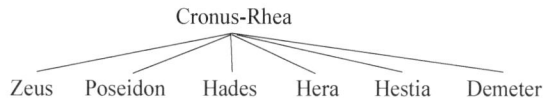

```
                        Cronus-Rhea
        _____|_____
       |        |         |        |         |          |
     Zeus   Poseidon   Hades     Hera     Hestia     Demeter
```

Step 5: Learning with a focus on Zeus-Hera: the third-generation deities

When Zeus became the undisputed ruler on Olympus, he made his sister Hera his queen, and distributed power among his brothers and sisters and sons and daughters. His brother Poseidon ruled over the seas and oceans and his brother Hades was the god of the underworld. His sister Hestia was the goddess of hearth, home and family that was essential for warmth, food preparations and completion of sacrificial offerings to deities. His sister Demeter was the goddess of grains and harvests, who was in charge of agriculture. His son Apollo was the god of the sun, music and poetry. His son Ares was the god of war. His daughter Artemis was the goddess of the moon. His daughter Athena was the goddess of wisdom, war and diplomacy. His daughter Aphrodite was the goddess of love and beauty.

Zeus had seven wives. His first wife was Metis. Zeus was plagued by the same concern and, after a prophecy that the offspring of his first wife, Metis, would give birth to a god "greater than he"—Zeus swallowed her. She was already pregnant with Athena. With the help of Hephaestus（火与锻造之神）, Athena leaped up from the of Zeus' head—fully-grown and dressed for war.

His second wife was his aunt Themis, goddess of Justice, Law and Order, who bore the three Horae（Hours 时序三女神）and the three Moirai（Fates 命运三女神）.

His third wife, was Eurynome, who bore the three Charites（Graces 美惠三女神）, goddesses of Charm, Beauty and Creativity.

His fourth wife was his sister, Demeter, who bore Persephone（冥后）.

His fifth wife was another aunt, Mnemosyne（记忆女神）, who slept with him for nine days and gave birth to nine Muses in charge of music, poetry, tragedy, comedy, history, etc.

His sixth wife was Leto, who gave birth to Apollo and Artemis（月亮女神）.

His seventh wife was Hera, queen, who gave birth to Ares（战神）, Hephaestus and Hebe（goddess of youth）.

Besides, Zeus had affairs with Maia, who gave birth to Hermes（众神的信使、商业神、偷盗之神）; Zeus had affairs with Alcmene, who gave birth to Heracles（大力神）; Zeus had affairs with Semele, who gave birth to Dionysus（酒神）; Zeus had affairs with Leda, who gave birth to Helen of Troy; Zeus had affairs with Dione, who gave birth to Aphrodite（爱与美之神）; Zeus had affairs with Europa, who gave birth to Minos.

Between Macedon（马其顿）and Thessaly（色萨利）of northern Greece there stood a lofty mountain range whose summit was called Mt Olympus where Zeus and other gods and goddesses lived. Though he was the king of gods and men, Zeus was not an autocrat by any standard. All the gods submitted to his final words, it was true, but Zeus made them all sit on a committee, a council of 12 members. First in the Olympian crowd sat Zeus. Next to him was Hera. There sat Poseidon, Hades, Apollo, Artemis, Athena, Ares, Aphrodite, Hephaestus, Hermes and Demeter. All the major gods and goddesses mentioned above assumed human forms of peerless beauty and grace. Often moved by human feelings and desires, they often gave way to anger and jealousy and became involved in endless quarrels and fights.

The genealogy of Greek gods is more than that. We have just covered ABCs of Greek mythology. I hope that this lecture can arouse your interest in it, and that you can learn more about it.

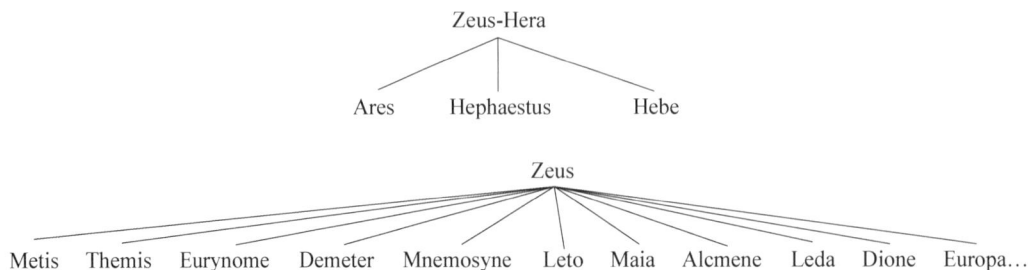

Step 6：Assignment：Exploring 10 idioms originating from Greek Mythology

You are asked to surf on the internet, explore 10 idioms from Greek Mythology and try to find out their stories and their meanings. They are Pandora's box, Apple of discord, Helen of Troy, Achilles heels, Gordian knot, Sphinx's riddle, Oedipus Complex, a Penelope's web, pile Pelion on Ossa and the pillars of Hercules.

Ⅱ. Analysis

思维导图是将思维形象化的一种方法,它图文并重,把各级主题的关系用相互隶属与相关的层级图表现出来。事实上,在思维导图中,每个信息都可以成为一个思考中心,并由此中心向外发散出许多关节点,每一个关节点代表与中心主题的一个连结,而每一个连结又可以成为另一个中心主题,再向外发散出许多关节点,呈现出放射性立体结构,由此可见,思维导图的特点具有发散性和层次性。本课基于思维导图,对希腊神话的神谱进行教学设计。一级主题是 Chaos,由此中心向外发散出 5 个关节点：Gaea, Tartarus, Eros, Erebus 和 Nyx。二级主题是 Gaea,由此中心向外发散出 3 个关节点：Uranus, Pontus 和 Ourea。三级主题是 Uranus 和 Gaea,由此中心向外发散出 3 个关节点：Titans, Cyclopes 和 Centimani。四级主题是 Cronus 和 Rhea,由此中心向外发散出 6 个关节点：Zeus, Poseidon, Hades, Hera, Hestia 和 Demeter。五级主题是 Zeus,由此中心向外发散出无数个关节点。使用思维导图最后能达到条分缕析和纲举目张的效果。

Part Two

Instructional Design of *Lexicology* and Case Analysis

Case 9 Instructional Design of *A Mastery of 3 ,000 Words Within 100 Days* Based on 3S and Analysis

Ⅰ. Instructional Design of *A Mastery of 3 ,000 Words Within 100 Days* Based on 3S

Step 1: Lead-in with three personal memorization experiences

在讲《3 000 单词百日通》之前,我先来讲我三次记忆的经历。第一次是记忆化学元素周期表的纵轴元素:氢锂钠钾铷铯钫,铍镁钙锶钡镭,硼铝镓铟铊,碳硅锗锡铅,氮磷砷锑铋,氧硫硒碲钋,氟氯溴碘砹,氦氖氩氪氙氡。我至今仍然能把它背下来,原因之一是当时我们的化学老师说:"你们上课要做'氢锂钠钾铷铯钫',因为这些元素比较活跃。你们也一样,上课要活跃,要认真听讲,积极思考,踊跃发言。不要做'氦氖氩氪氙氡',因为它们是惰性气体,不活跃。你们不能像'氦氖氩氪氙氡',上课懒洋洋的,伸懒腰,打哈欠,打瞌睡。"接着老师要求我们跟在他后面把纵轴元素说了三遍,结果我就记住了。第二次是记忆扬州大学第一位博士生导师任中敏教授的一段话。当时适逢我的母校扬州师范学院校庆 30 周年,任中敏教授应邀在中文系的阶梯教室做讲座。当时,许多校外专家、学者慕名而来,教室里面挤满了人,连教室外面窗台上都站满了人,我正好从那儿经过,看到这个情景,也挤过去凑个热闹,看看教室里究竟发生了什么。我透过窗台上人腿的空隙,看到任中敏教授,此时,他正在讲学术争鸣,他说:"学术争鸣,不要温柔敦厚,要你一刀,我一刀,刀来刀去,两刀相击,铿然有声,倏然有结果。"第三次是记忆巴黎公社是什么时候成立的,1871 年。其实,只要记住一个公社的"公"字,一切就迎刃而解了。左上方的一撇是"1",加右上方的一捺是"8",倒过来写个"7",右下方的一点是"1"。我对上面这三次经历总结一下,那就是,我们记忆东西时,要三个 c:concentration,curiosity,cue。第一是 concentration,在老师激发兴趣基础上,如果你聚精会神,记忆会比较容易。第二是 curiosity,如果你对什么好奇,记忆会比较容易。第三是 cue,如果你有些提示或暗示,记忆会比较容易。《3000 单词百日通》不是什么神话,但它是有前提的,那就是:"You must have concentration. You must have curiosity. You must have cues." 你的 concentration 和 curiosity 我无法主宰,但我可以给你提供一些 cues,有助于你记忆单词。这 cues 就是 sound, shape and sense。

Step 2：A mastery of 3,000 words within 100 days based on sound

我们要讲的第一个 cue 是 sound。我们来看八组单词。

第一组 large—little。这一组是讲开口元音和闭口元音所表示的意思差异。我们来感受一下，[ɑ:]是个开口元音，嘴要张得大，一般表示大、远、高、长或程度比较深等，如：far(远)，laugh(大笑)，snarl(咆哮)等。[i]是一个闭口元音，嘴要张得小，表示小、少、尖、细、碎、或程度比较浅，如：inn(小旅馆)，kid(小孩)，bit(一点)，pit(小坑)，tip(尖)，drip(一小滴)sip(小口喝)等。我们再来看一个例子，如：master—mister—minister 它们的本义是"大人物、小人物和小小人物"。至于 minister 现在表示"部长"这个意思，我们另当别论，因为，词在历史的发展过程中，有些意思扬升，有些意思降格，有些意思转移，有些意思扩大，有些意思缩小。这里是扬升了。事实上，今天的 mini-仍"小小的"意思，如：miniskirt(迷你裙)，mini-lecture(微型讲座)等。

第二组 deep—dip。这一组是讲长元音和短口元音所表示的意思差异。我们来感受一下，[i:]是长元音，[i]是短元音。一般说来，长元音表示程度比较深，短元音表示程度比较浅，此外，长元音表示速度比较慢，短元音表示速度比较快。如：droop—drop，前者表示"下垂、下沉"，速度较慢；后者表示"下降、落下"，速度较快；sleep—nap，前者入睡较慢，后者则较快。

第三组 band—bend—bind—bond—bund。这一组是讲元音表示意思的微调。band 是根带子，bend 把……弄弯，bind 把……捆绑，bond 表示抽象的捆绑在一起的东西：契约，bund 是表示具体的捆绑在一起的东西，像 a bundle of sticks(一捆树枝)，a bunch of flowers(一束花)，也表示连成一片的东西或地方，外滩就是连成一片的地方。再如：fact—fiction，fac 和 fic 都是表示"制造"，fact 造出来是真的，就是"事实"，fiction 造出来是假的，就是"虚构"。随便说一下，我对历史和文学的理解："History is facts and fiction. Literature is fiction and facts. (历史是事实加虚构；文学是虚构加历史)"。此外，有些动词的过去式和过去分词，通过改变元音，对意思进行微调，如：sing—sang—sung，begin—began—begun；arise—arose—arisen，write—wrote—written；blow—blew—blown，grow—grew—grown。有些名词的复数形式，通过改变元音，对意思进行微调，如：thesis—theses，man—men，tooth—teeth，mouse—mice 等。

第四组 bomb，bombard，blast，bang，bump，break。这一组是讲辅音表示一个词的基本意思。这一组词都是以爆破音开头，都与爆破、爆炸相关。bomb(爆炸、炸弹)，bombard(轰炸)，blast(爆炸、爆破)，bang(爆炸、猛打)，bump(碰撞、撞击)，break(撞破、打破)。再如：喉音一般表示用力或喘气，heavy(沉重)，hurry(快点)，help(救命啊)。

第五组 pat—bat。这一组是讲轻辅音和浊辅音所表示的意思差异。我们来感受一下，[p]是轻辅音，[b]是浊辅音。一般说来，轻辅音表示轻，这里就打得轻，浊辅音表示重，这里就打得重。

第六组 bind—wind。这一组是讲音近相通。他们都是双唇音，bind(捆绑)—wind(弯曲)。类似的还有，Bill—Will，mammilla—papilla。Bill (Will 或 William 的昵称)—Will，mammilla(乳头)—papilla(乳头)。音近相通这一点在翻译中也可以得到验证。第一、[b]可以音译为[p]、[m]和[w]。[b]音译为[p]，如：Bacon 音译为"培根"，Ban Ki-moon 音译为

"潘基文",等等;[b]音译为[m],如:Bangkok 音译为"曼谷",Bombay 音译为"孟买",等等;[b]音译为[w],如:Serbia 音译为"塞尔维亚",Bandung 音译为"万隆",Battambang 音译为"马德望",等等。第二、[p]可以音译为[b],如:Peter 音译为"彼得",Apollo 音译为"阿波罗",Peru 音译为"秘鲁"等等。第三、[m]可以音译为[w],如:salmon 音译为"三文鱼",Jumbo 音译为"巨无霸",Marlboro 音译为"万宝路"等等。第四、[w]可以音译为[m],如:sandwich 音译为"三明治"等。此外,音近相通还表现为双唇音与唇齿音相同,如:[b]和[p]通[f]这个音,如:basis(基础)—foundation(基础),brother(兄、弟)—frater(兄、弟),pater(爸爸)—father(父亲)。我们汉语里"爸爸"和"父亲"意思相同。最后要说的是,ma—ba—pa—wa,我们是一家人。

第七组 heaven—hell(天堂、地狱)。这一组是讲反义同源。由于他们同源,因此他们音相近。例如:blank—black(白、黑);gain—give(得、失);micro—macro(微、宏);hospitable—hostile(好客的、有敌意的);own—owe(有、欠);king—queen(国王、王后);push—pull(推、拉);sit—stand(坐、站);thick—thin(厚、薄);sub—super(上、下);wax—wane(盈、亏)等。

第八组-cide—杀。英语中的辅音与汉语的声母相近,如:suicide—自杀,homicide—他杀,matricide—杀母,patricide—杀父,infanticide—杀婴,fratricide—杀兄弟,sororicide—杀姐妹,genocide—种族灭绝,insecticide—杀虫,germicde—杀菌。类似的还有,back—背;bag—包;bind—绑;book—本;border—边;cut—砍;carve—刻;chop—切;cheat—欺;dad—爹;dump—堆;father—父;give—给;ghost—鬼;harm—害;howl—嚎;jail—监;lazy—懒;law—律;leak—漏;mother—母;mum—妈;mare—马;pat—拍;pour—泼;plain—平原;panic—怕;quick—快;scatter—撒;send—送;tow—拖;wind—弯等等。这一现象使人们想起《圣经》所描述的,人类最早是讲同一种语言,他们在巴比伦想建造一座通天塔,上帝为了阻止他们建造通天塔,搅乱人类的语言,使他们无法沟通,最后也就没有建成通天塔,但有可能原来同一种语言的残骸还遗留语言里,也有可能是一种巧合。

Step 3:A mastery of 3,000 words within 100 days based on shape

我们要讲的第二个 cue 是 shape。我们来看七个字母和一个单词。

我们知道,英语字母是来自拉丁字母,拉丁字母是来自希腊字母,希腊字母是来自腓尼基字母,当我们把字母追溯到腓尼基字母时,我们发现它们也是象形的。今天,现代英语字母中仍有一些象形的残骸。

第一个字母 A,在腓尼基语中,A 的顶部不是朝上,而是朝左,中间一横向两边延长一点点,像一个牛头,有的说表示"牛";有的说表示"牛头",代表 food(食物),民以食为天。

第二个字母 B,在腓尼基语中,B 的上面是个三角形,右边的那个边向下拖了一点,有的说表示"房子";有的说表示"窗户";还有的说表示"帐篷",总而言之代表 shelter(住所)。

第三个字母 C,在腓尼基语中,没有 C,只有 G。C 是后来从 G 慢慢演化出来的。上面是个角,表示"骆驼的驼峰",代表 transportation(交通)。因此,腓尼基语的 ABC 代表的是"食、住、行"。

第四个字母 D,在腓尼基语中,D 是个三角形△,表示"门"。由于门的重心在下面,因此,含有 D 字母的词常表示"向下",如:down(向下),damn(打入地狱),drip(滴下),drop

（落下）,dig（挖）,dampen（使消沉、使潮湿）,dive（跳水）,dump（倾倒）,detrain（下火车）,depress（压抑、使沮丧）,descend（下来）,decline（下降）,decrease（下降）,debase（降低、贬低）、degrade（降级）,demote（降级）,depreciate（降价、贬值）,devalue（贬值）。此外,表示"破坏、损坏"的 damage、destroy、devastate,也有向下的意思。

第五个字母 W,在腓尼基语中,表示水的字母是 M,后来慢慢演变为 W。W 像波浪,具有不稳定性和不确定性,这类的单词有：water（水）,wave（波浪）, wind（风）,whip（鞭子）等。正因为此,英语中的疑问词大多数是以 W 开始的,如：What, When, Where, Whose 等。

第六个字母 T,在腓尼基语中,表示钉在某个物体上的记号,具有稳定性,像 That, Then, There, Those 等词就非常确定。

第七个字母 P,这个字母颇为有趣。我们把手伸出,四指并拢,大拇指向下,看上去像字母 P,英语中的这些词都与手有关,如：palm（手掌）；push（推）；pull（拉）；press（按）；point（指）；pat（拍）；pack（捆,扎）；prise（撬）；pick（捡）；piece（拼）；pitch（扔）；pinch（捏）；play（打）；prick（扎）；pluck（摘）；plug（插）probe（探）；protect（护）；pounce（扑）；praise（p + raise 本义是用手"举起",引申为"表扬",）；applaud（a + pp + loud 两只手拍得很响）等等。

此外,英语单词中的 eye 也很象形。一般说来,英语单词中的 ee 和 oo 都跟眼睛有关,如：see, sleep, peep, look, shoot 等。

Step 4：A mastery of 3,000 words within 100 days based on sense

我们讲第三个 cue 是 sense。Sense 主要是通过语根来记忆单词。语根是个新的概念,是马秉义先生在《英语词汇系统简论》中提出来的,你们可能没听说过。简单地说,语根在词根和词缀上面的一级,换句话说,语根可以分解成词根和词缀。一般说来,一个语根有 50—60 个单词,最多的一个语根可以有 150 个单词左右。我们通过语根来记单词,可以把原来一盘散沙、毫无联系的单词,一个个串起来,使之更有系统性。我们今天就以单词最多的语根 ma 为例。ma 这个语根与我们汉语的"奶"字,非常相似。奶有三个基本意思：一是指人,如："奶奶"；二是指乳房,如："奶子"；三是指乳汁,如"喝奶"。ma 也有三个基本意思：同样指人、乳房和乳汁。我们下面一一来谈。

1. ma 指人

"ma"指人,既可以指人的全部,也可以指人的部分,还可以指人的比喻。

1）ma 指人的全部

所谓"ma"指人的全部,是指"ma"可以指一个完整的人,如：母亲（matter 和 mater）、主人（master）和榜样（model）。

（1）ma 指母亲（matter 和 mater）

ma 既是物之母 matter（物质）,也是人之母 mater（母亲）。作为物之母 matter（物质）,它的形容词是 material（物质的）；作为人之母 mater（母亲）,它的形容词 maternal（母亲的）,maternity（母性,母亲身份）,matrix（子宫）,matricide（杀母）。我们再举一个例子 Alma Mater（母校）。

一个女子在成为 mater 之后,管理一个家庭叫 matriarch（女家长）,管理更多的人或物叫 matron（女总管）。一个女子在成为 mater 之前,必须要成为 madam（夫人）,成为 madam 之前,是 maid(少女)和 maiden(少女)。那么,maid(少女)和 maiden(少女)怎么才能成为 madam? 那就 marry(结婚),在 marry 之前,要 mature(成熟),成熟的标志是 menstruation(月经)。顺便说一下,瓜果的成熟叫 mellow。成熟后显得 mild(温和的),接下来要与男子 meet(见面)。怎么才能见面呢? 要 move(移动,行走),migrate(移动),mobile(移动的)。见面后,要慢慢地进行 match(配对),再进行 mate(交配、配偶),最后才能 marry。marry 以后,make (a child)即生小孩,就成为 mater。顺便说一下,在西方,负责生殖的女神叫 Maia;生小孩的最佳时间为 May;结婚、生小孩的地点叫 mansion。古人因对生育迷惑不解故感到 magic/magical(魔术/神奇的),marvel/marvelous(神奇/妙极了),mystery/mysterious(神秘),miracle/miraculous(奇迹/奇妙的)。谈到 miracle,我们来看看另一个词 mirror,我们知道它现在的意思是镜子,而它的本意是“奇妙、神奇”。古人想:“我站在这里,怎么到镜子里面去了,这太神奇了”。我们再来看一个词 mirage(海市蜃楼),它的本义是表示“奇妙的景色”。

(2) ma 指主人(master)

早期,母亲在家里是家长,地位很高,是 master(主人)。正因为此,许多表示“大”、“主要”和“多”的词都与母亲有关。

表示“大”和“主要的”,如:magnify(放大),maximum(最大值),macro(宏观),maxim(最大/高的原则,准则),megastore(大型商店),mighty(力大的),major(较大的),mayor(主要人物,市长),main(主要的)等。

表示“多”,如:many(许多),massive(大量的),multiple(多的),much(许多),million(百万)march(行军)等。

其实,汉语中 ma 声的字也可以表示“大”和“多”。表示“大”,如:“马蜂、马勺、拇指、茫茫”等;表示“多”,如:“麻子、密密麻麻、蚂蚁、毛”等。

我们刚才讲到,一个女子在成为 mater 之前,必须要成为 madam(夫人),成为 madam 之前,是 maid(少女)和 maiden(少女)。这样就产生许多表示“小”与“少”的词,如:micro(微小),minor(小的),minute(细小的),minister(部长,原义为小小人物),miss(小姐),mister(原义为小人物,以后指父亲,可见父亲在家庭的地位不高),monk(和尚),monarch(君主,原义为一个人的统治),monologue(独白),monotheism(一神论),monogamy(一夫一妻制),merely(仅仅,只有)等。

有大有小就有中间,这样由此产生了许多表示“中间”的词,如:middle(中间),mean(平均数),median(中间的,中数),mediate(调停),medium(媒介),mediocre(中等的),medieval(中世纪的),Mediterranean(地中海),meddle(干涉)等。

由于事物具有相对性,古人搞不清“大”和“小”,因为许多“小”的东西,比“大”的东西还要大,如:“小象”要比“大老鼠”大。同样,古人也搞不清“中”的概念,这样就产生了“模糊”和“混淆”的词,如:melt(熔化),merge(合并),mist(薄雾,模糊不清),maze(迷宫、迷惑)、mask(面具,原义为迷惑),mash(把……捣烂成糊状),miscellaneous(混杂的),mix(混起来),mingle(混起来,合起来),mess(混乱),muddle(糊涂)等。由于“模糊”和“混淆”,就出问题,产生表示“错误”的“mis-”和表示“不良”、“不好”的“ma(1)-”。表示“错误”的词,如:misunderstanding(误解),mistake(错误),misspelling(拼写错误),misconception(错误概念)

等。表示"不良"、"不好"的词,如:malice(恶意),mad(神经错乱),malady(疾病),malaria(疟疾),malnutrition(营养不良)等。顺便说一下,"ma(1)-"的反义前缀是"bene-",这样可以形成一组反义词。malign—benign(恶性的—良性的),malediction—benediction(诅咒、恶言—祝福、良言),malignant—benignant(邪恶的—仁慈的),malefactor—benefactor(坏人、罪人—恩人、好人),malefaction—benefaction(坏事、犯罪行为—好事、恩惠),malevolent—benevolent(恶意的—善意的)等。

（3）ma 指榜样(model)

ma 是子女们一切活动的榜样、表率,这样由此产生了 model(模范),mode(模子),mo(u)ld(模子),modest(谦虚。本义是说话办事有模式,不过分、适度),moderate(适度的),moral(道德的。本义是指人们的生活方式),modern(现代。这个词变化较大,本义是指"适度"、"不过分"、"人们学习模仿的榜样"。"人们学习模仿的榜样"往往处在最前列,这样就演变成了"现代的"和"时髦的"。),module(模块),modulate(调节),modify(修饰),mimic(模仿)等。随便说一下,父亲叫 pater,他给子女们树的榜样叫 pattern。

2）ma 指人的部分

所谓"ma"可以指人的部分,是指"ma"指的手(man(u))和人的心(mind)。

（1）ma 指人的手(man(u))

ma 有一双勤劳的手,由此产生了 manual(手的,手册),manuscript(手稿),manacle(手铐),manufacture(手工生产,制造),manage(管理。本义是手工的,驯马人),manner(方式。本义是用手做事的方式),manure(肥料。本义是手工的,种地的,施肥的),mat(小垫子,本义为妈妈的手艺)等。

（2）ma 指人的心(mind)

ma 有一颗善良的心(mind),由此产生了 memory(记忆),mental(思想的、脑力的),memoir(回忆录),memorandum(备忘录),remember(记住)等。

3）ma 指比喻的人

所谓"ma"可以指比喻的人,是指"ma"指月亮(moon)。太阳是父亲,月亮是母亲。由 moon 产生了 month(月)和 Monday(星期一)是月亮日,顺便说一下,Sunday(星期日)是太阳日。再由此产生了表示测量的词汇:measure(测量),must(必须。本义是分给的一份,任务),dimension(尺寸),meter(米),diameter(直径),parameter(参数)和 symmetry(对称)等。

2. ma 指"乳房"

"ma"可以指"乳房",一些与乳房有关的词,如:mamma(乳房),mammary(乳房的),mammal(哺乳动物),mammilla(乳头)等。此外,还有一些类似乳房的词,如:mound(小山,小丘),mount(小山),mountain(大山)。山里有 mine(矿藏);mine 里面有 metal(金属);metal 可以造 machine(机器)等。

3. ma 指"乳汁"

"ma"可以指"乳汁"(milk),引申为食物,如:meal(饭),meat(肉),melon(瓜)。不仅有物质的食粮,还要有精神的食粮,如:music(音乐),Muse(音乐女神缪斯),melody(旋律)。乳汁的主要成分是 mare(水),如:marine(海的,水的),mariner(水手),submarine(潜水艇),

marsh(沼泽),moist(潮湿的),moss(苔藓),mushroom(蘑菇)等。由吃奶声,引申说话。吃奶要用 mouth(嘴),吃奶得到满足后的样子叫 merry(愉快的),小孩含乳发出的声音叫 mumble,murmur 和 mutter,它们分别表示"喃喃而语、咕哝","低语"和"咕哝、低语"。小孩吃奶后不作声叫 mute。

Step 5:Assignment:Reading *Words and Their Stories* about money

课后同学们阅读下面关于钱的故事,注意加粗的词和短语所表达的意思,下节课我来检查。

Money

I think people everywhere dream about having lots of money. I know I do. I would give anything to **make money hand over fist**(赚大钱). I would like to earn large amounts of money. You could win a large amount of money in the United States through **lotteries**(彩票). People pay money for tickets with numbers. If your combination of numbers is chosen, you win a huge amount of money—often in the millions. Winning the lottery is **a windfall**(发横财,侥幸所得).

A few years ago, my friend Al won the lottery. It changed his life. He did not have a rich family. He was not **born with a silver spoon in his mouth**(生于富贵之家). Instead, my friend was always **hard up**(缺钱) for cash. He did not have much money. And the money he did earn was **chicken feed**(小钱,很少的钱)—very little.

Sometimes Al even had to accept **hand-outs**(施舍、馈赠), gifts from his family and friends. But do not get me wrong. My friend was not a **deadbeat**(赖账的人). He was not the kind of person who never paid the money he owed. He simply **pinched pennies**(精打细算、非常节约). He was always very careful with the money he spent. In fact, he was often a **cheapskate**(守财奴、吝啬鬼). He did not like to spend money. The worst times were when he was **flat broke**(身无分文) and had no money at all.

One day, **Al scraped together**(费力地获得、凑足) a few dollars for a lottery ticket. He thought he would never **strike it rich**(发横财) or gain lots of money unexpectedly. But his combination of numbers was chosen and he won the lottery. He **hit the jackpot**(赢得一大笔钱、发大财). He won a great deal of money.

Al was so excited. The first thing he did was buy a costly new car. He **splurged**(挥霍、乱花) on the one thing that he normally would not buy. Then he started spending money on unnecessary things. He started to waste it. It was like he had **money to burn**(腰缠万贯、很有钱). He had more money than he needed and it was **burning a hole in his pocket**(挥金如土、把钱花光) so he spent it quickly.

When we got together for a meal at a restaurant, Al paid every time. He would always **foot the bill**(付账), and **pick up the tab**(承担全部费用). He told me the money made him **feel like a million dollars**(精神和健康处在极好状态). He was very happy.

But, Al spent too much money. Soon my friend was **down and out**(穷困潦倒的) again.

He had no money left. He was back to being **strapped for cash**（手头紧）. He had spent his **bottom dollar**（最后一点钱）, his very last amount. He did not even build up a **nest egg**（储备金）. He had not saved any of the money.

I admit I do feel sorry for my friend. He had enough money to live like a king. Instead, he is back to living **on a shoestring**（靠一点点钱）— a very low budget. Some might say he is **penny wise and pound foolish**（小事精明，大事糊涂）. He was wise about small things, but not about important things.

Many people believe that money makes the world go around. Others believe that money buys happiness. I do not agree with either idea. But I do admit that money can make people do strange things. Let me tell you about a person I once knew who liked to play card games for money. He liked to gamble.

My friend Bob had a problem because he liked to gamble **at all costs**（不惜代价）. He would play at any time and at any price. To take part in a card game such as poker, my friend would have to **ante up**（下赌注）. He would have to pay a small amount of money at the beginning of the game.

Bob always played with **cold, hard cash**（现钱、纸币和硬币）—only coins and dollar bills. Sometimes my friend would **clean up**（赢大钱、赚大钱）. He would win a lot of money on one card game. He liked to tell me that one day he would **break the bank**（把庄家的钱全部赢来）. What a feeling it must be to win all of the money at a gambling table!

Other times my friend would simply **break even**（不赢不输）. He neither won nor lost money. But sometimes Bob would **lose his shirt**（把钱输光）. He would lose all the money he had. He **took a beating**（损失惨重、输钱）at the gambling table. When this happened, my friend would have to go **in the hole**（负债）. He would go into debt and owe people money.

Recently, Bob turned to crime after losing all his money. In his job, he **kept the books**（管账）for a small business. He supervised the records of money earned and spent by the company. Although my friend was usually honest, he decided to **cook the books**（篡改账目）. He illegally changed the financial records of the company. This permitted him to make a **fast buck**（投机所赚的钱、轻易得来的钱）. My friend made some quick, easy money dishonestly.

I never thought Bob would **have sticky fingers**（手脚不老实、偷窃）. He did not seem like a thief who would steal money. But, some people will do anything **for love of money**（因为喜欢钱）.

Bob used the money he stole from his company to gamble again. This time, he **cashed in**（赚钱、赢钱）. He made a lot of money. Quickly he was **back on his feet**（东山再起）. He had returned to good financial health. His company, however, ended up **in the red**（负债、出现赤字）. It lost more money than it earned. The company was no longer profitable.

It did not take long before my friend's dishonesty was discovered. The company investigated and charged him with stealing. Bob tried to **pass the buck**（推卸责任）. He tried to blame someone else for the deficit. His lie did not work，however. He ended up in jail. Today，I would **bet my bottom dollar（孤注一掷、断言、确信）** that my friend will never gamble again. I would bet all I have that he learned his lesson about gambling.

Ⅱ．Analysis

本教学设计从音、形、义三个纬度来帮助学生记忆单词，以实现3 000单词百日通。从音的纬度看，音是有意思的。不同的音表示不同的义，如：辅音表示词的基本意思，元音表示意思的微调。从形的纬度看，形也是有意思的。不同的音表示不同的义，如：字母的形和单词的形，都表示一定的意思。从义的纬度看，单词的义不是孤立的，而是联系的；不是静止的，而是变化的。一方面，可以通过音、形、义各自的系统来帮助学生记忆单词；另一方面，可以把音、形、义三个系统打通，三管齐下有助于学生形成一个词汇系统，可以提高单词记忆的效果和效率。当然，单词的记忆非一日之功，它需要日积月累，尤其在初级阶段。3 000单词百日通不是什么神话，但它是有前提的，那就是："You must have concentration. You must have curiosity. You must have cues."只有这样，你的单词记忆才有可能突飞猛进。

Case 10 Instructional Design of *Characteristics of Affixes* Based on One-with-many Pattern and Analysis

Ⅰ．Instructional Design of *Characteristics of Affixes* Based on One-with-many Pattern

Step 1：Lead-in with many affixes with one meaning

上一节课，我们谈到了词缀的第一个特点：多缀一义，是指两个或两个以上词缀有相同的意思。例如：后缀-th、-ness、-ity、-ency、-sion、-osity、-ation等均可以表示"程度"，如：length（长度）、thickness（厚度）、density（密度）、consistency（浓度）、precision（精度）、luminosity（光度）limitation（限度）等。再如：-an、-ian、-al、-ant、-ent、-ar、-art、-ard、-ary、-ate、-or、-crat、-ee、-eer、-er、-ese、-eur、-ist、-ic等均可以表示"人"，如：American（美国人）、historian（历史学家）、criminal（罪犯）、servant（服务员）、student（学生）、scholar（学者）、coward（胆小鬼）、braggart（吹牛者）、secretary（秘书）、candidate（候选人）、educator（教育家）、democrat（民主党党员）、escapee（逃亡者）、engineer（工程师）、observer（观察家）、amateur（业余人员）、physicist（物理学家）、critic（批评家）等等。今天，我们继续讨论英语词缀的特点。除了"多缀一义"外，还有"一缀多义""一缀多性""一缀多形""一缀多源""一缀多位"和"一缀多类"的特点。下面我们就一一来谈。

Step 2：Characteristics of affixes with a focus on one affix with many meanings

所谓"一缀多义"，是指同一词缀有许多意思。例如：-ism有十三个意思，它们分别是(1)表示"主义"，如：feudalism（封建主义），romanticism（浪漫主义），colonialism（殖民主义）；(2)表示"学""法""论"，如：magnetism（磁力学），stimulism（兴奋疗法），fatalism（宿命论）；(3)表示"宗教"，如：Buddhism（佛教），Judaism（犹太教），Islamism（伊斯兰教）；(4)表示"语言",如：colloquialism（口语），euphemism（委婉语），witticism（妙语）；（5）表示"风格"如：archaism（古风），Americanism（美国风格），orientalism（东方人的风格）；（6）表示"性质""特征"，如：philistinism（庸俗性），humanism（人性），antagonism（对抗性）；（7）表示"学派"，如：impressionism（印象派），cubism（立体派），Platonism（柏拉图学派）；（8）表示"疾病"，如：rheumatism（风湿病），mutism（哑症），alcoholism（酒精中毒症）；（9）表示"偏见""歧视"，如：sexism（性别歧视），racism（种族歧视），ageism（年龄歧视）；（10）表示"制度"，如：federalism（联邦制），parliamentarianism（议会制），multipartism（多党制）；（11）表示"动作、行为"，如：criticism（批评），baptism（宗教洗礼），vandalism（故意破坏）；（12）表示"情况""状态、现象"，如：multi-culturalism（多文化并存现象），bachelorism（独身状态），me-tooism（人云亦云现象）；（13）其他，如：patriotism（爱国心），organism（有机体），mechanism（机械装置），journalism（新闻业）等。

Step 3：Characteristics of affixes with a focus on one affix with many parts of speech

所谓"一缀多性"是指一个词缀可以表示多种词性。如：-ate 可以用作名词后缀、动词后缀和形容词后缀。

1. -ate 用作名词后缀

-ate 用作名词后缀可以表示五个意思。（1）表示"会""馆"，如：senate（参议院）、consulate（领事馆）等；（2）表示"职位""地位"或"身份"，如：directorate（指导者或董事、处长、导演等的职位）、marquisate（侯爵地位或身份）等；（3）表示"……酸盐""……酸酯"，如：sulphate（硫酸盐、硫酸酯）、acetate（醋酸盐、醋酸酯）等；（4）表示"动作涉及的对象""产物"，如：precipitate（沉淀物）、filtrate（滤出物）等；（5）表示"一群人"，如：electorate（全体选民）等。

2. -ate 用作动词后缀

-ate 用作名词后缀可以表示四个意思。（1）表示"成为""使成为"，如：maturate（成熟、使成熟）、validate（使生效）等；（2）表示"产生""使形成""使呈……形式"，如：ulcerate（使溃疡、形成溃疡）、triangulate（使成三角形）等；（3）表示"供给""以……处理"，如：aerate（通过呼吸供氧气给）、vaccinate（给……接种疫苗）等；（4）表示"使与……化合"，如：oxygenate（氧化）、acidulate（酸化）等。

3. -ate 用作形容词后缀

-ate 用作形容词后缀可以表示三个意思。（1）表示"……的""和……有关的"，如：collegiate（大学的）、accurate（精确的）等；（2）表示"充满……的""有……的"，如：affectionate（充满深情的）、passionate（充满热情的）等；（3）表示"有……形状的""像……的"，如：stellate（星形的、像星的）、cordate（心脏形的）等。

同类的还有，-al 既可用作形容词后缀，表示"……的"，如：traditional（传统的），educational（教育的），也可用作名词后缀，表示"动作""过程"，如：arrival（到达），refusal（拒绝）等；-ful 既可用作形容词后缀，表示"充满……的""有……性质"，如：careful（仔细的），useful（有用的），也可用作名词后缀，表示"充满所需的量"，如：handful（一把），houseful（一屋子）等；-er 既可用作名词后缀，表示"……的人""……物""用于……机械或工具，如：

worker（传统的）、boiler（锅炉）等,也可用作动词后缀,如:waver（动摇）,wander（漫无目标地走）等;-ly 既可用作形容词后缀,表示"像……的""有……性质的""每一特定时间发生一次的",如:manly（男子气概的）、weekly（每周的）,也可用作副词后缀,表示"方式""状态""时间""地点""程序""程度""方向"等,如:greatly（伟大地、非常）、firstly（首先）、unexpectedly（出乎意外地）等。

Step 4:Characteristics of affixes with a focus on one affix with many forms

所谓"一缀多形"是指一个词缀可以有多种形式,即一个词缀由于受到音的同化,出现了一些变体形式。

前缀 ad-表示"（运动）的方向""变化""添加",如:advance（前进）、advert（提出看法）、adjourn（休会）。如果 ad-出现在 c、k、q 字母前面,其中的 d 字母一律同化为 c,如:accept（接受）、acknowledge（承认）、acquire（获得）;如果 ad-出现在 b、f、g、l、n、p、r、s、t 等字母前面,其中的 d 字母均同化为后接的相应字母。如:abbreviate（缩写）、affix（附加、附加物）、aggress（侵略）、allomorph（词素变体）、annex（附加、并吞）、appendix（附录）、arrive（到达）、assimilate（同化）、attach（系、附加）等;如果 ad-出现在 ch、sc、sp、st 前面,ad 变为 a-,如:achieve（取得）、ascend（上升）、aspirate（发送气音）、astern（向船尾）等。

同类的还有,前缀 in-表示"不""非""无",如:incorrect（不正确的）,如果 in-出现在 b、p、m 字母前面,其中的字母 n 同化为 m,如:imbalance（不平衡）、impossible（不可能）、immoral（不道德）等。如果 in-出现在 n、l、r 等字母前面,其中的 n 字母同化为 g、l、r,如:ignoble（不体面的）、illegal（非法的）、irresponsible（不负责的）等。前缀 ob-表示"反""逆""倒""非",如:object（反对）、obstacle（障碍）、obtriangular（倒三角形的）。如果 ob-出现在字母 f、p 的前面,其中的 b 字母同化为 f 和 p。如:offend（冒犯）、oppose（反对）等。

Step 5:Characteristics of affixes with a focus on one affix with many sources

所谓"一缀多源"是指一个词缀来自不同的词源,有的来自拉丁语、有的来自希腊语,有的来自日尔曼语。如:表示"放进""放在……上面""使处于……境地""登上"的前缀 en-来自拉丁语,如:encage（把……关在笼子里）,enslave（使做奴隶）,entrain（使上火车）,enrich（使丰富）;表示"内""在……之内"的前缀 en-来自希腊语,如:energy（能量）、enthusiasm（热情）;表示"小"的后缀-en 来自日尔曼语,如:chicken（小鸡）、maiden（少女）等。

同类的还有,表示"民族的""具有……的特点""稍微有点……""大约"的形容词后缀-ish 来自日尔曼语,如:Scottish（苏格兰的）、Spanish（西班牙的）、snobbish（势利小人的）、selfish（自私的）、longish（稍微有点长）、reddish（微长的）、elevenish（大约十一）、thirtyish（大约三十的）等,表示动词的后缀-ish 来自拉丁语,如:abolish（废除）,accomplish（完成）等;表示"前任""以前的"的前缀 ex-来自拉丁语,如:ex-wife（前妻）、ex-president（前总统）;而表示"出"的前缀 ex-来自希腊语,如:exodus（出埃及记）、export（出口）等。

Step 6:Characteristics of affixes with a focus on one affix with many positions

所谓"一缀多位"是指一个词缀既可以用作前缀,又可以用作后缀。如:en 既可以用作前缀,又可以用作后缀。en-用作前缀上文已有所涉及,这里不再赘述,关于-en 用作后缀,再补充几点。-en 加在形容词或名词后面构成动词,表示"使""使成为""使具有",如:deepen

（深化）、worsen（使……更糟）、strengthen（加强）等。-en 加在物质名词后面构成形容词,表示"由……制的或构成的""……样的",如:wooden（木头的）、golden（金色的）等。在某些名词后面构成复数,如:oxen（公牛）、children（小孩）等。-en 还可以构成某些不规则动词的过去分词,如:spoken（speak 的过去分词）、fallen（fall 的过去分词）等。

同类的还有,an 既可以用作前缀,又可以用作后缀。an-用作前缀时,表示"无",如:anandrous（无雄蕊的）、anarchy（无政府）等。-an 用作后缀时,既可以用作形容词后缀,表示"属于……的""带有……性质的",如:European（欧洲的）、urban（城市的）;也可用作名词后缀,表示"……地方的人",如:American（美国人）、civilian（平民）等。

Step 7:Characteristics of affixes with a focus on one affix with many categories

所谓"一缀多类"是指一个词缀属于不同的类型的词缀,既属屈折词缀又属派生词缀。如:在 They are *building* a house.（他们在建房）中的-ing 是个屈折词缀,因为这里的 building 是个现在分词,词性没有发生改变;而在 This is a *building*.（这是一幢大楼）中的-ing 就是个派生词缀,因为这里的 building 是个名词,与动词 build 分属不同的词类。

同类的还有,在 They were *excited* by the news.（这个消息使他们很激动）中的-ed 是个屈折词缀,因为这里的 excited 是个过去分词,词性没有发生改变;而在 They were very *excited*.（他们很激动）中的-ed 就是个派生词缀,因为这里的 excited 是个形容词,与动词 excite 分属不同的词类。在 happier 中的-er 是个屈折词缀,表示形容词的比较级,而在 teacher 中的-er 就是个派生词缀,表示"……的人",构成名词。

综上所述,我们不难看出英语词缀的除了"多缀一义"外,还有"一缀多义""一缀多性""一缀多形""一缀多源""一缀多位"和"一缀多类"的特点。这些特点的发现将有助我们对英语词缀的其他方面进一步探索,同时,也为词汇教学或词汇学教学提供一些参考。

II. Analysis

本教学设计是基于"一缀多＊"模式,讲授英语词缀的特点。本教学设计以"多缀一义"的特点导入,体现了"以旧带新"。接着巧妙把英语词缀特点"一缀多义""一缀多性""一缀多形""一缀多源""一缀多位"和"一缀多类"联在一起,给人一气呵成之感。整个教学设计思路清晰,层层深入,具有完整性和系统性。这样的教学设计既有助于学生教学内容的掌握,也有助于学生思维的培养,真可谓一箭双雕。

Case 11   Instructional Design of *Semantic Field* Based on 3C and Analysis

I. Instructional Design of *Semantic Field* Based on 3C

Step 1:Lead-in with a brief introduction to the origin of field

本节课我们来探讨语义场。在讲语义场之前,我们先来看看场这一概念。场（field）原是物理学的一个术语,特指一个范围。物理场即指相互作用场,如:磁场、电场、引力场等。

语言学借用"场"的概念来研究语义,于是就出现了语义场(semantic field)。关于语义场理论,我们可以追溯到 19 世纪中期的普通语言学的奠基人、德国语言学家洪堡特(W. Humboldt),而真正提出语义场概念的是 20 世纪 30 年代的德国和瑞士的一些结构主义语言学家,如:伊普森(Ipsen)、乔利斯(Jolles)、波尔齐格(Porzig)和特里尔(J. Trier)等。其中最突出的首推特里尔,其理论被人们广泛地认为是开创了语义学史上的新阶段。这些结构主义语言学家摒弃了过去既难深入又易偏颇的、孤立的、原子主义的研究方法,主张用联系的、发展的观点去研究,强调语言体系的统一性和环境对意思的影响。

Step 2:The teaching of *Semantic Field* with a focus on the first C:Concept

那么,究竟什么是语义场呢?语义场又称为词汇场(lexical field)和领域(domain),是指归属于一个共同概念之下的、意思上紧密相连的(不论是表共性的还是表差异的)一组词的聚合体。它有两层意思:其一是一种语言中的某些词,可以在一个共同概念的支配下,结合在一起组成一个语义场。这种共同概念既可以由上义词表示,语义场由下义词组成;也可以用语义特征来表示。如:在 vegetable 这个共同概念下,spinach,cauliflower,cabbage,pepper,onion,tomato,cucumber 等词共同组成一个语义场;再如:由 honesty,sincerity,chastity,fidelity 等词组成的语义场,可由 virtue 这个语义特征加以概括。其二是属于同一语义场的词,不仅仅在语义上相关,而且在语义上相互制约,相互规定。也就是说,要确定某个词的意思,必须首先比较该词与同一语义场中其他词在语义上的联系,以及该词在语义场中所占的位置。例如:由 fast 与 slow/sober/loose/disloyal/faded/slowly/eat 等词构成的多种不同的反义义场。要确定 fast 一词的意思,首先要了解 fast 与 slow 等词所表示的反义关系。针对形容词 slow 来说,fast 的意思是"快的";针对形容词 sober 来说,fast 的意思是"放荡的";针对形容词 loose 来说,fast 的意思是"紧的、牢的";针对形容词 disloyal 来说,fast 的意思是"忠实的";针对形容词 faded 来说,fast 的意思是"不褪色的";针对副词 slowly 来说,fast 的意思是"快地";针对动词 eat 来说,fast 的意思是"绝食"等。

然而,人们在研究语义场时,最重要的是给语义场确定一个界限,因为只有确定了语义场的界限,才能确定所要研究的语义场的规模,才能进行比较科学的描写,否则就容易引起混乱。例如:要研究英语中 dwelling place 这一义场,我们首先要搞清楚 dwelling place 这一义场是否只是指人的 dwelling place,如:house, apartment, villa, chateau, hut, cabin 等,是否包括动物的 dwelling place,如:nest, cage, stable, pigsty 等。如果是人的 dwelling place,是否包括一些临时性的 dwelling place,如:hotel, inn, shelter, asylum 等和一些或多或少与 dwelling place 有关的地方,如:hospital, prison 等,是否包括死人的 dwelling place,如:tomb, coffin, mausoleum 等。

Step 3:The teaching of *Semantic Field* with a focus on the second C:Categorization

众所周知,任何一种语言都包含着大量的语义场。这些语义场由于彼此之间的意思不同,词义的关系也不一样,因而分成许多类型。在英语中,主要分成四种类型:上下义义场(hyponymy),整体与部分义场(part/whole relationship),同义义场(synonymy)和反义义场(antonymy)。

我们首先来谈谈上下义义场。上下义义场是语义场中最常见的一类,它是指一词在上,表示总的概念,两个或三个以上的词在下,表示具体概念。在上者称作总义词(general terms)或上义词(superordinates 或 higher terms),在下者称作特义词(specific terms)或下义词(hyponyms 或 lower terms)。上下义义场又分为二元的和多元的。二元的是指一个上义词只包括两个下义词,如: parent 包括 father 和 mother; sibling 包括 brother 和 sister。多元的是指一个上义词包括三个或三个以上的下义词。如: colour 包括 red, orange, yellow, green, indigo, blue, purple 等。由于一词多义和不同的环境,有时同一个词既可以充当上义词,也可充当下义词。如:

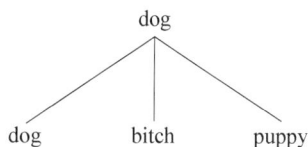

```
              dog
            /  |  \
          /    |    \
        dog  bitch  puppy
```

很显然,dog 这个词出现在不同的层次,当它在较高层次时,是上义词,表示狗的总称,当它在较低层次时,是下义词,表示公狗。

我们接下来谈谈整体与部分义场。当某一个词所指的事物是另一个词所指的事物的一部分时,两者之间便构成整体与部分义场。我们把表示部分的词称作组成词,把表示整体的词称作整体词。这种义场可包括两类。一类是有序类,即这些语义场中各词义之间有一种顺序关系。如: week 这个语义场中的 Sunday, Monday, Tuesday, Wednesday, Thursday, Friday, Saturday;和 year 这个语义场中的 January, February, March, April, May, June, July, August, September, October, November, December。另一类是离散类,即这些语义场中各词义之间无须按一定的次序排列。如: human body 的语义场包括 head, neck, shoulder, chest, belly, arm, wrist, hand, leg 等。

值得一提的是,上下义义场与整体与部分义场既有共同点,又有不同点。共同点是它们都是包含关系,即上义词和整体词是包含部分,下义词和组成词是被包含部分。不同点是:如果 A(上义词)和 B(下义词)组成上下义义场,那么 B 是一种 A。如: red 是一种 colour, spinach 是一种 vegetable。而如果 A(整体词)和 B(组成词)。组成整体与部分义场,那么 B 是 A 的一部分,而不是一种 A。例如: January 是 year 的一部分,而不是一种 year, head 是 human body 的一部分,而不是一种 human body。

下面我们来谈谈同义义场。所谓同义义场是指一组理性意思基本相同,并在某种程度上可以互换,而在发音、拼写、内涵、习惯用法等方面不同的词组成的语义场。同义义场又分为绝对同义义场和相对同义义场。绝对同义义场比较稀少,它是指语义上毫无区别,可在任何上下文毫无区别地互相代替的词组成的语义场。如: mother tongue—native language(母语), malnutrition—undernourishment(营养不良),breathed consonant—voiceless consonant(轻辅音)等。而相对同义义场则比较丰富,它是指语义基本相同或相似,但在程度上、感情色彩上、语体风格上和搭配关系上有不同的词组成的语义场。现将相对同义义场的几个类型分述如下:

在程度上不同的同义义场。组成这类语义场中的名词有相同的外延意思,但程度上有所不同。如: anger, rage 和 fury 这三个词都是讲 the emotional excitement induced by intense displeasure,但 anger 是一般用词,没有具体的程度(no definite degree of intensity),rage 强调失去自控(a loss of self-control),fury 表示的意思最强烈近乎发疯(a rage so violent that it may approach madness)。

在感情色彩上不同的同义义场。这类语义场是由那些语义基本相同,而感情色彩不同的同义词构成的。如:philanthropist 和 do-gooder 两个词都有"行善"的意思,前者指同情帮助穷人或处境困难的人的慈善家,含褒义;后者是不现实的人道主义者,一般带有过于天真或浮躁、鲁莽、徒劳无功的空想改良家,含贬义。再如:statesman 和 politician 这两个词的字面意思都指"政治家",前者是表示善于管理国家的明智之士,含褒义,后者指为谋取私利而搞政治、耍手腕的政客,含贬义。

在语体风格上不同的同义义场。语体风格上不同的同义义场是指那些理性意思基本相同,而语体风格上不同的同义词组成的语义场。美国语言学家 Martin Joos 在 Five Clocks(《五种时间》)一书中把词义的语体风格分为 frozen(庄严)、formal(正式)、consultative(交谈性)、casual(随便)和 intimate(亲昵)等五种。根据这五种语体风格,我们可以给表示 horse 这一组同义义场的词分别贴上相应的标签,charger 为庄严,steed 为正式,horse 为交谈性,nag 为随便,plug 为亲昵。

在搭配关系上不同的同义义场。该类语义场是由搭配关系不同的同义词构成的。例如:表示"指责"概念的同义义场中的词有 accuse,charge,rebuke 和 reproach 等,但与它们搭配的介词有所不同,accuse 跟 of 搭配,charge 跟 with 搭配,rebuke 跟 for 搭配,reproach 跟 with 或 for 搭配。

最后,我们来谈谈反义义场。反义义场是指意思相反、相对或相矛盾的,属于同一词性和同一范畴的一组词构成的语义场。它可以分为两极义场、互补义场和换位义场。

两极义场。两极义场是指由语义相对,形成两极的词构成的语义场。如:hot-cold, rich-poor 等。这类语义场有两个特点,一是语义的归一性(semantic polarity)和相对性(relativity),即语义的两极相比较而存在。我们可以说:A man may be rich or very rich. One man may be richer than another.二是语义对立的渐进性(gradual),也就是说,既可以在反义义场的两极中间插进表示不同程度性质的词,体现出对立的层次性。如:在 hot 和 cold 之间,可以插入 warm, tepid, lukewarm, cool 等词,也可以在反义词的两极增加不同程度的词,体现出对立的层次性。如:在 hot 和 cold 的两极可以增加 boiling, sweltering, chilly 和 freezing。

互补义场。这类义场是指语义上相互排斥的词组成的语义场,即非此及彼或非彼及此。例如:dead—alive, If he is not dead, he is alive. /If he is not alive, he is dead,这类反义义场还有:male—female, single—married, present—absent 等。一般说来,这类义场中间不可能插入表示层次性对立的词,也就是说没有中间状态。

换位义场。换位义场是指语义上既相互对立,又相互依存的一组词组成的语义场,一方的存在以另一方的存在为前提,双方形成对立的统一体。如:buy—sell, lend—borrow, husband—wife, employer—employee 等,因此,If A lends $100 to B, then B borrows $100 from A. If A is B's husband, then B is A's wife.

Step 4：The teaching of *Semantic Field* with a focus on the third C：Characteristics

语义场的特点很多,总括起来,主要有七个,即层次性、传递性、交错性、相对性、变化性、模糊性和民族性。

1. 层次性

语义场有明显的层次性,它可以从上到下地观察,最高层次的词最具有概括性,次一个层次的词较为具体,再下一个层次更加具体,这样可以不断地分析下去。例如：

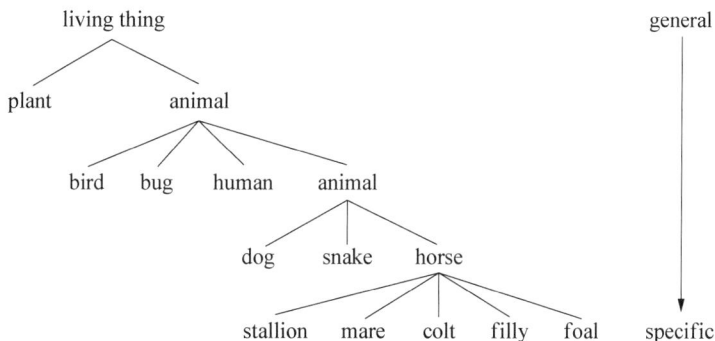

语义场层次性的特点是由客观事物的系统性决定的,同时,也反映了人类认识客观事物的成果。

2. 传递性

语义场的另一特征,是其传递性,即如果 A 在 B 中,B 又在 C 中,那么,A 就在 C 中。这种传递性主要表现在两个方面：一是在上下义义场中,如果 B 是一种 A, C 是一种 B,则 C 是一种 A,例如：animal 是一种 living thing, dog 是一种 animal,那么 dog 是一种 living thing；另一个是在整体与部分义场中,如果 B 是 A 的一部分,C 又是 B 的一部分,那么 C 是 A 的一部分,例如：season 是 year 的一部分,month 是 season 的一部分,那么,month 是 year 的一部分。

3. 交错性

语义场有大量错综复杂的情况,因而具有交错性的特点。它体现在两个方面：其一,一词一义相对于不同的词构成不同的语义场。如：parent 既可跟 father 和 mother 构成上下义义场,也可跟 child 构成反义义场；其二,一词多义跟不同的词构成不同的语义场。如：前面提到的 fast 可跟 slow 等词构成一系列的反义义场。同时,它既可跟 quick, rapid, speedy 构成一组同义义场,也可跟 firm, fixed 构成一组同义义场,还可跟 devoted, loyal 等构成另一组同义义场。再如：cow 这个词既可以在较高层次表示牛的总称,又可以在较低层次表示具体的母牛。

4. 相对性

语义场的相对性有两层意思,一是指上下义关系不是绝对的、固定不变的、而是相对的,如：

如图所示,bird 相对于 animal 来说,出现在较低层次,是下义词,而相对于 sparrow, parrot 和 fowl 等词是上义词；fowl 也是一样,相对于 bird 是下义词,相对于 chicken 等词是上义词。

```
                              animal
                 ┌──────────┬────┴─────┬──────────┐
               bird        bug      human      animal
          ┌─────┼─────┐
       sparrow parrot  fowl
                    ┌────┼────┐
                 chicken turkey quail
```

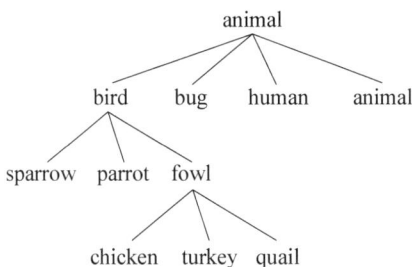

二是语义场在描述不同事物时,依据的标准是不同的,即是相对而言的。例如:在 big—small 这个语义场中,大小是相对的,有时,小的事物比大的事物还要大。如:a small elephant 要比 a big mouse 大,而 a small mouse 比 a big mosquito 还要大。

5. 变化性

任何一种语言从历时的角度看总是在不断变化发展的,其中以词汇表现得尤为突出,它不仅表现为旧词的消失和新词的产生,而且表现为词义范围的变化。这些变化势必引起语义场的变化。例如:nice 一词原来是"愚蠢的、傻里傻气的",与 foolish, stupid 构成同义义场,在现代英语中 nice 演变成了"好的"这个意思,跟 good, fine 构成同义义场;再如 bird 这个词原来专指"幼鸟",现在演变成了"鸟"的总称,词义扩大了。由于词义的变化,一些词由一个语义场转到另一个语义场。

6. 模糊性

语义场的模糊性是指由于人们对客观世界中有些事物至今还没有明确的概念,使之产生了模糊性,如:olive(橄榄)是该放在水果义场还是放在蔬菜义场,sled(雪橇)是该放在交通工具义场还是放在体育器材义场,这些都很模糊。

7. 民族性

由于各个民族有不同的文化风俗习惯,因此各种语言的语义场必定带有自己的民族性。例如:在汉语中,牙医与医生可构成一个上下义义场,而在英语中 dentist 与 doctor 之间并不构成上下义义场,因为 dentist 并不是 doctor,而是负责照看牙齿的人。再如:在汉语中,"给……印象"与"表达"绝对不能构成一组反义义场,而在英语中,impress 和 express 却可构成一组反义义场。只要我们分析一下这两个词的构成,就可以明白了。前缀"im-"和"ex-"的意思分别是 in(进)和 out(出),词根 press 的意思是 push(推、压),因此,impress 的意思就是"压进去""给……印象",express 的意思是"推出来"即"表达"。这种英汉两种语言语义场的不对应现象,正是语义场民族性的体现。此外,英汉两种语言语义场的缺位现象,也是语义场民族性的体现。如:汉语里的"长处"和"短处"构成一组反义义场,而英语中只有 shortcoming,却没有 longcoming,因此也就谈不上构成反义义场了。

以上是我们对英语语义场的探讨,应该强调的是语义场理论不仅实用性强,而且应用范围广。因此,我们应加强这方面的研究,以便更好地为语言教学、翻译、写作和词典编纂服务。

Step 5:Assignment:reading *We Need More* with a focus on antonymous semantic field

本节课的课后作业是读 We Need More。这是我写的一段文字。阅读时要特别注意反义义场,同时也也从道德层面慢慢体会这段文字。

We need more love, not hate; we need more faith, not heresy; we need more sincerity, not hypocrisy; we need more smile, not sorrow; we need more concern, not indifference; we need more humility, not pride; we need more kindness, not envy; we need more sympathy, not apathy; we need more charity, not greed; we need more truth, not deception; we need more beauty, not ugliness; we need more understanding, not misunderstanding; we need more wisdom, not folly; we need more forgiveness, not vengeance; we need more optimism, not pessimism; we need more justice, not injustice; we need more democracy, not autocracy; we need more freedom, not enslavement; we need more knowledge, not ignorance; we need more concentration, not distraction; we need more industry, not laziness; we need more tranquility, not chaos; we need more action, not idleness; we need more facts, not fiction; we need more courage, not cowardice; we need more generosity, not stinginess; we need more humor, not anxiety; we need more cooperation, not competition; we need more flowers, not thorns; we need more hope, not despair; we need more concord, not discord; we need more conscientiousness, not cynicism; we need more encouragement, not discouragement; we need more health, not disease.... With these, we can create a paradise in our hearts.

Ⅱ. Analysis

教学设计的一个重要特点是简约性。本教学设计的理念为 3C,就体现了简约性这样一个特点。第一个 C 是 Concept,即语义场的概念。它是指归属于一个共同概念之下的、意思上紧密相连的(不论是表共性的还是表差异的)一组词的聚合体。第二个 C 是 Categorization,即语义场的分类:语义场主要分成四种类型:上下义义场、整体与部分义场、同义义场和反义义场。第三个 C 是 Characteristics,即语义场的特点:层次性、传递性、交错性、相对性、变化性、模糊性和民族性。通过这三个 C,学生从宏观上马上就能了解这节课的重点是什么,这样要言不烦、一言中的。最后学生掌握语义场三个方面也就瓜熟蒂落、水到渠成。

Part Three

Instructional Design of *Translation* and Case Analysis

Case 12 Instructional Design of *Inversion* Based on System Theory and Analysis

I. Instructional Design of *Inversion* Based on System Theory

Step 1: Lead-in with a brief introduction to translation techniques with inversion as a focus

在任何一篇段落与语篇的翻译中,都会涉及多种翻译技巧。如:词义选择、减译、增译、替代、词序调整等。我们今天要翻译的这个段落也不例外。

大自然对人的恩赐,无论贫富,一律平等。所以人们对于大自然,全都一致并深深地依赖着。尤其在乡间,上千年来人们一直以不变的方式生活着。种植庄稼和葡萄,酿酒和饮酒,喂牛和挤奶,锄草和栽花;在周末去教堂祈祷和做礼拜,在节日到广场拉琴、跳舞和唱歌;往日的田园依旧是今日的温馨家园。这样,每个地方都有自己的传说,风俗也就衍传了下来。

在这个段落中,许多词义需要选择,如:"上千年来"中的"上千",是译为"thousands of"?还是译为"more than/over a thousand"?还是译为"about/around a thousand"?还是译为"nearly a thousand"?又如:"酿酒和饮酒"中的"酒",是译为"wine"?还是译为"beer"?还是译为"liquor"?还是译为"spirits"?再如:"拉琴"中的"琴",是译为"violin"?还是译为"accordion"?还是译为"erhu"?还是译为"musical instrument(s)"?

教师要求学生思考刚才的几个问题并讨论。思考时,要结合原文,尽可能吃透原文,还要比较这些译文。讨论时,可以各抒己见。

我们怎么翻译"在周末去教堂祈祷和做礼拜"中的"祈祷和做礼拜"?在这个上下文中能不能减去不译?这里涉及到一个减译的问题。同样,"上学去读书"中的"去读书"能不能也减去不译?

我们再看下一句,在"尤其在乡间,上千年来人们一直以不变的方式生活着"中,要不要根据上下文把相关内容增译上去?在"种植庄稼和葡萄,酿酒和饮酒,喂牛和挤奶,锄草和栽花;在周末去教堂祈祷和做礼拜,在节日到广场拉琴、跳舞和唱歌"中,是"谁"在干这些事?

要不要根据上下文把"谁"增译上去？关于替代，如："大自然对人的恩赐，无论贫富，一律平等。所以人们对于大自然，全都一致并深深地依赖着。"中的第二个"大自然"要不要代词来替代？如果要，用什么来替代，是用"it"，还是用"her"？这些大家都要仔细的思考。

接下来，我们来看看词序调整。它是我们最常见、最常用的翻译技巧之一，同时也我们这一节课要讲解的重点和难点。

Step 2：Inversion in the coordinate structure without any restraint from the original

在原文中有"贫富"和"跳舞和唱歌"等并列结构短语，应该怎么译？是译为"poor or/and rich"，还是译为"rich or/and poor"？是译为"dance and sing/dancing and singing"，还是译为"sing and dance/singing and dancing"？教师鼓励学生思考并加以判断。很显然，应为后者。这里一点需要强调：在汉英两种语言中，都有一些并列结构短语，已经形成了各自固定的语序，互不相同。在翻译这些并列结构短语时，必须按照英语表达习惯，进行必要的调整，不受原文的束缚。类似的并列结构短语还有很多，如：

1. 新郎新娘：the bride and the groom

2. 衣食住行：food, clothing, shelter and transportation（饮食：food and drink）

3. 左顾右盼：look right and left

4. 身心：mind and body

5. 南北：north and south（东南西北：north and south, east and west）

6. 不论晴雨：rain or shine

7. 钢铁：iron and steel

8. 我和你：you and I（me）

9. 祸福：weal and woe

10. 往返/来回：back and forth

11. 血肉：flesh and blood

12. 工农业：agriculture and industry

13. 迟早：sooner or later

14. 水火：fire and water（水陆：land and water）

15. 敌我矛盾：contradictions between ourselves and enemy

16. 新老：old and new

17. 死活：life and death

18. 三三两两：by twos or threes

19. 田径：track and field

20. 此时此地：here and now

21. 得失：loss and gain

22. 断断续续：on and off

23. 公私：private and public

24. 手臂：arms and hands

25. 文学艺术：art and literature

26. 山水：waters and mountains

27. 腹背：back and belly

28. 口蹄疫：foot and mouth disease

29. 远近 near and far

同学们把这些常见、常用不受原文束缚的并列结构短语"记"下来，既要"记"到笔记本上，更要"记"在大脑里，以便日后使用。

Step 3：Inversion in terms of logical relationship

我们下面再来看原文中的一段话："种植庄稼和葡萄，酿酒和饮酒，喂牛和挤奶，锄草和栽花。"如何翻译这段话？老师鼓励学生思考并让学生试译这句话。

接着，教师给学生提供两个译文。这两个译文是目前八级辅导材料和核心期刊提供的参考译文。一是："They plant crops and grapevines, brew wine to drink, feed cows to milk, and weed gardens to grow flowers."另一是"They grow crops and grapes, brew the wine for drink, raise cows for milk, weed their gardens for cultivation of flowers."学生可以把自己的译文与教师提供的两个译文比较一下，并进行讨论交流。

应该说这两个译文，无论是结构还是选词，都已经下了相当的功夫，译得不错。但仔细研究这两个译文，会发现一些美中不足的地方，即：这两个译文都是按照其原文顺序亦步亦趋进行翻译，逻辑关系有些紊乱。如果我们摆脱原文顺序的束缚，按照逻辑关系调整词序，那又该怎样调整词序？同学们思考思考，讨论讨论。

我们先试着调整词序，然后再进行翻译，最后老师拿出自己译文，供同学们参考。（教师展示自己的译文）

"They weed gardens and cultivate flowers; plant grapevines and grow crops; feed and milk cows; and brew and drink wine."

请同学们注意，老师的译文只是若干译文中的一种，代表的是老师的理解与翻译，不一定是好的。你们一定要学会甄别优劣。正如孔子所说："师不必贤于弟子，弟子不必不如师"。再说，译文永远是"没有最好，只有更好。"我们在汉译英时，可能会遇到汉语中逻辑关系的先后安排与英语的习惯不同。这时，我们需要从两个方面来考虑：一是从所描述的事情的类别、强弱/轻重、大小等来考虑；另一是从行为发生的时间以及它们的因果关系来考虑，调整译文中句子的成分和某些词语的顺序。如：

第一，按照类别的词序调整

1. 君子之交淡如水，小人之交甘如醴。君子淡以亲，小人甘以绝。

The friendship between men of virtue is light like water, yet affectionate; the friendship between men without virtue is sweet like wine, yet easily broken.

2. 不登高山，不知天之厚也；不临深渊，不知地之厚也。

One can never be aware of the height of the sky or the depth of the earth, if he does not climb up a high mountain or look down into a deep abyss.

例1的译文把对"君子"的描述放在一起，把对"小人"的描述放在一起，这样显得条分缕析、泾渭分明，给人一气呵成之感。同样，例2的译文把"不登高山"和"不临深渊"放在一起，把"不知天之厚也"和"不知地之厚也"放在一起,这样显得干净利索、简洁明快,给人自然流畅之感。

第二,按照强弱/轻重的词序调整

3. 救死扶伤：heal the wounded and rescue the dying

4. 无地和少地的农民：those peasants who have little or no land

5. 它有一部分领袖人物不属于这个集团,而且被这个集团所打击、排斥或轻视。Some leaders do not belong to this clique by which they are slighted, pushed aside or attacked.

6. 丰收年多积累一点,灾荒年或半灾荒年就不积累或少积累一点。Accumulate more in good years and less or none in years when the crops half fail or totally fail.

7. 许多这些探险都以失败、死亡、灾难和失望而告终。Many such expeditions ended in disappointment, failure, disaster and death.

8. 一切都失去了——自由、信仰、友谊、希望等等。Since hope was lost, friendship was lost, faith was lost, liberty was lost—all was lost.

一个短语或一个句子,有两个或几个并列的词语时,其含义常有强弱、轻重之分。汉语的顺序排列,一般是把强的、重的放在前面,把弱的、轻的放在后面。英语正好相反,一般是把弱的、轻的放在前面,把强的、重的放在后面。例 3 ~ 例 6 就属于这样的情况。我们刚才是讲的一般情况。有时候,汉语的逻辑性不强,可能强弱、轻重还有点乱,这时,我们要按照英语的"由弱到强"和"由轻到重"的顺序进行排列,例 7 和例 8 就属于这样的情况。

第三,按照大小的词序调整

9. 中小学：elementary and high schools

10. 中小型企业：small and medium-sized enterprises

11. 年月：month and year

12. 设在位于纽约市中心一座摩天大楼第四十层楼里的那间办公室就是他工作的小天地。The office on the fortieth floor of a skyscraper in the center of New York City is the world he works in.

13. 他一九四五年八月二十二日早晨八点乘飞机离开华盛顿。He left Washington by air at 8 on the morning of August 22,1945.

在有表示时间、空间或范围的并列结构或句子中,汉语一般把表示大的单位放在前面,小的单位放在后面;英语正好相反,一般是把表示小的单位放在前面,把大的放在后面。不论是例 9—例 11 中的并列结构,还是例 12 和例 13 的句子,翻译时词序均需要按照大小进行调整。

第四,按照时间先后的词序调整

14. 手疾眼快：quick of eye and deft of hand

15. 经风雨见世面：face the world and brave the storm

我们前面刚讲过,有时候,汉语的逻辑性不强,这时,我们应该按照时间先后顺序来翻译。在例 14 中,从逻辑上讲,总是先看见后动手;在例 15 中,从逻辑上讲,是 face the world 在前,brave the storm 在后。

第五,按照因果的词序调整

16. 不论什么人,凡对于这个革命统一战线的巩固工作有所贡献者,我们就欢迎他,他就是正确的;凡对于这个革命统一战线的巩固工作有所损害者,我们就反对他,他就是错误的。Whoever contributes to the consolidation of this revolutionary united front is doing right, and we welcome him; whoever harms this consolidation is doing wrong, and we oppose him.

这里的"正确"和"欢迎","错误"和"反对"都是因果关系,因此也要做适当的调整,以便符合英语的表达习惯。

刚才我们讲解了五种按照逻辑关系的词序调整,他们分别是:按照类别的词序调整、按照强弱/轻重的词序调整、按照大小的词序调整、按照时间先后的词序调整和按照因果的词序调整。

Step 4:Inversion in terms of adverbials

原文中有这样一句话:"上千年来人们一直以不变的方式生活着"。仔细地阅读这句话,我们发现它有三个状语"上千年来""一直"和"以不变的方式"。我们还是先来看看目前八级辅导材料和核心期刊提供的三个参考译文。

译文一:"People have kept the same lifestyle for a millennium or so. ";

译文二:"Their ways of life have been kept intact/have remained unchanged for thousands of years. ";

译文三:"People have been living in the same way for over a thousand years. "

那么,这三个状语到底应该怎么翻译? 具体地说,这里我们有四个问题:其一是第一个状语"上千年来",由于对"上"的理解有不同,有三种译文。哪一个相对比较准确? 其二是第二个状语"一直"该怎么翻译? 其三是第三个状语"以不变的方式"该怎么翻译? 其四是这三个状语该怎么排序? 要求学生思考、讨论并发表自己的看法。

根据网上的《汉典》,"上"的第十五个定义,是表示"达到一定的程度或数量",这样可以看出,译文一相对准确。我们再看它的位置,三个译文无一例外地都进行了词序调整,把它从原文的句首放到句尾。这可能是出于语言的表达习惯的考虑。当然,状语的词序调整,也有出于句子的平衡或上下文的关联等方面的考虑。

我们接着来看第二个状语"一直",三个译文不约而同地都用"完成时",而没有用"always"或"constantly"等副词表示"一直"。这说明有时候,我们可以用时态表示状语如"现在"和"过去"。类似的情况如:

1. 他现在讲英语没有过去讲得多。He does not speak as much English as he did.

2. 对他的帮助,我过去很感激,现在依然很感激。I was, and remain very grateful for his help.

我们再来看第三个状语"以不变的方式"。有的把它译为动宾结构中的"定语"(the same);有的把它译为复合结构中的"宾语补足语"(intact);有的把它译为系表结构中的"表语"(unchanged);还有的把它直接译为"状语"(in the same way)。由此可见,状语的翻译颇为灵活,千万不能亦步亦趋。

这里还有一个状语的排序问题,即多个状语的词序调整问题。一般说来,汉语里状语的顺序为：时间状语、地点状语和方式状语；而英语里状语的顺序为：方式状语、地点状语和时间状语。这一点，我们看一下译文3，就明白了。类似的例子还有：

1. 他每天早晨在室外高声朗读。He reads aloud in the open every morning.

2. 我们上周在她家饱餐一顿。We ate to our hearts' content at her home last Sunday.

我们刚才讲了状语的词序调整。请一个同学把状语的词序调整总结一下。

汉译两种语言的状语位置较为复杂，一方面汉英两种语言的状语位置都不那么固定，可能是出于语言的表达习惯或句子的平衡或上下文的关联等方面的考虑，要对状语的词序进行调整；另一方面是因为汉英两种语言的状语位置差别很大，也要对状语的词序进行调整。

Step 5：Inversion in terms of attributes

我们还是来看原文，其中有一句："往日的田园依旧是今日的温馨家园"。虽然"往日的"可以译为"in former days"、"in the past"、"old（en）"、"yesterday"等，"今日的"可以译为"present-day"、"nowadays"、"today"等，但是考虑到原文中的"往日的"与"今日的"对称，这样选择"yesterday"和"today"较妥。"yesterday"和"today"这两个词都既可以用作名词也可以用作副词，用作名词时，"往日的"和"今日的"，可以用所有格来翻译；用作副词时，可以把它们放在所修饰的名词后面，也就是定语的词序调整。我们看到"今日的温馨家园"时，可能会想到一本宣传中国的杂志叫《今日中国》和中央电视台播的一个节目叫《今日关注》，他们分别译为"China Today"和"Focus Today"，因此这句话我们可以译为："The garden-like farmland yesterday remains their sweet home today."这种副词用作定语的例子还有：

1. 他作了一次国外旅行，刚刚回来。He has just returned from his trip abroad.

2. 这是唯一的出路。This is the only way out.

3. 那边的工厂是我们学校办的。The factory there is run by our school.

实际上，定语的词序调整在汉译英时非常常见。这里我们再补充几种。

第一，在某些固定结构中，单个形容词用作定语时，习惯上放在所修饰名词的后面。例如：

4. 军事法庭：Court Martial

5. （世界卫生组织）总干事：Director-General（of the WHO）

6. 当选总统：the president elect

7. 确定继承人：an heir apparent

8. 桂冠诗人：a poet laureate

第二，在一些科技名词中，单个名词用作定语时，习惯上放在所修饰名词的后面。例如：

9. 氯化钠：sodium chloride

10. 碳酸钙：calcium carbonate

11. 硝酸银：silver nitrate

12. 二氧化碳：carbon dioxide

第三，在日常生活中，也有单个名词用作定语时，习惯上放在所修饰名词的后面。例如：

13. 中石油：Petrol China/PetroChina

14. 希望工程：Project Hope

15. 圣诞老人：Father Christmas

16. 男婴：baby boy

第四,汉译英时,用介词短语作定语、用分词短语作定语以及用句子作定语均要调整词序。例如：

17. 据说那一带的树多数都10米多高。It is said the trees in that area are mostly over ten meters tall.

18. 相关部门昨天讨论了这件事。The department concerned discussed the matter yesterday.

19. 环绕原子核运动的粒子：particles moving around their atomic nucleus

20. 氧是一种能和许多物质化合的气体。Oxygen is a gas which unites with many substances.

我们这节课主要学了跟这篇短文相关"词序调整"这一翻译技巧,共有四个大类,即：不受原文束缚的并列结构短语的词序调整、按照逻辑关系的词序调整、状语的词序调整和定语的词序调整。"词序调整"还有一些类型尚未涉及。实际上,"词序调整"极其普遍,诸如：

复合词的词序调整,如：降雨(rainfall)、耗时的(time-consuming)等。

称呼语的词序调整,如：王教授(Professor Wang)、胡主席(President Hu)等。

主谓结构的词序调整,如：新年快乐(Happy New Year!)、激情似火(burning passion)等。

重新确立主语的词序调整,如：我们的事业取得了一个又一个的胜利(We have achieved one victory after another in our cause.)；他的英语讲得好(He speaks good English.)等。

被动语态的词序调整,如：改革开放取得了重大突破(Major breakthroughs were made in reform and opening-up.)；支农惠农政策不断加强(Policies were constantly strengthened to support and benefit agriculture, rural areas and farmers.)等。

基于语篇的词序调整,如：他出现在台上,观众给予热烈鼓掌。(He appeared on the stage and was warmly applauded by the audience.)；口试时,问了十个问题,她全都答对了。(She was asked ten questions in the oral exam and answered every one of them correctly.)等。

词序调整远远不是。还有更多的东西需要我们以后进一步学习、练习、思考和探究。翻译是无止境的,希望同学们能够"窥斑见豹、触类旁通",更要学会站在巨人的肩膀上,这样会站得更高、看得更远、想得更深!

Ⅱ. Analysis

词序调整是一个重要的翻译技巧,我们的译文之所以诘屈聱牙、生硬别扭、晦涩难懂,原因之一是我们在翻译时以词对词,以句套句,没有进行适当的词序调整,这一现象在大四的译文中仍很普遍。

这是大四学生快要考英语专业八级前的一节《汉译英》的教学设计,这时的学生由于英语专业八级压力和就业的压力,对按照现有的课本,按部就班地讲解段落与语篇翻译,可能已经缺乏兴趣和耐心。鉴于此,本节课的教学设计思路分为三步。第一步,选择贴近学生现实需要的段落或语篇,尽可能把《汉译英》教学内容与英语专业八级考试有机地结合起来；第二步,进一步巩固本课程的教学理念:"得法于课堂,得益于课外",本节课具体的法是"词序调整";第三步,从所学的段落或语篇出发,教师对"词序调整"的方方面面进行选择、引导、分类、拓展和总结;学生对"词序调整"的方方面面进行感知、参与、思考、讨论和甄别。

了解"词序调整"这一翻译技巧。首先了解"词序调整"这一翻译技巧的普遍性,大多数句子翻译都用到这一技巧;其次了解"词序调整"这一翻译技巧的类型,从而使学生关于"词序调整"的知识条理化和系统化;最后在了解"词序调整"这一翻译技巧的基础上,逐步形成"词序调整"意识。

本教学设计的理念是系统论。它以系统作为研究对象,运用完整性、集中性、等级结构等概念,研究适用于一切综合系统或子系统的模式、原则和规律的学问。本教学设计主要采用它的等级结构或层次结构,即一个系统可以分解成若干个子系统,向下还可以再分更小的系统,同时一个系统又可以和另外一些系统组成一个大系统。几个大系统可以组成一个更大的系统。词序调整这个系统向下可分为"不受原文的束缚的词序调整、按照逻辑关系的词序调整、状语的词序调整、定语的词序调整"等子系统。在"按照逻辑关系的词序调整"这个子系统中,又分为"按照类别的词序调整、按照强弱/轻重的词序调整、按照大小的词序调整按照时间先后的词序调整"等更小系统。这样有助于学生比较容易地掌握所学内容。

参考译文:

All people, rich or poor, are equally blessed by Nature, and they deeply depend on her. This is true, especially in the countryside where their lifestyle has remained unchanged for nearly a thousand years. They weed gardens and cultivate flowers; plant grapevines and grow crops; feed and milk cows; and brew and drink wine. On weekends they go to church, and on holidays they play musical instruments, sing and dance in the plaza. The gardenlike farmland yesterday remains their sweet home today. Thus, every place boasts its own folklore in such a way that its customs are handed down from generation to generation.

Case 13 Instructional Design of *Strategies for English-to-Chinese Transliteration* from Phonological Perspective and Analysis

I . Instructional Design of *Strategies for English-to-Chinese Transliteration* from Phonological Perspective

Step 1: Lead-in with three phonological rules

With the economic globalization, intercultural communication is becoming increasingly important. One of the bridges that facilitate intercultural communication is translation, in which there exist many areas that require in-depth research. As a form of translation, transliteration is a mapping from one system of writing into another, word by word, or ideally letter by letter. Transliteration attempts to use a one-to-one correspondence so that an informed reader should be able to roughly reconstruct the original spelling of unknown transliterated words. There are many transliterated words in Chinese. How they have been transliterated into Chinese, to be more specific, what strategies have been employed in English-to-Chinese transliteration is open to further inquiry. We'll show you some strategies for English-to-Chinese transliteration from phonological perspective so as to gain insight into the Chinese and English languages and to facilitate intercultural communication.

Phonology deals with the function of sounds and their patterns of combination. The former is to distinguish meaning and the latter can be reduced to three rules: sequential rules, assimilation rule and deletion rule.

According to *A New Concise Course in Linguistics for Students of English* (Second edition) by Dai Weidong (2010), sequential rules refer to the rules that govern the combination of sounds in a particular language, that is, the phonological system determines which phonemes can begin a word, end a word, and follow each other. There are many sequential rules in English. For example, if a word begins with /l/ or /r/, then the next sound must be a vowel. Another example, if three consonants should cluster together at the beginning of a word, the combination should obey the following three rules:

(1) The first phoneme must be /s/;

(2) The second phoneme must be /p/, /t/ or /k/;

(3) The third phoneme must be /l/, /r/ or /w/.

That is why we have these English words, like "spring, strict, square, splendid, scream."

Assimilation rule refers to the rule that assimilates one segment to another by "copying" a feature of a sequential phoneme, thus making the two phones similar. Assimilation of neighboring sounds is, for the most part, caused by articulatory or physiological processes. When we speak, we tend to increase the ease of articulation. This "sloppy" tendency may become regularized as assimilation rule.

Assimilation rule accounts for the varying pronunciation of the alveolar nasal /n/ in some sound combinations. The rule is that within a word, the nasal /n/ assumes the same place of articulation as the consonant that follows it. We know that in English the prefix "in-" can be added to an adjective to make the meaning of the word negative, e. g. *discrete—indiscrete*, *correct—incorrect*. But the /n/ sound in the prefix in- is not always pronounced as an alveolar nasal. It is so in the word *indiscrete* because the consonant that follows it, i. e. /d/, is an alveolar stop, but the /n/ sound in the word *incorrect* is actually pronounced as a velar nasal, i. e. /ŋ/; this is because the consonant that follows it is /k/, which is a velar stop. So we can see that while pronouncing the sound /n/, we are "copying" a feature of the consonant that follows it. The sound assimilation is actually reflected in the spelling in most cases. Instead of *inpossible*, the negative form of possible is *impossible*, as the /n/ sound is assimilated to /m/. For the same reason, the negative form of *plausible*, *legal*, *regular* are *implausible*, *illegal*, and *irregular*.

Deletion rule refers to the fact that when a sound is to be deleted although is orthographically represented. While the letter "g" is mute in "sign", "design" and "paradigm", it is pronounced in their corresponding derivatives:"signature", "designation" and "paradigmatic". The rule then can be stated as: delete a /g/ when it occurs before a final nasal consonant. This accounts for some of the seeming irregularities of the English spelling, like the letter *b* in words like *comb* and *tomb*.

Since there are sequential rules, assimilation rule and deletion rule in English, we try to apply these rules to English-to-Chinese transliteration and come up with some transliteration strategies so as to gain insight into the Chinese and English languages and to facilitate intercultural communication. Based on three phonological rules mentioned above, we are going to talk about four strategies for English-to-Chinese transliteration, which are epenthesis, segmental adaptation, deletion and segmental split strategies.

Step 2: Epenthesis strategies for English-to-Chinese transliteration

The first strategy we are going to deal with is epenthesis strategy. In phonology, epenthesis is the addition of one or more sounds to a word, especially to the interior of a word. In English-to-Chinese transliteration, epenthesis strategy refers to the strategy for addition of one or more sounds to a word, especially to the interior of a word, which can be subdivided into two types: anaptyxis and excrescence strategies. According to *Table of English Sounds with Their Chinese Equivalents* by Lu (2007), most vowels can stand independently and become words without any addition of sounds, like /eɪ/ transliterated into "埃" and /ɒ/ into "奥" while most consonants can hardly stand independently and require addition of sounds to become words, like /t/ that requires "e" transliterated into "特" and /p/ that requires "u" transliterated into "普". That is why more anaptyxis strategy is employed than excrescence strategy.

Anaptyxis strategies refer to the strategy for addition of a vowel. One of the different features between English and Chinese is that Chinese characters are monosyllabic and are open while many English words are multi-syllabic and are closed, in other words, most of Chinese characters end with a vowel while most English words end with a consonant. In this case, anaptyxis strategies are employed in English-to-Chinese transliteration. According to *Table of English Sounds with Their Chinese Equivalents* by Lu (2007), there are three types of inserting vowels. The first type is inserting "u" after bilabials and labial-dentals; the second type is inserting "e" after alveolar plosives and velar plosives; and the third type is inserting "I" after alveolar fricatives, dental fricatives, palatal fricatives and palatal affricates.

There are two strategies for inserting "u" after bilabials and labial-dentals. One is the strategy for inserting "u" after bilabials /b/, /p/ and /m/; and the other is the strategy for inserting "u" after labial-dentals /f/ and /v/.

The first strategy is inserting "u" after bilabials /b/, /p/ and /m/, like "Jobs" /dʒɒbz/ transliterated into "乔布斯", "Hobson" /ˈhɒbsn/ into "霍布森", "Plimsol" /ˈplɪmsəl/ into "普

利姆索尔", Priestley /ˈpriːstlɪ/ into "普利斯特利", "Hopkins" /ˈhɒpkɪnz/ into "霍普金斯", "Sharp" /ʃɑːp/ into "夏普", "Harlem" /ˈhɑːləm/ into "哈莱姆", "Hamlin" /ˈhæmlɪn/ into "哈姆林" and "Ransom"/ˈrænsəm/ into "兰塞姆". The second strategy is inserting /ʊ/ after labial-dentals /f/ and /v/, like "Swift" /swɪft/ transliterated into "斯威夫特", "Cardiff" /ˈkɑːdɪf/ into "卡迪夫", "Grove" /grəʊv/ into "格罗夫" and "Steve"/stiːv/ into "史蒂夫". What is mentioning here is that "Yale" /jaɪl/ is transliterated into "耶鲁" by inserting "u" after alveolar liquid /l/, which is not very common in English-to-Chinese transliteration.

There are two strategies for inserting "e" after alveolar plosives and velar plosives. One is the strategy for inserting "e" after alveolar plosives. The other is the strategy for inserting "e" after velar plosives.

The first strategy is inserting "e" after alveolar plosives /t/ and /d/, like "Kate" /keɪt/ transliterated into "凯特", "Strong" /strɒŋ/ into "斯特朗", "Alfred" /ælfrɪd/ into "阿尔弗雷德" and "Gerald" /dʒerəld/ into "杰拉尔德". The second strategy is inserting "e" after velar plosives /k/ and /g/, like "Olympic" /əʊˈlɪmpɪk/ transliterated into "奥林匹克", "Blake" /bleɪk/ into "布莱克", "Greenland" /ˈgriːnlənd/ into "格林兰" and "Ogden" /ˈɒgdən/ into "奥格登".

There are four strategies for inserting "i" after alveolar fricatives, dental fricatives, palatal fricatives and palatal affricates, to be more specific, inserting "i" after alveolar fricatives /s/ and /z/; inserting "i" after dental fricative /θ/; inserting "i" after palatal fricative /ʃ/; inserting "i" after palatal affricates.

The first strategy is inserting "i" after alveolar fricatives /s/ and /z/, for example, "Alice" /ˈælɪs/ is transliterated into "爱丽丝", "Boris" /bɒrɪs/ into "鲍里斯", "Scott" /skɒt/ into "司各特", "Slater" /ˈsleɪtə/ into "斯莱特", "Jazz" /dʒæz/ into "爵士", "Yuppies" /ˈjʌpɪz/ into "雅皮士". The second strategy is inserting "i" after dental fricative /θ/, like "Wordsworth" /ˈwɜːdzwəθ/ transliterated into "沃兹沃思" and "Kenneth" /ˈkenɪθ/ into "肯尼思". The third strategy is inserting "i" after palatal fricative /ʃ/, like "Bush" /bʊʃ/ transliterated into "布什" and "Mackintosh" /ˈmækɪntɒʃ/ into "麦金托什". The fourth strategy is inserting "i" after palatal affricates /tʃ/ and /dʒ/, like "Church" /tʃɜːtʃ/ transliterated into "秋奇" and "Goodrich" /ˈgʊdrɪtʃ/ into "古德里奇", "Coleridge" /ˈkəʊlrɪdʒ/ into "科尔里奇" and "Partridge" /ˈpɑːtrɪdʒ/ into "帕特里奇".

In addition, vowels can also be inserted before consonants. For example, Dean /diːn/ is transliterated into "迪安", where /æ/ is inserted; and Boon /buːn/ is transliterated into "布恩" where /e/ is inserted and Payne /peɪn/ into "佩恩" where /e/ is inserted.

Now we'll come to excrescence strategy, which refers to the strategy for addition of a consonant. There is a common feature in excrescence strategy, that is, transliterating the words in Chinese way though the letters are silent in them. By surveying *A New English-Chinese Dictionary* (1985), it is found that there are four types of inserting consonants. One type is to insert /h/, like John /dʒɒn/ transliterated into "约翰", Birmingham /ˈbɜːmɪŋəm/ into "伯明翰" and Buckingham /ˈbʌkɪŋəm/ into "白金汉"; another type is to insert /w/, like Powel /ˈpəʊəl/ transliterated into "鲍威尔", Owen /ˈəʊɪn/ into "欧文" and Howard /ˈhaʊəd/ into "霍华德"; the other type is to insert /g/, like Langland /ˈlæŋlənd/ transliterated into "兰格兰", Singer /ˈsɪŋə/ into "辛格" and Zenger /ˈzeŋə/ into "曾格".

Step 3: Segmental adaptation strategies for English-to-Chinese transliteration

OK! Let's talk about segmental adaptation strategies, which refer to the strategies for adapting certain sound segment to Chinese pronunciation in English-to-Chinese transliteration. One principle must be observed: the sound that is adapted must belong to the same category. Segmental adaptation strategies are divided into vowel adaptation strategies and consonant adaptation strategies.

Vowel adaptation strategies refer to those for adapting vowels in English-to-Chinese transliteration, like adapting long vowels to short ones, adapting front and central open vowels to back ones. For example, "Beadle" /ˈbiːdle/ is transliterated into "比德尔", "Leakey" /ˈliːkɪ/ into "利基" and "Reade" /riːd/ into "里德", where /iː/ is changed into /ɪ/; "Booth" /buːθ/ is transliterated into "布思" and "Gould" /guːld/ into "古尔德" where /uː/ is changed into /ʊ/.

Consonant adaptation strategies refer to those for adapting consonants in English-to-Chinese transliteration, to be more specific, voiced consonants can be adapted to voiceless consonants and vice versa; bilabials, alveolar liquids and nasals can be adapted within themselves respectively; besides, bilabials and labio-dentals can be adapted in terms of labials, so can dentals and alveolars in terms of dentals.

Consonant adaptation strategies in terms of voicing refer to the strategies that voiced consonants can be adapted to voiceless consonants and vice versa. For example, "Utopia" /juːˈtəʊpɪə/ is transliterated into "乌托邦" where /p/ is changed into /b/; "Truman" /ˈtruːmən/ is transliterated into "杜鲁门" and "Huntington" /ˈhʌntɪŋtən/ into "亨廷顿" where /t/ is changed into /d/; "media" /miːdɪə/ is transliterated into "媒体", where /d/ is changed into /t/; "Peter" /ˈpiːtə/ is transliterated into "彼得" where /p/ is changed into /b/ and /t/ into /d/; "Waters" /ˈwɒtəz/ into "沃特斯" where /z/ is changed into /s/; Similarly, "volt" /vɒlt/ is transliterated into "伏特", "Virginia" /və(ː)ˈdʒɪnjə/ is transliterated into "弗吉尼亚", "Vatican" /ˈvætɪkən/ is transliterated into "梵蒂冈", "Harvard" /ˈhɑːvəd/ is transliterated into "哈佛", where /v/ is transformed into /f/.

Consonant adaptation strategies in terms of bilabials refer to the strategies that bilabials can be inter-transliterated into one another. For example, "Bombay" /ˈbɒmbeɪ/ is transliterated into "孟买" and "Bangkok" /ˈbæŋkɒk/ into "曼谷", where /b/ is changed into /m/. "Sandwich" /ˈsænwɪdʒ/ is transliterated into "三明治", where /w/ is changed into /m/. "Salmon" /ˈsæmən/ is transliterated into "三文鱼", "Jumbo" /dʒʌmbəʊ/ into "巨无霸" and "Marlboro" into "万宝路", where /m/ is changed into /w/; "Ban Ki-moon" /bænkɪmuːn/ is transliterated into "潘基文", where /b/ is changed into /p/ and /m/ into /w/. "Serbia" /ˈsɜːbɪə/ is transliterated into "塞尔维亚", where /b/ is changed into /w/.

Consonant adaptation strategies in terms of alveolar liquids refer to the strategies that /r/ is changed into /l/ in English-to-Chinese transliteration for they have something in common. When we articulate /l/, the tip of the tongue touches the upper gum. When we articulate /r/, the tip of the tongue is close to the upper gum. So in some cases, we can transform /r/ to /l/. For instance, "radar" /ˈreɪdaː/ is transliterated into "雷达", "rifle" /ˈraɪfl/ is transliterated into "来福枪", "romantic" romantic is transliterated into "罗曼蒂克", "Arab" /ˈærəb/ is transliterated into "阿拉伯", "aspirin" /ˈæspərɪn/ is transliterated into "阿斯匹林", "Reuters" /ˈrɒɪtəz/ is transliterated into "路透社", "Pandora" /pænˈdɔːrə/ is transliterated into "潘多拉", "heroin" /ˈherəʊɪn/ is transliterated into "海洛因", "Motorola" /ˈməʊtəʊrəʊlə/ is transliterated into "摩托罗拉", "Rolex" is transliterated into "劳力士", "Green" /griːn/ is transliterated into "格林", "Brandy" /ˈbrændɪ/ is transliterated into "白兰地", etc.

Consonant adaptation strategies in terms of nasals refer to the strategies that nasals can be inter-transliterated into each other. For example, "King" /kɪŋ/ is transliterated into "金" and "Lincoln" /ˈlɪŋkən/ into "林肯", where /ŋ/ is adapted to /n/. "Kemble" /ˈkembl/ is transliterated into "肯布尔" and "Lambert" /ˈlæmbɜːt/ into "兰伯特", where /m/ is adapted to /n/. "Conrad" /ˈkɒnræd/ is transliterated into "康拉德" and "Constable" /ˈkɒnstəbl/ into "康斯特布尔", where /n/ is adapted to /ŋ/.

Consonant adaptation strategies in terms of nasals refer to the strategies that some bilabial can be transliterated into labio-dental and that some labio-dental can be transliterated into bilabial. For example, "Buddhism" /ˈbʊdɪzəm/ is transliterated into "佛教", where /b/ is changed into /f/. "Valentine" /ˈvæləntaɪn/ is transliterated into "瓦伦丁", and "Victor" /ˈvɪktə/ into "维克多" where /v/ is changed in /w/.

Consonant adaptation strategies in terms of dentals refer to the strategies that dentals can be transliterated into alveolars. For example, Faith /feɪθ/ is transliterated into "费思" and Thad /θæd/ into "萨德", where /θ/ is changed into /s/. "Rutherford" /ˈrʌðəfəd/ is transliterated into "拉瑟福特" and "Southey" /ˈsaʊðɪ/ into "索塞", where /ð/ is changed into /s/.

Step 4: Deletion strategies for English-to-Chinese transliteration

Deletion strategies refer to those for deleting certain sounds in order to avoid making transliterated words too long. The sounds that can be deleted are some unstressed or unimportant ones. Deletion strategies can be subdivided into strategy for deletion of vowels and strategy for deletion of consonants.

Strategy for deletion of vowels is employed in English-to-Chinese transliteration when an unstressed sound segment occurs in English words. The typical example is that an unstressed /ə/ is often deleted, like America /əˈmerɪkə/ transliterated into "美利坚", "Iris" /ˈaɪərɪs/ into "爱

丽斯" and "Cyrus" /ˈsaɪərəs/ into "塞勒斯". Another case is that when /aɪn/ and /eɪn/ are in unstressed syllables, they can be changed to /an/ and /en/, where /ɪ/ is deleted. For instance, "Einstein" /ˈaɪnstaɪn/ is transliterated into "爱因斯坦" and "Bernstein" /ˈbɜːnsteɪn/ transliterated into "伯恩斯坦", where /ɪ/ is deleted.

Strategies for deletion of consonants can be divided into strategies for deletion of consonant in the middle of a word and strategies for deletion of consonant at the end of a word.

Strategies for deletion of consonant in the middle of a word can be divided into strategies for deletion of a plosive and strategies for deletion of other consonant. A plosive will be unreleased when it appears before another plosive, or a nasal, or an alveolar fricative. In this case, the plosive is omitted in the transliteration. The same is true of strategies for deletion of other consonant. For example, "Eastman" /ˈiːstmən/ is transliterated into "伊士曼" where /t/ is omitted. The same thing happens to "Westcott" /ˈwestkət/ and "Montgomery" /mənt'ɡʌməri/ when they are transliterated into "威斯克" and "蒙哥马利" respectively, where /t/ is omitted. "Shakespeare" /ˈʃeɪkspɪə/ is transliterated into "莎士比亚", where /k/ is deleted. "Walpole" /ˈwɔːlpəʊl/, "Engels" /ˈeŋɡəls/ and "Reginald" /ˈredʒɪnəld/ are transliterated into "沃波尔", "恩格斯" and "雷金纳德" respectively, where /l/ is omitted.

Strategies for deletion of consonant at the end of a word are relatively complicated. Sometimes, a consonant at the end of a word is deleted and sometimes more than one consonant at the end of a word is deleted. For example, in terms of strategy for deletion of a consonant at the end of a word, "Juliet" /ˈdʒuːljət/ is transliterated into "朱丽叶" where /t/ is deleted; "David" /ˈdeɪvɪd/ and "Stanford" /ˈstænfəd/ are transliterated into "大卫" and "斯坦福" where /d/ is deleted; "Vandenberg" /ˈvændənbɜːɡ/ is transliterated into "范登堡", where /ɡ/ is deleted; "Columbus" /kəˈlʌmbəs/ is transliterated into "哥伦布", where /s/ is deleted; Moses /ˈməʊzɪz/ is transliterated into "摩西", where /z/ is deleted; "Elizabeth" /ɪˈlɪzəbəθ/ is transliterated into "伊丽莎白", where /θ/ is deleted. In terms of strategy for deletion of more than one consonant at the end of a word, we' look at the following examples. "MacDonald" /məkˈdɒnəld/ is transliterated into "麦克唐纳", where /ld/ is deleted. "Los Angeles" /lɒsˈændʒələs/ is transliterated into "洛杉矶", where /ləs/ is deleted.

Step 5：Segmental split strategies for English-to-Chinese transliteration

Segmental split strategies, as the name suggests, refers to the strategies for splitting a speech sound into two sounds in English-to-Chinese transliteration. There are two segmental split strategies, which can be subdivided into vowel split strategy and consonant split strategy.

Vowel split strategy refers to the strategy for splitting a vowel into two in English-to-Chinese transliteration. For example, gene /dʒiːn/ is transliterated into "基因", where /iː/ is split into /dʒi:/ and /i:n/. Similarly, "Sophia" /ˈsɒfaɪə/ is transliterated into "索菲亚" where /ɪ/ is split into /aɪ/ and /ɪə/.

Consonant split strategy refers to the strategy for splitting a consonant into two in English-to-

Chinese transliteration. For example, "Anna" /ˈænə/ is transliterated into "安娜", where /n/ is split so that we can have /ˈæn/ + /nə/; "Janice" /ˈdʒænɪs/ is transliterated into "詹妮丝", where /n/ is split so that we can have /ˈdʒæn/ + /nɪs/; "Bonnie" /ˈbɒnɪ/ is transliterated into "邦妮", where /n/ is split so that we can have /ˈbɒn/ + /nɪ/ and etc.

In the process of absorbing loanwords, Chinese people recreate the borrowing words from the point of view of the sound system and vocabulary. As a basic means of borrowing words, transliteration pours fresh blood into modern Chinese, enriches the expression of Chinese, and brings in foreign culture and development of technology. Since language is developing, transliteration is not a simple replacement between two languages, but a creative job. Its ultimate goal is to create exchange intermediary for the target language, which plays a key role in modern life. Therefore, in the process of language communication and development, as the most convenient and the most commonly used method, borrowing words has become very popular.

We have just discussed the English-to-Chinese transliteration, especially different transliteration types and transliteration strategy from a phonological point of view and concluded some transliteration strategies: epenthesis, deletion, syllable split, and segmental adaption. Because there are many differences between English and Chinese in their sound systems, we need to follow certain rules to get scientific and unified transliteration. But, the strategies mentioned above can not summarize all the transliteration strategies, which still remain to be studied in the future. The field of transliteration still has a lot of research space, and the combination of phonology and transliteration is open to more exploration.

II. Analysis

本教学设计从音位学角度讨论英译汉的音译策略,其特点是思路清晰、条理分明。音位学有三个规则:顺序规则、同化规则和省略规则。这三个规则均可应用到英译汉音译中,与之相应的音译策略包括增音策略、换音策略、删音策略和切分音策略。增音策略可细分为增辅音策略和增元音策略;换音策略可细分为换元音策略和换辅音策略;删音策略可细分为删元音策略和删辅音策略;切分音策略可细分为切分元音策略和切分辅音策略。由于本教学设计涉及的内容相对比较专业,有效性应作为第一要素考虑。离开了有效性,任何教学设计都是空谈,而有效性的一个重要标志就是清晰明了。

Part Four

Instructional Design of *Research Methods* and Case Analysis

Inquiry-based Instructional Design of *Definition of Research* and Analysis

Ⅰ. Inquiry-based Instructional Design of *Definition of Research*

Step 1: Inquiry into *Definition of Research* in terms of "研"

今天我们来对"研究"进行一番"研究"。古今中外,有不少人曾对"研究"进行过界定。由于这些界定不是针对某一特定的学科,而是泛指一切形式和意义的研究。这里我们不妨把它们称之为广义的研究。

我们先来看汉语中的"研究"这两个字,它们是出"研"和"究"构成。我们先来看"研"。

根据东汉许慎《说文解字》,"研","磨也。从石,开声。"意为"把石头细磨使成粉末"(grinding stone or rock into fine powder)。可以设想一下,要"把石头细磨使成粉末",就像把"铁棒磨成针"一样,这得要花功夫,且这不是一般的功夫,而是苦功夫(painstaking effort)。这苦功夫既有质的要求,也有量的要求。

所谓苦功夫质的要求是指研究者在研究期间,要做到三个 c。第一个 c 是 concentration 即要专心致志,而不要心不在焉;要全神贯注,不要三心二意。例如:从前有一个下棋能手名叫秋,他的棋艺非常高超。秋有两个学生,一起跟他学习下棋,其中一个学生非常专心集中精力跟老师学习。另一个却不这样,他认为学下棋很容易,用不着认真。老师讲解的时候,他虽然坐在那里,眼睛也好像在看着棋子可心里却想着:"要是现在到野外射下一只鸿雁,美餐一顿该多好。"因为他总是胡思乱想心不在焉,老师的讲解一点也没听进去。结果,虽然两个学生同是一个名师传授,但是,一个进步很快,成了棋艺高强的名手,另一个却没学到一点本事。第二个 c 是 categorization,即要分门别类把一些事物按照特性和特征分别归入各种门类。原来杂乱无章的东西,经过分门别类后思路更为清晰、内容更为精炼。如:整个英语修辞格可以分为相似、相关和相反。在相似的修辞格里有音的相似,如:rhyme(押韵)、alliteration(押头韵);形的相似,如:parallelism(平行结构)、parody(仿拟);义的相似,如:simile(明喻)、metaphor(暗喻)。相关的修辞格,如:metonymy(借代)、synaesthesia(通感)。相反的修辞格,如:oxymoron(矛盾修辞法)、antithesis(对比)。第三个 c 是 connection,即要把所学的东西打通,联系起来。如:大豆可以榨豆油,可以发豆芽,可以做酱油,可以做豆酱,可以做豆浆,可以做豆腐,可以做豆腐干,可以做豆腐皮,可以做臭豆腐。同样,莫言诺贝尔文学奖演讲(英文版),可以作为阅读材料在《英语阅读》课上用;可以作为翻译材料在《汉译英》课上用;可以作为教学设计材料在《英语教学设计》课上用;可以作为语料在《语料库语言学》课上用;可以作为跨文化交际材料,在《跨文化交际》课上用等等。

所谓量的要求是指要有三个 lots:lots and lots and lots of time 即要花许许多多的时间。许许多多的时间从哪儿来? 首先,把现有的时间要充分利用起来,要耐得住寂寞,练就一身坐冷板凳的硬功,如果这一点做不到,再多的时间也没有用。其次,要计划好时间,特别是工作以外的时间,养成良好的习惯,保证每天有一定时间用于研究、读书学习,且雷打不动,争取做到几十年如一日;再次,还要学会忙里偷闲,抓紧点滴时间,我们中国古人有三上,即:枕上、厕上、马上,类似的英美人有在三 B 上,即在 bed 上、在 bath 上和在 bus 上,这样可以积少成多,集腋成裘。例如:马克思在写《资本论》时,花了大量的时间,倾注了大量的心血,据说,在伦敦大英博物馆的圆形阅览室,由于马克思成年累月地在那里阅读、写作,竟然在坚硬的水泥地面上磨出了两个脚印。可以想象一下,这需要多少时间,需要多大功夫。

Step 2:Inquiry into *Definition of Research* in terms of "究"

"究",根据东汉许慎《说文解字》,"穷也。从穴,九声。",意为"穷尽"(exhaustiveness)。"穷尽"可分为绝对穷尽和相对穷尽两种。

所谓绝对穷尽是指囊括所有的可能性。如:时间。它只有四种可能性:无始无终、无始有终、有始无终和有始有终。其中无始无终叫做宙,是绝对无限时间;无始有终叫做有尽、有始无终叫做无穷和有始有终叫做须臾,这三者是相对有限时间。我要特别强调一下我们每个人的生命,我们上的每一节课,叫做须臾,一眨眼就过去了,因此要好好珍惜。空间也有四种自然形态:无外无内、无外有内、有外无内、有外有内。其中无外无内叫做宇,是绝对无限空间;无外有内叫做宏,有外有内叫做中,有外无内叫做微,后三类形态是相对有限空间。

所谓相对穷尽是指在现有条件下(由于主观和客观条件的制约),囊括所有的所有的可能性。然而,随着时空的变化,可能有新的可能性。例如:这是我 2008 年对"外国语学院"译文的穷尽。由于"外国语学院"是由"外国语"和"学院"组成,我们必须要弄清楚它们各自的译法。首先,来看一下"外国语"的译法,译得最多的为"foreign languages",如:(北京大学)外国语学院译为"School of Foreign Languages"。此外,还有六种译法:(1) foreign studies,如:天津外国语学院译为 Tianjin Foreign Studies University;(2) international studies,如:四川外国语学院译为 Sichuan International Studies University;(3) foreign languages and literatures,如:(西北师范大学)外国语学院译为 College of Foreign Languages and Literatures;(4) international communication,如:(北京科技大学)外国语学院译为 School of International Communication;(5) foreign languages and cultures,如:(成都理工大学)外国语学院译为 College of Foreign Languages and Cultures;(6) foreign language,如:(广州大学)外国语学院译为 Foreign Language School。再来看一下"学院"的译法,译得较多的为 school 和 college,还有些译为 university,institute,faculty 和 department。鉴于上文未提及 institute,faculty 和 department 的例子,我们再举几个例子。如:(福建师范大学)外国语学院译为 Foreign

Languages Institute；（湖北大学）外国语学院译为 Faculty of Foreign Studies；（安庆师范学院）外国语学院译为 Foreign Language Department。此外，"学院"一词所处的位置，有的是放在后面译为... university/college/school/institute/faculty；有的是放在前面译为 university/college/school/faculty of ...，经过排列组合，这样共在网上搜到 22 种译法。以后是不是就 22 种，就不一定了。只能说到目前为止的相对穷尽。

Step 3：Inquiry into *Definition of Research* in terms of "re-"

英语中的"研究"叫 research，它是由 re 和 search 两个部分组成。

根据 *The Concise Oxford Dictionary*，re-表示 frequentative or intensifying（反复或强化或精细化）。我们首先来谈"反复"，众所周知，绝大部分研究都不是一次就能完成的，需要反复。我认为这里的"需要反复"有四层意思。第一层意思是从认识论的角度看，首先，人们对客观事物的认识不可能一次就完成，需要多次反复才能完成，这是因为一方面客观事物本身的内部矛盾有一个逐渐显露的过程，它的发展是曲折复杂的；另一方面人的认识要受到主客观条件的制约，在认识过程中不可避免的要有这样或那样的疏忽，因此也就不可避免的要出现片面性和主观性。其次，人们对事物的认识必然经过一个由表层到深层，由现象到本质，由片面到全面，由感性到理性的逐步发展变化的过程，这个过程同样也需要反复才能完成。第二层意思是在研究某个问题的过程中，又发现了新的问题，这个新的问题同样需要反复研究。第三层意思是指旧的问题解决了，新的问题又产生了，这些新产生的问题需要反复研究。第四层意思是其他研究人员按前人的研究思路和方法，反复他的研究，以验证他的研究结果。

我们的研究不仅需要"反复"，而且还需要"强化"。例如：如果我们想提高学生的写作水平，可以强化输出，让学生多写；也可以强化输入，让学生多读，还可以既强化输入又强化输出，让学生多读多写。再如：现在学生上课玩手机的现象比较严重，如果我们想让学生上课好好听讲，也可以使用强化方法，我们既可以用平时成绩加分的方法，鼓励学生上课认真听讲；用平时成绩扣分的方法，惩罚学生上课不认真听讲。此外，如果我们做研究，还需要"精细化"。一般说来，人文社会科学需要的精细化程度没有自然科学那么高。

Step 4：Inquiry into *Definition of Research* in terms of "search"

我们来看 search，根据 *The Concise Oxford Dictionary*，search 表示 look for what may be found or find something of which presence is suspected，probe，make investigation，也就是说，我们在研究中需要搜寻、查找、探究和调查。

1. 需要搜寻和查找

在研究过程中需要搜寻、查找即查找各种文献资料。查找各种文献资料在研究过程中极其重要，它可以帮助研究人员（1）产生研究问题；（2）了解前人所做的相关研究；（3）提供可借鉴的研究方法；（4）提供可解释研究结果的背景资料；（5）吸收他人的教训，避免同类错误的发生。

1）产生研究问题

研究问题的产生源于问题的提出，研究者在查找大量的文献的过程中，可能会发现各种各样的问题：有的是缺少某一方面的研究；有的是研究结果有矛盾之处；有的是某一方面有待于继续研究等，进而提出问题，最终形成研究问题。

2）了解前人所做的相关研究

通过查找文献,研究者可以了解前人在某一领域已做了哪些研究;研究到了什么程度;采用了什么研究方法:是定性的,还是定量的;得出了什么结论;还有哪些不足等等。只有了解前人所做的相关研究,才能给自己的研究准确定位,而不至于重复别人的研究。

3）提供可借鉴的研究方法

研究方法在整个研究中起着至关重要的作用,有时甚至可以直接影响到研究的信度和效度。研究者从文献中可以了解前人是如何选择研究对象、如何选择研究工具、如何收集数据、如何分析数据等,看看有哪些值得借鉴。

4）提供解释研究结果的背景资料

文献可以为研究者在解释研究结果时提供一些背景资料。例如:研究者的某项研究是在前人研究的基础上,向前推进了一步,得出了新的结论;或者前人之所以没有得出象研究者这样的结论是因为前人研究的样本太小,或没有精确的量化数据。研究者在解释其新结论时,需要提供一些背景资料,而这些背景资料都是来自文献。

5）吸取他人的教训,避免同类错误的发生

任何研究都不是完美无缺的,总有这样或那样的局限性。其局限性可能表现在样本上,如:样本太小、样本没有随机抽样、参加者都是志愿者;其局限性也可能表现在收集的数据中,如:数据缺值太高;其局限性还可能表现在研究工具上,如:尽管英语专业4、8级是全国唯一的权威性的测试,但我们并不知道它们的信度和效度。因此,研究者在查找文献时,要吸取他人的教训,尽量避免同类错误在自己日后的研究中发生。

在搜寻或查找时,要寻找可以找到的东西,换句话说,要能发现结果。如果搜寻或寻找不到,那就不要搜寻或寻找。例如:chicken-and-egg question(先有鸡还是先有蛋的问题),类似的还有,mother-and-daughter question(先有母亲还是先有女儿的问题)就不要研究了。其次要找到有疑点的东西,其实,只要我们留心,我们处处都可以发现有疑点的东西。我们的衣食住行,有不少可以发现有疑点的东西;我们的信仰信念也有不少可以发现有疑点的东西;我们的教育教学也有不少有疑点的东西。发现这些有疑点的东西,我们接下来就要进行探究。

2. 需要探究

所谓需要探究是指需要探个究竟,追根求源,到底是怎么回事。例如:America 为何译为"美利坚"? 笔者曾对此进行过探究。最初 America 一词被译为"阿美利坚"和"亚美利坚"。后来一些翻译家在音译名词时制定了一条规则:即为了使音译名词不必过长,某些处于非重读音节的音可以不译出来。由于America [əˈmerɪkə]中的[ə]处于非重读音节,因此可以不译出来。同样,我们没有把 England 译为"英格兰德",而是译为"英格兰";没有把 Elizabeth 译为"伊丽莎白丝",而是译为"伊丽莎白"。第二个音节[me]译为"美"可以理解。第三个音节[rɪ]为何译为"利"? 这里笔者得解释一下,在古汉语中,"l、n、r"这三个音相通,具体到 America 这个词,是 r 通 l,即[lɪ]译为"利"。同样,Mary 译为"玛丽",lemon 译为"柠檬"是 l 通 n,McDonald 译为"麦当劳"是 n 通 l。第四个音节[kə]为何译为"坚"? 在古汉语中,k、g 和 j 这三个音相通,这里是 k 通 j,这样[kə]也就译为"坚",同样 club 译为"俱乐部",也是 k

通 j。

我们再来探究一下明代奇书《金瓶梅》书名的来历。有人说：《金瓶梅》是取名西门庆所宠的三大淫妇：潘金莲、李瓶儿和庞春梅。英文中有个短语叫 go down（堕落）。They are going down. 这句话可音译为："她们够淫荡"。有人说：《金瓶梅》是指"金瓶插梅"，一般人家用瓷瓶插梅，西门庆家太富有了，他家用金瓶插梅。也有人说：《金瓶梅》是指《金瓶霉》，你看连金瓶都发霉，可见社会之腐朽。还有人说：《金瓶梅》是对男人的三大警钟。金代表财，瓶代表酒，梅代表色，它要男人戒财、戒酒、戒色。

3．需要调查

所谓调查是指研究者对某一范围中的某一类或某一对象进行直接接触、询问和现场观察，以了解调查对象的历史、现状和其他情况，从而获得事实、数据的一种方法。广义的调查可包括观察、访谈、实验和问卷调查。因此，需要调查是指研究者在研究过程中需要观察、访谈、实验和问卷调查。

1）观察

观察是指研究者通过感觉器官和科学仪器对周围存在的事物、现象、过程和人在自然的条件下进行有目的、有计划的感知和描写，从而获得经验事实的一种研究方法。它要求研究者在观察时必须遵循科学性、隐蔽性和系统性。所谓科学性是指要用随机抽样的方法，确定观察时间，以获得比较正确反映客观事物的数据；所谓隐蔽性是指尽量不对现场产生干扰，尽量让被观察对象保持常态，以免产生假象，或影响正常工作；所谓系统性是指研究者对所要观察的对象既要宏观把握、大局在胸，又要细致入微、明察秋毫。观察的特点为客观、便利和经济。

2）访谈

访谈是指研究者通过有计划地与访谈对象面对面谈话来了解情况、征求观点、反映态度、收集资料的方法。访谈就其方式可分为非正式访谈和正式访谈。非正式访谈就象日常自然的谈话，是一种随意的、自由的、开放式的、非指示性的和非结构性的谈话方式；正式访谈是一种结构式的访谈，研究者一般事先准备好访谈的问题，按照这些问题对访谈对象进行访谈。访谈的特点是可以全面深入地了解情况，有较强的灵活性，并适用于各类访谈对象。

3）实验

实验是指研究者根据研究目的，运用一定人为手段主动干预或控制实验对象的发生、发展过程，并通过把有干预情况下所获得的事实与未干预情况下同类现象变化的事实进行比较，确认事物间因果关系的方法。实验是发现科学真理的基础，也是检验真理的唯一标准。根据是否有对照组和是否随机抽样，实验可分为前实验、准实验和真实验。前实验既没有对照组，也没有随机抽样；准实验有对照组，但没有随机抽样；真实验既有对照组，又有随机抽样。实验的特点是比较科学、严谨。

4）问卷调查

问卷调查是指研究者将所要调查的问题编成一种统一的问卷表格，发给问卷对象填写，并及时收回调查资料的一种方法。根据回答问题的方式，问卷可分为开放式问卷和封闭式问卷两种。所谓开放式问卷是指在问卷中只向调查对象提问，不提供预先列出的答案，而由问卷对象自由回答的一种问卷;所谓封闭式问卷是指在问卷中把提出的问题和供选择的答案一起列出,由问卷对象从给定的答案中选择出一项或几项答案填上的一种问卷。它的特点是比较经济、操作简便。

Step 5：Inquiry into *Definition of Research* in terms of "研究"

《辞海》把"研究"一词定义为"用科学的方法探究事物的本质和规律"。这里增加了新的东西:科学的方法、探究事物的本质和规律。关于科学的方法,我们下面要详谈,这里先暂时不谈。我们来谈一谈研究是探究事物的本质和规律。这里我们先谈一谈探究事物的本质。要探究事物的本质,我们必须从现象入手。我们常说"要透过现象看本质"。现象是事物的外部表现,是局部的、个别的、具有丰富性和变化性,可以在一定程度上反映事物的本质。本质是事物的根本特征,是一般的、抽象的,具有深刻性和稳定性,通过一定的现象体现出来。事实上,客观事物是非常复杂的,我们探究事物的本质时,是不可能一下子完全认识事物的本质,只能无限接近事物的本质。我们接着谈谈探究事物的规律。所谓规律是指自然界和社会诸现象之间必然、本质、稳定和反复出现的关系,换句话说,事物诸现象之间的共性,相同或相似性。《黄帝内经》上说:"智者察同,愚者察异"。这里的同就是规律。我们来看看手机和粉笔有什么相同的东西。马克思是位智者,从政治经济学的角度,他看到了他们之间的共性:他们都是商品,都凝集人类的一般劳动。从哲学的角度,他看到了他们之间的共性:他们都是由物质构成的。乔姆斯基是位智者,他研究普遍语法(Universal Grammar),人类所特有的存在于正常人的大脑中的语言知识体系。

Step 6：Inquiry into *Definition of Research* in terms of "research"

在应用语言学领域,Hatch 和 Farhady (1982)把"研究"定义为: a systematic approach to finding answers to questions(用系统的方法探求问题的答案)。这个定义比较好,揭示了研究的三要素:问题、系统的方法和答案。

第一个要素:问题

根据文秋芳教授等,所要研究的问题必须有意义(significant)、有新意(original)、有可行性(feasible)。所谓有意义的问题是指这个研究问题要么有理论意义,要么有实践意义,要么有方法论意义,要么三者兼而有之,即既有理论意义、又有实践意义、又有方法论意义。所谓有理论意义是指研究问题要么证明某一理论、要么证伪某一理论、要么拓展某一理论、要么修正某一理论、要么澄清某一理论、要么提出新的理论。在理论意义当中,相对比较容易的是证明某一理论,其次是拓展某一理论,最难的是提出某一理论。所谓实践意义是指能提高二语的教与学、提高编写双语词典的质量和翻译质量等。所谓有方法论意义是指与前人的研究方法不一样。例如:前人用定量研究,而你用的定性研究;或者前人用定量研究,而你既用定量研究,又用的定性研究。有新意的问题是指这个问题与前人的研究的问题在一个或几个方面的不同,可能是学习的环境不同了,也可能学习者的类型不同了,可能研究设计不同了,也可能研究处理的方法不同了,可能是数据收集的方法不同了,也可能数据分析的方法不同了,总之,有新意并不是指整个都是新的,而是一个程度问题。可行性的问题是指研究人员在一定的时间范围内,利用现有的人力、物力和财力能够解决研究问题,而不是研究"是先有鸡还是先有蛋"这类无法解决的问题。

难怪爱因斯坦说"提出一个问题往往比解决一个问题更为重要。解决一个问题也许只需要数学上的运算或实验的操作,而提出新的问题,新的可能性,从新的角度看旧的问题却需要创造性的想象力,这标志着科学的真正进步。"

第二个要素: 系统的方法

系统的方法是指研究应遵循一整套明确、合理的步骤,即发现问题、提出假设、收集数据、分析数据、得出结论。例如:大约 20 年前,扬州生意最红火的一家美容厅:慧文美容厅发生了一起杀人案。在这家美容厅工作的四个女孩子同时被杀了。为什么要杀害这四个女孩子? 一种可能性是因为慧文美容厅生意最红火,赚的钱最多,有人谋财害命;另一种可能性是因为慧文美容厅的四个女孩子都非常漂亮,有人谋色害命;还有一种可能性是因为慧文美容厅生意最红火,有些生意不好的美容厅,出于嫉妒,把四个女孩子杀了。接下来,公安局派警察到现场来侦察并收集相关的蜘丝马迹。然后把所侦察并收集相关的蜘丝马迹带到公安局进行分析。最后,这个案子破下来了。这里慧文美容厅发生了一起杀人案就是发现问题;杀害四个女孩子的三种可能性就是提出假设;公安局派警察到现场来侦察并收集相关的蜘丝马迹,就是收集数据;警察把所侦察并收集相关的蜘丝马迹带到公安局进行分析,就是分析数据;最后,这个案子破下来了,就是得出结论。这些步骤有时在数据收集前就确定了,有时在研究过程中才确定。这两种情况,不管哪一种,都应把选择研究对象的步骤、收集数据的步骤和分析数据的步骤记录下来,并向其他研究者报告。此外,还要解释为什么使用这些步骤,以便其他研究者能重复或效仿。

第三个要素: 答案

所谓答案是指有效答案,这里的有效是指效度,即这个答案是某个研究问题的唯一答案。如果某个研究问题有其他答案,其效度就要低。如:有一项研究旨在研究二语学习中的性别差异。研究发现在英语水平测试中,英语专业的女生比男生考得好,研究者由此得出结论:在二语学习方面,女生比男生聪明。很显然,关于这一现象,我们可以有十余种解释,如:女生比男生花的时间多;女生比男生把考试当回事;最聪明的男生去学理工科,而没有学英语专业,等等。既然其他的解释也讲得通,那么,这一结论的效度就低。

应该强调的是,这三个要素之间彼此是联系。一方面,所有的研究都始于问题,没有问题便没有研究;另一方面,有了问题,还必须采用系统的方法,否则就不能得到有效的答案。

Step 7: Zhou's definition of research upon the previous definitions

根据前人的研究,我把研究定义为: a scientific approach to finding answers to questions,即用科学的方法探求问题的答案。其中的 a scientific approach(科学的方法)比系统的方法涵盖更广,内容更丰富。根据 Tuckman 和文秋芳,科学的方法有六个特点:系统性(systematic)、逻辑性(logical)、实证性(empirical)、简约性(reductive)、客观性(objective)和可重复性(replicable)。

科学方法的第一个特点是系统性,它是指研究应遵循一整套明确、合理的步骤,即发现问题、提出假设、收集数据、分析数据、得出结论。上文已经提到,内容大同小异,这里就不赘叙了。

科学方法的第二个特点是逻辑性。它是指整个研究都要合乎逻辑规则,它体现在三方面。其一,所采用的步骤必须合乎逻辑,以满足内部效度的要求;其二,所得出的结论必须合乎逻辑;最后,由样本推及到研究总体时,必须合乎逻辑,以满足外部效度的要求。随便说一下,在逻辑学中,有三个重要概念:概念、判断和推理。在我们的研究中,概念要前后一致;判断要遵守三个定律:同一律即 A is A.、矛盾律即 A can't be both B and not-B. 和排中律 A is either B or not-B.;推理常用的是:归纳推理即 from specific to general、演绎推理即 from general to specific 和类比推理即 from specific to specific。

科学方法的第三个特点是实证性。它是指研究的资料和数据是来自现实生活,而不是来自其他文献,这些资料和数据一般都是研究者亲自收集。此外,研究者就外部效度,即样本推及到研究总体的程度来评价这些数据和资料。

科学方法的第四个特点是简约性。它是指研究者在分析数据时,把纷繁复杂、杂乱无章的东西分成容易理解的类别范畴。在分成各种类别范畴时,虽然一些特殊性和独特性会丧失,但可看出总的关系。这种简约性使研究不仅起到描写作用,而且起到解释作用。

科学方法的第五个特点是客观性。它是指研究者在研究当中坚持实事求是,一切以客观实际为准绳,根据客观事实的本来面目加以考察,排除一切主观偏见和预断,以获得对某一现象的正确认识。它要求人们在研究中必须遵循和坚持价值中立的原则。只有客观地研究和把握事实,才有可能实现理论上的突破与创新。

科学方法的第六个特点是可重复性。它是指研究应遵循一整套明确、合理的步骤,其他研究者能重复或效仿。值得一提的是,任何研究方法都不是完美无缺的,尤其是把人作为研究对象更是如此。因此,千万不要把科学的方法理解为完美无缺的方法。实际上,研究者在研究过程中常常承认自己在研究中的局限性,以便后人重复研究时,加以避免。

II. Analysis

本教学设计以"探究"为理念,从"古今中外"四个纬度对"研究"的界定进行探究。一个好的教学设计,不是说这个教学设计完美无缺、没有问题,而是说这个教学设计给人多少启发。同样,本教学设计给人以下几点启发。启发一、抓住教学内容的关键点:研究和 research,这是这一教学设计的起点,也是这一教学设计的终点;启发二、教学设计结构完整、有序,环环相扣,一步一步向深度推进;启发三、教学设计怎样在前人的基础上,进一步完善;启发四、教学设计的思维应具有广泛性:"古今中外"。

Case 15 Methodology-based Instructional design of *Three Issues Concerning Research Methods in Applied Linguistics* and Analysis

I. Methodology-based Instructional design of *Three Issues Concerning Research Methods in Applied Linguistics*

Step 1:Lead-in with two short stories about different views about the same thing

在讲《应用语言学研究方法三题》之前,我先来给大家讲两个小故事。第一个是英语的。

In the small villages of Eastern Europe, the rabbi was the undisputed leader of the Jewish people of his village. Not only was he the master of religious wisdom and law, but he often served as the arbiter of civil disputes as well. Once upon a time, two individuals had a major dispute and agreed to go to the rabbi for resolution. The first party to the dispute came to the rabbi and carefully outlined his side of the argument. The rabbi listened intently and finally said, "My friend, you are right." The man went away satisfied. Later in the day, the other party to the dispute arrived and told the rabbi his side of the issue. The rabbi again listened carefully, was impressed with the arguments, and replied after some thought, "you are right." Later, the rabbi's wife, who had overheard the rabbi's conversations with both men, said to him, "Rabbi, you told both the first party and the second party that they were right. How can this be?" to which the rabbi replied, "And you are right, too!"

第二个故事是汉语的。

　　墙壁上,一只虫子在艰难地往上爬,爬到一大半,忽然跌落了下来……这是它又一次失败的记录……然而,过了一会,它又沿着墙根,一步一步地往上爬了……

　　第一个人注视着这只虫子,感叹地说:"一只小小的虫子,这样的执著、顽强;失败了,不屈服;跌倒了,从头干;真是百折不回啊! 我遭到了一点挫折,我能气馁、退缩、自暴自弃吗? 难道我还不如这一只虫子?!"他觉得自己应该振奋起来。他果然振奋起来了。

　　这只虫子再一次从墙壁上跌落下来……

　　第二个人注视它,禁不住叹气说:"可怜的虫子! 这样盲目地爬行,什么时候才能爬到墙顶呢? 只要稍微改变一下方位,它就能很容易地爬上去;可是,它就是不愿反省,不肯看一看。唉—可悲的虫子! 反省我自己吧:我正在做的那件事一再失利,我该学得聪明一点,不能再闷着头蛮干一气了——我是个有思维头脑的人,可不是虫子……我该感谢你,可怜的虫子,你启迪了我,启迪了我的理智,叫我学得聪明一些……"果然,他变得理智而聪明了。

　　第三个人询问智者:"观察同一只虫子,两个人的见解和判断截然相反,得到的启示迥然不同。可敬的智者,请您说说,他们哪一个对呢?"智者回答:"两个人都对。"询问者感到困惑:"怎么会都对呢?""对虫子的行为,一个是褒扬,一个是贬抑,对立是如此鲜明。然而,您却一视同仁,您是好好先生吗? 您是不愿还是不敢分辨是非呢?"……智者笑了笑,回答道:"太阳在白天放射光明,月亮在夜晚投洒清辉——它们是'相反'的;你能不能告诉我:太阳和月亮,究竟谁是谁非? 假如你拿着一把刀,把西瓜切成两半——左右两边是'对立'的。你能不能告诉我:'是'和'非'分别在左右的哪一边? 不分是非的好好先生不足为训。但是,世界并不是简单的'是非'组合体。同样观察虫子,两个人所处的角度不同,他们的感觉和判断就不可能一致,他们获得的启示也就有差异。你只看到两个人之间的异,却看不到他们之间的同。"

这两个小故事告诉我们同一道理,那就是:世界并不是简单的'是非'组合体,并非非此即彼、黑白分明。由于不同的人所生长的环境不同、经历不同、视角不同,他们所看到的东西肯定是千差万别的,正所谓的仁者见仁,智者见智。这从一个侧面证明了苏轼的诗:横看成岭侧成峰,远近高低各不同。不识庐山真面目,只缘身在此山中。

同样,不同的研究方法可能导致不同的研究结果。我们回到今天要探讨的应用语言学研究方法中的三个问题。其一是应用语言学的研究过程,一般说来,应用语言学的研究过程共分为四步:第一,确定研究问题;第二,形成假设;第三,验证假设;第四,得出结论。其二是不同的研究方法可能导致不同的研究结果。其三是任何一种研究方法都有其局限性,即世界上没有十全十美的研究方法,它们总有这样或那样的问题。下面我们来一一探讨。

Step 2:The first issue concerning research methods:research process

一般说来,应用语言学的研究过程共分为四步:第一,确定研究问题;第二,形成假设;第三,验证假设;第四,得出结论。

1. 确定研究问题

我们经常听到有人说,"英语难学。学了这么多年,英文报纸、杂志还看不懂,跟外国人交流还有问题。"我们也经常听到有人说,"汉语难学,那书写简直像画画,还有那四声,太难区分了。"这样,我们就有"是英语难学还是汉语难学?"这个问题。有了问题后,接下来就要看一看这个问题是否值得研究。就应用语言学而言,看一个问题是否值得研究,根据文秋芳等,要看三个方面。第一,是否有意义;第二,是否有新意;第三,是否有可行性。所谓有意义是指这个问题要么有理论意义,要么有实践意义,要么两者兼而有之,即既有理论意义,又有实践意义。所谓有理论意义是指研究问题要么能证明某一理论、要么能证伪某一理论、要么能对现行理论进行修改或补充、要么能澄清某个有争议的问题、要么能提出新的理论模式。所谓实践意义是指能提高二语的教与学、提高编写双语词典的质量和翻译质量等。所谓有新意是指这个问题与前人的研究的问题在一个或几个方面的不同,可能是学习的环境不同,也可能学习者的类型不同,可能研究设计不同,也可能研究处理的方法不同,可能是数据收集的方法不同,也可能数据分析的方法不同,总之,有新意并不是指整个都是新的,而是一个程度或方面的问题。所谓可行性是指研究人员在一定的时间范围内,利用现有的人力、物力和财力能够解决研究问题,而不是研究"是先有鸡还是先有蛋"这类无法解决的问题。如果一个问题具备了以上这三个条件,就可以把它确定为研究问题。

下面来看一看这个问题是否有意义。就理论意义而言,我们认为,至少可以帮助我们进一步认识这两种语言,同时可以澄清或有助于澄清这个问题:"究竟是英语难学,还是汉语难学?"。但有一点是可以肯定的,它有实践意义,如果是汉语比英语难学,那么我们可以鼓励现在的学生,增强他们学英语的信心。可以设想一下,这么难的汉语你都学会了,英语肯定能学好。如果是英语比汉语难学,可以打破原来汉语难学的成见,从而更快、更好把汉语和中国文化介绍给世界,让世界了解中国,最终促进中外文化交流。关于这个研究问题是否有新意,我们可以到中国知网查阅年相关文献,发现英汉比较方面的研究很多,但比较英汉两种语言易难方面的研究还没有。因此,可以断定这个研究问题是有新意的。关于这个研究问题的可行性,应该说研究人员在一定的时间范围内,利用现有的人力、物力和财力通过访谈、问卷或查阅文献等方法是能够探讨这一研究问题,并得出相应的结论。

2. 形成假设

确定了研究问题后,就可以进入下一个步骤,形成假设。

根据这个研究问题,我们可以形成五种假设性:

假设一: 英语比汉语难学。

假设二: 汉语比英语难学。

假设三: 英语和汉语一样难学。

假设四: 英语和汉语一样难容易。

假设五: 很难说是英语难还是汉语难。

形成假设后,我们可以进入下一个步骤,验证假设。

3. 验证假设

如何验证假设,必须有数据。数据从哪儿来? 必须要收集。就上述这个研究问题,至少有两种方法收集数据:一是通过问卷调查或访谈从直接使用英汉两种语言的人那儿收集数据,另一是从英汉两种语言中收集数据。

1）从英汉两种语言使用者那儿收集数据

要从英汉两种语言使用者那儿收集数据,即对他们进行问卷调查或访谈,就必须选择研究对象。应该强调的是,不是所有的人都可以成为研究对象,研究对象必须有学习英汉两种语言的经历,最好要熟悉这两种语言,否则"是英语难学还是汉语难学?"就无从谈起。相对说来,英语专业的教师和学生,中文专业的教师和学生,还有母语为英语来中国学汉语的外国留学生和外教,这些人作为研究对象较为合适。

确定好研究对象后,就可以进行问卷调查或访谈。我前一段时间做了探索性的小规模研究(pilot study),对十二位访谈对象进行了非结构化访谈。所谓非结构化访谈是一种比较灵活、给访谈者许多自由、访谈问题没有固定顺序的访谈。这种访谈极像自由聊天,甚至访谈对象都没有意识到自己在接受访谈,它的最大特点是极富人情味,没有拘束,容易谈深入。在访谈对象中,有两位是高校英语教师,五位是英语语言文学专业硕士研究生,一位高校的中文教师,两位汉语语言文字学方向研究生和两位外籍教师。

由于采用的非结构化访谈,研究者在访谈过程中,既没有录音,也没有记录,这样,访谈对象可以在自由、轻松的环境里表达自己的观点。研究者在访谈后随即对访谈内容进行回忆与整理,以免遗忘与遗漏。

2）分析数据

收集好数据后,就要分析数据。分析数据时,要看定量研究还是定性研究。如果是定量研究,可以根据情况采用 SPSS(社会科学统计软件),进行描述性统计,或推断性统计。如果是定性研究,要把相关数据进行筛选、整理、分类、综合和比较。

3）研究结果与讨论

就小规模访谈结果,详见表1。

表1 小规模访谈结果

访谈对象	英语教师	英语研究生	汉语教师	汉语研究生	外教	合计
英语比汉语难人数			1			1
汉语比英语难人数	2	5		1	2	10
英汉语一样难人数						0
英汉语一样易人数						0
很难说哪个难人数				1		1
总人数	2	5	1	2	2	12

从表1可以看出,共有十人认为"汉语比英语难"。其中有两位英语教师,五位英语语言文学的研究生,一位汉语语言文字方向的研究生和两位外教。一位汉语教师认为"英语比汉语难"。一位汉语的研究生认为"很难说哪个难"。在问及原因时,认为"汉语比英语难"的访谈对象谈得很散、很多。总括起来有了四个:一是语音,尤其是四声很难区别;二是词汇,很难写、很难认;三是语法,结构松散,无法可依;四是文化,中国历史悠久,汉字传承数千年的文化,其底蕴之丰富,可以说是博大精深。至于汉语成语,它的文化内涵就更丰富了。中文教师说:"英语比汉语难学。我曾经为了职称连续考了两年英语,都没过关,第三年改考日语,一次就通过了。此外,英语很难听懂,至于用英语与外国人交流就更难了,再加上英语单词那么多,又那么难记,刚记住过一会儿就忘了。还有语法,一会儿什么时态,一会儿什么语态,一会儿什么复数,头都搞大了。"认为"很难说哪个难"的研究生说:"哪种语言难学,哪种语言容易学这东西很难说。毛主席就曾经说过:'语言这东西不是随便可以学好的,非下苦功不可。'不过,我想学好一种语言取决于两个因素,一是取决于学习者所处的环境,二是取决于学习者。一般说来,处在中国的环境里,学汉语容易,处在英美国家的环境里,学英语就容易。至于学习者,有人对英语感兴趣,英语就容易学,有人对汉语感兴趣,汉语就容易学。此外,有人有学语言的天赋,不能一概而论,也不好一概而论。"

4.得出结论

如果我们仅根据探索性的小规模研究访谈结果,可以暂时得出结论:汉语比英语难学。由于访谈对象不十分具有代表性,且规模较小,这一结论有待验证。

Step 3:The second issue concerning research methods:the same research question leading to different conclusions because of different methods

不同的研究方法可能导致不同的研究结果。前面使用的是访谈,从英汉两种语言使用者那儿收集数据。暂时得出的结论是:汉语比英语难。下面使用方法的是比较,从英汉两种语言那儿收集数据。具体地说,是通过英汉两种语言的语音、词汇和语法的比较,收集相关数据,来得出结论。

1.英汉两种语言语音的比较

1)音位的比较

语言中区分意思的最小单位是音位(phoneme)。关于英语中究竟有多少音位,各家说法不一,有的学者认为英语共有 44 个音位,其中元音(vowel)20 个,辅音(consonant)24 个,如周考成先生;也有学者,如劳允栋先生认为英语共有 55 个音位,其中元音 25 个,辅音 30 个。根据金定元先生,汉语中共有 31 个音位,其中元音为 6 个,辅音为 25 个。但不管怎么说,英语的音位数量要比汉语多。

2) 音节的比较

英语中的音节比较复杂,且变化较多,有人做过统计,英语的音节变化约有三四千种。此外,就英语中的词而言,有单音节词、双音节词和多音节词,最多的音节可多达 10 余个,如:antidisestablishmentarianism(反对政府与宗教分离的主张)。而汉语的字都是单音节。根据《现代汉语词典》,汉语共有 1382 种音节,汉语的音节是由声母(initials of the Chinese Phonetic System)、韵母(finals of the Chinese Phonetic System)和声调(tone)组成的。其中声母是 21 个,由辅音担任,韵母是 35 个,由单元音、双元音或三元音担任,也可由元音加辅音担任。汉语的字都是单音节。无论从音节的数量上看,还是从音节的变化上看,英语的音节都远远超过汉语。

3) 重音的比较

英汉两种语言均有重音,根据陈宏薇等(2004:35),英语的单词有重音,且其排列有规律。如:双音节词和三音节词的重音一般在第一个音节上(family /ˈfæmɪlɪ/),三个音节和三个音节以上的词,重音一般在倒数第三个音节上(psychology /saɪˈkɒlədʒɪ/)等。多音节词中除了主重音(primary stress),还有次重音(secondary stress)(magazine /ˌmægəˈziːn/),有的词有双重音(double stress)(Chinese /ˈtʃaɪˈniːz/)。汉字是单音节,只有一个重音。

如果仅仅从音位的数量、音节的数量以及重音的数量来看,很显然,英语多于汉语,这很可能会造成英语比汉语难。但由于汉语的音节变化少,汉语有大量的同音字,再加上四声,这给汉语学习也带来了不少困难。因此,在语音方面,英汉两种语言的难度是平分秋色,各有千秋。

2. 英汉两种语言词汇的比较

1) 词汇一级结构的比较

词汇一级结构为英汉两种语言书写的最小结构,英语为字母(letter),共 26 个,且有大小写之分;汉语为笔画(stroke),如:丶、丿、丨、乛等共 24 个,无大小写之分。其复杂程度显然是英语比汉语难,且数量也比汉语多。

2) 词汇二级结构的比较

词汇的二级结构为词素。它是语言中最小的、有意义单位。英语为词素(morpheme),从结构上说,词素可分为能独立成词的自由词素(free morpheme)和与其他词素在一起构成一个词的粘着词素(bound morpheme)。从语义上说,词素可分为词缀词素(affix morpheme),简称词缀和词根词素(root morpheme)简称词根。我们且不谈英语中 1430 多个的词根,其中自由词根 1000 多个,粘着词根 380 多个。就词缀(包括前缀和后缀)也有 337 个。众所周知,一个人如能知道英语中这些词根和词缀,这对记忆单词大有好处。如果只知道 26 个字母,而不知道这些词根和词缀,那记单词肯定麻烦,令人头疼。汉语中与英语的词素相对应的是偏旁部首(radical)。从结构上说,有些偏旁部首可独立成字,与英语中自由词素相仿,有些偏旁部首不能独立成字,必须与其他字在一起构成一个新字。在《新华字典》上,共有 189 偏旁部首。就数量而言,汉语中的偏旁部首明显比英语中词根和词缀少得多。

3) 词汇三级结构的比较

在词汇三级结构上,英语中为词(word)。汉语为字(Chinese character)。英语中的词是数以百万计,陆国强估计英语有一百多万个词,汪榕培估计英语有二百多万个词。而汉语中的字只有数以万计,《新华字典》就收了一万多字。为什么英语的词要比汉语的字多那么多?我们不妨来看一下部分英汉动物名称的比较。先看汉语中的部分动物。

表 2　汉语中部分动物

1	2	3
个性的字/下义词	共性的字/上义词	共性的字/性别
公鸡 母鸡	鸡	公 母
公马 母马	马	
公鹿 母鹿	鹿	
公羊 母羊	羊	
公猪 母猪	猪	
公牛 母牛	牛	
公狗 母狗	狗	

从表 2 中的 1、2 两纵列可以看出,"鸡"既是"公鸡、母鸡"的上义词,又是表示共性的字;"公鸡、母鸡"既是"鸡"的下义词,又是表示个性的字。下面的"马""鹿""羊""猪""牛""狗"都是一样,既是"公马、母马"等的上义词,又是表示共性的字;"公马、母马"等既是"马"等的下义词,又是表示个性的字。从表 2 中的 1、3 可以看出,"公鸡、母鸡""公马、母马""公鹿、母鹿""公羊、母羊""公猪、母猪""公牛、母牛""公狗、母狗"都有"公""母"这两个字。因此,这里的"公母"是表示共性的字。"鸡""马""鹿""羊""猪""牛""狗"是表示个性的字。这就是说,在汉语中,共性加上个性就可以组合成新概念,且组合能力非常强。这样上述 23 概念中只用了 9 个字。再看英语中的部分动物。

表3　英语中部分动物

个性的词/下义词	共性的词	上义词	共性的字/性别
cock	无	chicken	（male & female）无
hen			
stallion	无	horse	
mare			
buck	无	deer	
doe			
ram	无	sheep	
ewe			
boar	无	pig	
sow			
bull	无	cow	
cow			
dog	无	dog	
bitch			

从表3可以看出,虽然"chicken"是"cock、hen"的上义词,但是chicken并不表示cock、hen的共性;下面的"horse""deer""sheep""pig""cow""dog"都是一样,虽然它们都是上义词,但是它们都不表示共性。英语没有这种共性与个性的关系,几乎每个事物都要造一个词,这样23概念中有21个词。此外,现代英语为了应付不断涌现的新事物、新思想、新概念,也在不断造新词。要么是借助拉丁词根,要么重新组合已有的单词,结果越是专业的词汇,就越长,也越难记。

综上所述,在词汇方面,无论是一级结构,还是二级结构、三级结构,英语的数量都大大超过汉语,这说明在这一方面,英语比汉语难。

3. 英汉两种语言语法的比较

一般说来,语法规则是越简单越好,不规则的变化是越少越好。汉语是孤立语,没有词形变化,没有严密逻辑性和规律性,靠词序和虚词表达语法意义。英语是屈折语,词形有变化。如:名词单复数及其所有格有变化;动词的单数第三人称一般现在时、过去式、过去分词、现在分词等有变化;形容词和副词的比较级和最高级有变化,且这当中还有许多不规则变化。由此可见,英语语法比汉语语法难。

4. 得出结论

根据以上英汉两种语言比较,我们可以暂时得出另一个结论:英语比汉语难学。

应该指出的是,产生不同结果的原因可能是是多方面的,如:研究者(或研究对象)对研究问题的理解侧重不同。比如运用访谈的方法时,访谈者偏重的是语言学习过程的难易度;而在对语言本身进行比较时,研究者关注的是语言本身的复杂性。从这点上讲,不同研究方法可能产生了不同的结果,即使同一研究方法也可能产生了不同的结果,这就是为什么有些研究需要反复进行验证。

Step 4：The third issue concerning research methods：no perfect research method

那么，究竟是英语比汉语难，还是汉语比英语难？一时还难以定夺。我们设想这样一个的研究方法：实验。具体做法是：让一位英语专家和一位汉语专家同时教几十位来自非洲某个国家的土著学生。这两位专家的语言水平以及教学水平相同。这些非洲学生年龄相仿，智力相当，他们的母语既跟英语无关，也跟汉语无关，且都没有学习这两种语言的经历。经过一段时间（一年、两年或更长的时间）的实验，再对这些土著非洲学生进行调查，看看他们的回答，以此来断定哪种语言难学。这个研究方法只是一种理想化的研究方法，在实践中很难实现。这是因为正如世界上找不到两片相同叶子，世界上也找不到两个语言水平与教学水平相同的教师，更何况是涉及两种语言水平与教学水平呢？再说这些非洲学生，尽管他们的母语跟英语和汉语无关，且都没有学习这两种语言的经历，但他们可能有其他经历，这些经历可能会有助他们学习英语或汉语。

一方面，由于应用语言学研究的对象是人，人的各种现象非常复杂，各种变量难以控制。另一方面，金无足赤，人无完人，不是完人的人设计出研究方法，总归有这样或那样的问题，这是正常的，也是在所难免的。我们要做的是：首先要尽可能控制干扰变量，努力使研究方法科学合理，其次要坦言承认研究方法的局限性，这才我们应有的科学精神和实事求是的态度。当然，我们也不要因为各种现象非常复杂，各种变量难以控制，以及研究方法天生的不足，而使我们的研究畏首畏尾，裹足不前。从本质上说，人们从不同视角，使用不同的方法对应用语言学的问题进行研究，有助于拓宽人们的视野与思维，虽然人们的每一个成果都不可能最终解决这些问题，但对这些问题认识又向前迈了一步，更加逼近真理。其实，这正是应用语言学研究方法的目的所在，也是任何研究方法的目的所在。

Step 5：Assignment with a preview of *Variables*

我们今天所探讨的英语和汉语，用一句行话来说，叫变量。那什么是变量？它又有哪些种类呢？不同变量之间又有什么关系呢？请大家预习相关内容，我们下一节课再讲变量。

Ⅱ．Analysis

这是一个基于研究方法的教学设计，具体地说，是探讨应用语言学研究方法中的三个问题：一是应用语言学的研究过程；二是不同的研究方法可能导致不同的研究结果；三是任何一种研究方法都有其局限性。一般说来，应用语言学的研究过程共分为四步：第一，确定研究问题；第二，形成假设；第三，验证假设；第四，得出结论。不同的研究方法可能导致不同的研究结果，产生不同结果的原因可能是是多方面的：有的是研究设计的不同；有的是研究对象不同；有的是研究工具不同；有点的是收集数据的方法不同；有的是分析数据的方法不同。有时，即使同一研究方法也可能产生了不同的结果，这就是为什么有些研究需要反复进行验证。任何一种研究方法都有其局限性，即世界上没有十全十美的研究方法，它们总有这样或那样的问题：有研究对象的、有样本大小的、有研究工具的、有数据收集的、有数据分析的。说到底，是我们的人不是十全十美的。不是十全十美的人，创造出来的研究方法肯定不是十全十美的。整个教学设计条分缕析，逻辑性较强，一环扣一环。三个问题既彼此独立，又相互联系，形成一个有机的整体。

Part Five

Instructional Design of *Linguistics* and Case Analysis

Instructional Design of *Linguistics* Based on Arousal of Students' Interest and Analysis

Ⅰ. Instructional Design of *Linguistics* Based on Arousal of Students' Interest

Step 1: Lead-in with some interesting episodes in *Linguistics*

今天,我和大家一起学习一门新课,叫"Linguistics"(语言学)。这是一节引论课,通过这节课,我们对"Linguistics"这门课有个大概了解。长期以来,人们普遍认为:"Linguistics"是一门理论性很强(theoretical),比较抽象(abstract),比较枯燥(boring)的课程。这是真的吗?实际上,"Linguistics"这门课理论性很强,实用性(practical)也很强;这门课比较抽象,也比较具体(concrete);这门课有些地方比较枯燥,有些地方也比较有趣(interesting)。因此,我们这里先用林语堂先生的一句话开头:"A good introductory remark should be like a woman's skirt, short enough to arouse interest, but long enough to cover the essentials."。都说"书山有路勤为径,学海无涯苦作舟",但我更要说:"书山有路趣为径,学海无涯乐作舟"。我们不妨来看网上流传几个有趣的语言片段。

片段一:"English"的读法。小时侯上学,把"English"读为"应给利息"的同学当了银行行长;读为"阴沟里洗"的成了小菜贩子;读为"因果联系"的成了哲学家;读为"硬改历史"的成了政治家;读为"英国里去"的成了海外华侨。而我,不小心读成了"应该累死",结果成了一名英语老师。说实在的,尽管英语教师有些累、有些苦,还是有不少乐趣。像今天我们在这里不急不慢、气定神闲地侃侃"English"的读法,本身就是一件趣事。再说了,生活中,哪个工作不苦,哪个工作不累。我们要学会苦中作乐,更要学会干一行,爱一行。

片段二:中国式英语的创意。smilence = smile + silence(笑而不语),chinsumer = Chinese + consumer(在国外疯狂购物的中国人),Gunvernment = gun + government(枪杆子里面出政权),Stupig = stupid + pig(蠢猪),togayther = together + gay(终成眷属),animale = animal + male(男人天性)。我曾经与我们学院的外教讨论过这些词的意思,他的第一反应就是很有趣,也有道理。

片段三:英语单词内部所隐藏的。就算是 believe,中间也藏了一个 lie;就算是 friend,还是免不了 end;就算是 lover,还可能会 over;就算是 wife,心里也夹杂着 if;欣慰的是:即便是 forget,也曾经 get,就算 impossible,但还藏着 possible,如果现在 unhappy,谁又能保证以后不会 happy?

这三个小片段有所侧重,第一个侧重音;第二个侧重形;第三个侧重义。在语言的音、形、义三个系统中,有音趣、形趣和义趣,它需要我们去挖掘,只有这样,我们才会感到学有所得,学有所益,学有所趣。

Step 2:Arousing students' interest in linguistics in terms of sound

众所周知,语言首先是口头的,而不是书面的。没有语音这个外壳,语言就不复存在。这里我们首先来谈谈语言中的音趣。语言中的音趣很多,这里举几个例子可以窥斑见豹。

英汉语中都存在大量的绕口令,由于绕口令是将若干发音相同、相近的词有意集中在一起,组成简单、有趣的语韵,要求快速念出,所以读起来使人感到节奏感强,妙趣横生。如:While we were walking, we were watching window washers' wash Washington's windows with warm washing water. 再如:When a doctor doctors(给……治病)another doctor, does the doctor doctor the doctored doctor the way the doctored doctor wants to be doctored or does the doctor doctor the doctored doctor the way the doctoring doctor wants to doctor the doctor? 又如:How many cans(罐头)can(能)a canner can(做罐头)? A canner can can as many cans as he can. 汉语毫不逊色,下面的例子不仅是个绕口令,还是个对联:长长长长长长长;长长长长长长长 横批:长长长长。其读法为:chang zhang chang zhang chang chang zhang,zhang chang zhang chang zhang zhang chang。chang zhang zhang chang。

再如,英汉两种语言中都存在大量的同音异义现象,英语这方面的例子非常多,可以信手拈来,如:son 和 sun,piece 和 peace,to、too 和 two,meet、meat 和 mete,right、write、wright 和 rite 等。与英语相比,汉语中的同音异义现象可以说是有过之而无不及,这一点在赵元任先生的《施氏食狮史》达到登峰造极的地步。这篇《施氏食狮史》共由 92 个相同音的字组成,他是这样写的:"石室诗士施氏,嗜狮,誓食十狮。施氏时时适市视狮。十时,适十狮适市。是时,适施氏适市。氏视是十狮,恃矢势,使是十狮逝世。氏拾是十狮尸,适石室。石室湿,氏使侍拭石室。石室拭,氏始试食是十狮。食时,始识是十狮,实十石狮尸。试释是事。"有人采用意译的方法,把这篇《施氏食狮史》译成英语。其译文如下。

The Lion-Eating Poet in the Stone Den

In a stone den lived a poet whose surname was Shi. He loved to eat lions and decided to eat ten. He often went to the market for lions. One day at ten o'clock, ten lions just arrived at the market. At that time, Shi just arrived at the market, too. Seeing those ten lions, he killed them with arrows. He brought the corpses of the ten lions to the stone den. The stone den was damp. He asked his servants to wipe it. After the stone den was wiped, he tried to eat those ten lions. When he ate, he realized that those ten lions were in fact ten stone lion corpses. Try to explain this.

英国翻译家 Nicholas Williams 采用动态功能对等,把《施氏食狮史》译成英语,译文如下:

Songster Smith of the stone cell, savoring swine, swore to sup on seven swine. Sometimes Smith, striding to the city, saw some swine. At seven, seven swine scampered to the city. Smith serendipitously saw the seven swine, so Smith speared to slay the seven swine. Smith snatched the seven swine stiffs, and sped to Smith's stone cell. Smith's stone cell seeming slippery, Smith suggested servants sweep the stone cell. The stone cell swept, Smith set to swallowing the seven swine. Straightaway Smith saw, sadly, the seven swine stiffs were simply seven stone swine stiffs. Seek to solve such a story!

Nicholas Williams 创造性地把原文是"shi",译为以"s"音开头的词,且对原文做了较大的更改,如:姓氏"施"译为了"Smith","狮"译为"Swine","十"译为了"seven"等。从语义角度,译文与原文相差甚远。但在此案例中,什么姓氏,什么动物,什么数量都无关紧要,真正重要的是能保留原文的效果,使译文读者能像原文读者一样,作出同样或相似的反应。

Step 3:Arousing students' interest in linguistics in terms of form

语言中另一重要的系统是形。语言中的形可以包括字母的形、单词的形、短语的形、句子的形和语篇的形等。这样我们来挖掘字母中的形趣、单词的形趣、短语的形趣、句子的形趣和语篇的形趣,从而激发大家的兴趣,联想与想象。

首先,挖掘字母的形趣。象形不是汉语所独有。我们知道,英语字母是来自拉丁字母,拉丁字母是来自希腊字母,希腊字母是来自腓尼基字母,当我们把字母追溯到腓尼基字母时,我们发现它们也是象形的。今天,现代英语字母中仍有一些象形的残骸。例如:字母 W 像波浪,具有不稳定性和不确定性,这类的单词有:Wave,Water,Wind,Whip 等。正因为此,英语中的疑问词大多数是以 W 开始的,如:What,When,Where,Whose 等。与 W 相反,字母 T 具有稳定性,像 That,Then,There,Those 等词就非常确定。再如:把手伸出,四指并拢,大拇指向下,看上去像字母 P,英语中的这些词都与手有关。push(推);pull(拉);press(按);point(指);pat(拍);pack(捆、扎);prise(撬);pick(捡);piece(拼);pitch(扔);pinch(捏);play(打);prick(扎);pluck(摘);plug(插)probe(探);protect(护);pounce(扑);praise(p + raise 本义是用手"举起",引申为"表扬");applaud(a + pp + loud 两只手拍得很响)等等。

其次,挖掘单词的形趣。我们可以使用模写来挖掘单词的形趣。所谓"模写"是指根据特定情景之需,把英语单词拼写成相对标准语不正规的变体,从而达到描摹逼真的效果。如:The pilot radioed Seattle's FAA control centre that the mountain had exploded, to get everyone from there, because the blast was big, Big, BIG. 这里的 blast 是指美国华盛顿州 Mount St Helens 火山发生大爆炸。三个"big",先全部小写,然后 B 大写,然后三个字母全大写,三个"big"书写上逐步升级,表明其语义程度逐步升高,即声音越来越大。

再次,挖掘短语的形趣。我们使用字母易位来挖掘短语的形趣,如:mother-in-law 可易位为 woman Hitler 和 the warm lion;Statue of Liberty 可易位为 built to stay free;New York Times 可易位为 Monkeys write 或 Monkey writes。The Golden Notebook 可易位为 The token Nobel? Good!

此外,挖掘句子的形趣。我们使用回文来挖掘句子的形趣。如:Ma is as selfless as I am. 又如:Madam, I do get a mate. God, I'm Adam. 更有趣的是,西方人在大选期间,为了拉选票,用回文做口号:RISE TO VOTE SIR。

最后,关于语篇的形趣,我们来看一下《华山图》。

山山

座上

山八青山

华晓上天

山美谁天高山

华道皆响水流

山川人人浅浅深山

过在自由声声鸟百

山雾霭自叫荒径只

真亦幻亦攀步步身

这首诗横念竖念都无法成句,必须自高处沿右侧蜿蜒而下,七步一歇,往复回环,行至山足,再沿左侧拾级而上,盘旋攀越,登临绝顶,便成一道情景交融的优美诗篇:

山上青山天上天,高山流水响浅浅。

深山百鸟声声叫,荒径只身步步攀。

亦幻亦真山雾霭,自由自在过山川。

人人皆道华山美,谁晓华山八座山。

Step 4:Arousing students' interest in linguistics in terms of meaning

语言中的义趣更是琳琅满目,令人目不暇接。其中有一词多义的义趣、矛盾修辞法的义趣、排比的义趣、双关的义趣等等,不一而足。

我们先来看一词多义的义趣。这首诗是有一年我所见到扬州树人集团初一招生的场景。当时扬州是狂风暴雨,来送考生参加考试的汽车把路上堵得水泄不通,有些考生都无法进考场,考试竞争非常激烈,10 个才录取一个。看到这一情景,我的心情非常沉重。于是就写下了这首《Heavy Is My Heart》

Heavy Is My Heart

The rain is heavy.

Heavy is my heart.

The wind is heavy.

Heavy is my heart.

The traffic is heavy.

Heavy is my heart.

The competition is heavy.

Heavy is my heart.

这里的 heavy 表示雨"大"、表示风"高"、表示交通"繁忙"、表示竞争"激烈"、也表示心情"沉重"。

语言中的义趣还表现"矛盾修辞法"上。我这儿有个谜语,大家来猜一猜。这个谜语是这样的:一个"似男人非男人"的人,"看见又看不见"一只"似鸟非鸟"的东西栖息在一个"似竹非竹"的东西上面,这个"似男人非男人"的人拿了一块"似石非石"的东西,向那只"似鸟非鸟"的东西砸去,最后那只"似鸟非鸟"的东西就飞走了。同学们可以讨论讨论这个谜语。最后,我来公布了谜底,它讲的是:一个"似男人非男人"的人说的是一个太监(eunuch),这个太监是独眼龙(one-eyed),一只眼睛好,一只眼睛不好,因此他"看见又看不见"。一只"似鸟非鸟"的东西是"蝙蝠"(bat),众所周知,蝙蝠既似鸟又非鸟。这只蝙蝠栖息在芦竹(reed)上面,芦竹是"似竹非竹"。这个太监拿了一块浮石(pumice)向蝙蝠砸去,因为浮石很轻,"似石非石"。最后,蝙蝠飞走了。谜底的英文是:A one-eyed eunuch saw a bat sitting on the reed. He picked up a piece of pumice and threw at the bat. And it flew away.

下面我们来看排比的义趣,题目叫《问秋》。

什么季节最忙? 秋天,多事之秋;什么季节最公平? 秋天,平分秋色;什么季节最简单? 秋天,一叶知秋;什么季节最长? 秋天,一日不见如隔三秋;什么季节最爽? 秋天,秋高气爽;什么季节最险? 秋天,秋后算账;什么季节最暧昧? 秋天,暗送秋波;什么季节最成功? 秋天,春华秋实。

(What is the busiest season? Autumn, for it is full of events. What is the fairest season? Autumn, for it divides things equally. What is the simplest season? Autumn, for the fall of one leaf is enough to tell autumn's arrival. What is the longest season? Autumn, for a one-day separation seems as long as three autumns. What is the most invigorating season? Autumn, for its sky is clear and its air is crisp. What is the most risky season? Autumn, for someone will settle accounts with you after autumn harvest, which means that someone will take revenge on you or punish you afterwards. What is the most subtle season? Autumn, for its limpid ripples, referring to the limpid eyes of a beautiful woman, are secretly or stealthily sent, which means that a beautiful woman sends silent and endearing messages with bewitching eyes or casts sheep's eyes. What is the most successful season? Autumn, for flowers in spring result in fruits in autumn.)

我们再来看双关的义趣。

Everybody, Somebody, Anybody, and Nobody

Once upon a time, there were four people named Everybody, Somebody, Anybody and Nobody.

There was an important job to be done and Everybody was asked to do it. Everybody was sure Somebody would do it. Anybody could have done it, but Nobody did it.

Somebody got angry about that, because it was Everybody's job. Everybody thought Anybody could do it but Nobody realized that Everybody wouldn't do it.

It ended up that Everybody blamed Somebody when Nobody did what Anybody could have done.

由于 Everybody，Somebody，Anybody，和 Nobody 既是不定代词又是名词,读起来让人忍俊不禁。

Step 5：Arousing students' interest in linguistics in terms of sound，form and meaning

三国时期,周瑜和诸葛孔明各司其主,因孔明才学渊博,计高一筹,使周瑜十分嫉妒,总想加害孔明。有一天,周瑜想出了一条妙计,设宴相请,并以对诗为名进行加害。孔明早已觉察周瑜的心思,便故意说:"谁输了就砍谁的头。"周瑜暗自大喜,忙说:"君子无戏言,戏言非君子。"鲁肃见他俩击掌为定,急得出了一身冷汗,埋怨孔明聪明一世,糊涂一时,轻易地入了圈套。而孔明假装不知,泰然自若。周瑜见孔明中计,十分高兴,首先出诗一首:"有水也是溪,无水也是奚。去掉溪边水,加鸟便是鸡,得志猫儿雄过虎,落毛凤凰不如鸡。"

孔明听了,心中暗想,自己身为刘备的军师,今日落入周瑜之手,岂不是"落毛凤凰"吗? 便立即吟诗以对曰:"有木也是棋,无木也是其。去掉棋边木,加欠便是欺。龙游浅水遭虾戏,虎落平阳被犬欺。"

周瑜闻言大怒,鲁肃早已留意这场龙虎斗,见周都督意欲爆发,急忙劝解道:"有水也是湘,无水也是相。去掉湘边水,加雨便是霜,各人自扫门前雪,莫管他人瓦上霜。"

风波平息了,周瑜怒气未消,他更换内容,又吟诗一首:"有手便是扭,无手便是丑。去掉扭边手,加女便是妞,隆中有女长得丑,百里难挑一个妞。"孔明见周瑜奚落自己的夫人,也就毫不客气,反唇相讥,遂吟诵道:"有木也是桥,无木也是乔。去掉桥边木,加女便是娇。江中吴女大小乔,曹操铜雀锁二娇。"孔明的嘲讽,激得周瑜怒火万丈,暴跳如雷,暗令伏兵团团围住,孔明毫不惊慌,稳如泰山。鲁肃立即上前劝阻:"都督息怒!我有一诗奉献:'有木也是槽,无木也是曹。去掉槽边木,加米便是糟。今日这事在破曹,龙虎相残大事糟。'"鲁肃以诗指点,周瑜恍然大悟,遂喝退刀斧手,与孔明共议破曹妙计,干出了后来流传千古的火烧赤壁的大事业。

这些诗让我们领略到中国古人的智慧、涵养和素质,使我们现代人为之汗颜。从语言学的角度看,这些诗中包含有音趣、形趣和义趣。

Step 6：Assignment：Reading a short passage about *Crazy English*

Let's face it—English is a crazy language.

There is no egg in eggplant nor ham in hamburger; neither apple nor pine in pineapple. English muffins weren't invented in England nor French fries in France. Sweetmeats are candies while sweetbreads, which aren't sweet, are meat.

We take English for granted. But if we explore its paradoxes, we find that quicksand can work slowly, boxing rings are square and a guinea pig is neither from Guinea nor is it a pig.

And why it is that writers write but fingers don't fing, grocers don't groce and hammers don't ham? If the plural of tooth is teeth, why isn't the plural of booth beeth? If you have one goose, two geese, why not one moose, two meese, or one index, two indices?

Doesn't it seem crazy that you can make amends but not one amend, or that you can comb through the annals of history but not a single annal? If you have a bunch of odds and ends and get rid of all but one of them, what do you call it?

If teachers taught, why didn't preachers praught? If a vegetarian eats vegetables, what does a humanitarian eat? If you wrote a letter, perhaps you bote your tongue?

Sometimes I think all the English speakers should be committed to an asylum for the verbally insane. In what other language do people recite at a play and play at a recital; ship by truck and send cargo by ship; have noses that run and feet that smell; park on driveways and drive on parkways?

How can a slim chance and a fat chance be the same, while a wise man and wise guy are opposites, and quite a lot and quite a few are alike? How can the weather be hot as hell one day and cold as hell another?

You have to marvel at the unique lunacy of a language in which your house can burn up as it burns down, in which you fill in a form by filling it out and in which an alarm clock goes off by going on.

English was invented by people, not computers, and it reflects the creativity of the human race (which of course, isn't a race at all). That is why, when the stars are out, they are visible, but when they lights are out, they are invisible. And why, when I wind up my watch, I start it, but when I wind up this essay, I end it?

II. Analysis

书山有路"趣"为径,学海无涯"乐"作舟。只要有了兴趣,学生的一切学习都迎刃而解。所谓兴趣是指人们对事物的一种向往、迷恋、积极探索追求的心理倾向,是学习的情感动力,是求知欲的源泉。正因为此,我们都说"兴趣是最好的老师"。在实际教学中,教师如果想要激发学生对《语言学》的兴趣,自己首先要对《语言学》感兴趣。如果教师自己对《语言学》就没有兴趣,一切都无从谈起。本课基于激发学生的兴趣,对《语言学》进行教学设计。众所周知,语言学是对语言研究的学问。语言由音、形、义三个部分组成。因此,本教学设计通过绕口令和同音异义激发学生对音的兴趣;通过字母的形、单词的形、短语的形、句子的形和语篇的形激发学生对形的兴趣;通过一词多义、矛盾修辞法、排比、双关等激发学生对义的兴趣。事实上,在任何一种语言中,不管是英语还是汉语,都有许多有趣的现象,只要我们做个有心人,只要我们留心,就一定能挖掘更多、更好、更有趣的东西,一定能化理论为实践,化抽象为具体,化枯燥为有趣。

参考文献

［1］戴炜栋,何兆熊.新编简明英语语言学[M].上海:上海外语教育出版社,2012.

［2］王守仁,赵文书,康文凯.泛读教程[M].上海:上海外语教育出版社,2014.

［3］吴慧颖.中国数文化[M].长沙:岳麓书社,2013.

［4］周维杰.过程教学法在翻译教学中的应用[J].四川外国语学院学报,2002－1.

［5］周维杰.基于"问题教学法"的Getting the best value for time 的教学设计,载胡效亚主编《扬州大学研究性教学案例选编》[M].南京:江苏教育出版社,2012.

［6］周维杰.英语教学设计·实践篇[M].上海:上海译文出版社,2014.